Teacher Development
Induction, Renewal
and Redirection

Peter J. Burke
Wisconsin Improvement Program

 The Falmer Press

(A member of the Taylor & Francis Group)
New York, Philadelphia and London

USA   The Falmer Press, Taylor & Francis Inc., 242 Cherry Street, Philadelphia, PA 19106-1906

UK   The Falmer Press, Falmer House, Barcombe, Lewes, East Sussex, BN8 5DL

First published 1987

Library of Congress Cataloging in Publication Data

Burke, Peter, 1945–
  Teacher development.

  Bibliography: p.
  Includes indexes.
  1. Teachers—Training of. 2. Continuing education.
I. Title.
LB1715.B855   1987   371.1′46   86–29357
ISBN 1–85000–143–X
ISBN 1–85000–144–8 (pbk.)

Jacket design by Caroline Archer

Typeset in 11/13 Bembo by
Imago Publishing Ltd, Thame, Oxon.

Printed and bound in Great Britain by
Redwood Burn Limited, Trowbridge, Wiltshire

Contents

Acknowledgements

Lanore A. Netzer and Glen G. Eye of the University of Wisconsin-Madison, now both Emeritus Professors, were instrumental in the conceptualization, development, and composition of this book. It would not exist without their forethought, guidance, and involvement. Sincere gratitude is expressed for their continual support and encouragement.

Dr. James C. Stoltenberg, Emeritus Dean of Education, at the University of Wisconsin-Platteville, also had an involvement in the early stages of the manuscript. His support and advice are appreciated. The work of the Collegial Research Consortium, especially that of Dr. Ralph Fessler, Johns Hopkins University, and Dr. Judith Christensen, National College of Education, Evanston, Illinois, added greatly to recent revisions on the text. The work of this group has been invaluable in the revised organization of this book.

Finally, a special acknowledgement is due to Karen Jolly, Sandi Grimm, and Pam Hellenbrand who shared the responsibility for the word processing of the several stages of the manuscript. Their patience and endurance necessary to bring the project to its fruition are sincerely appreciated.

Preface

Teacher education has expanded beyond the scope of four years of preservice preparation followed by forty years of inservice teaching. The professional growth of a teacher is now a career-long process of development beginning with undergraduate studies and culminating in retirement. Teachers exhibit different needs at different times in their professional lives, and these needs prompt a differentiated approach to their professional development. It is axiomatic that the professional practitioner must pursue learning beyond initial certification. This book is based upon the need for continuous staff development for teachers and other education personnel.

Access to a career in education, as well as in other fields, is dependent upon the award of a certificate by the legal licensing agency, usually the state. The certificate is evidence that the individual has met the program requirements of an accredited institution of higher education. The major assumption about the licensing or certificating process is that it provides a basic *minimum* of *preparation* for the profession. This assumption is a recognition that the professional practitioner must pursue learning continuously beyond initial certification. The need for continuing staff development is the basis for this book, particularly that need for teachers and other education personnel.

The expectation of continuousness in mastering the direction of the learning of others is all-encompassing in nature. It requires more than knowledge of subject matter to be taught and the use of teaching skills. The teacher is expected to be knowledgeable and skillful even though (i) students are diverse in capacity to learn; (ii) school systems are variable in programs and organization; (iii) societal characteristics often are unpredictable; (iv) governmental controls are inflexible; and (v) educational expectations of people often are unstable. Yet, in the presence of these conditions, the teacher must accomplish the goals and purposes of education. These are the compelling forces that keep continuous teacher *development* in central focus. The author of this book feels such continuousness can be more of a challenge than a burden. Continuousness in development is seen as including (i) the period of basic *academic* and *pedagogical preparation*; (ii) successful *induction* into teaching positions and tasks throughout the career; (iii) continuing personal and professional *renewal* in knowledge and teaching skills; and (iv) *redirection* of tasks and expertise as the changeable society dictates.

The term *development* is a central focus in the book title. The terms induction, renewal, and redirection are in the sub-title because they indicate the three major thrusts that assure comprehensive developmental processes and achievements. Preparation is seen not only as an initiating or a pre-conditioning activity but also as an ongoing and vitalizing support to the three thrust areas that combine in teacher and staff development. The meaning of *development* will be presented last so the combining of the activities of *induction, renewal,* and *redirection* will be seen in their relating and supporting functions. The figure 1 shows the relationship pictorially.

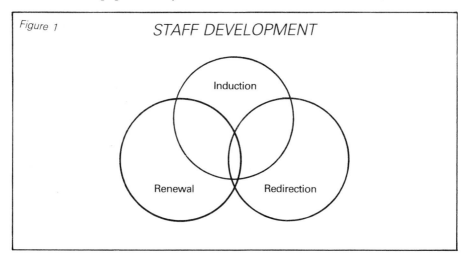

Figure 1 — STAFF DEVELOPMENT — Induction — Renewal — Redirection

Induction

The most common perception of induction is that it occurs as one enters a new position. It often is considered as a brief period of introduction to the first teaching experience, such as a one-day pre-school workshop for new teachers in a district. This narrow view ignores many early and important steps preceding the entrance to a first position such as (i) formal studies related to educational programs and organizations; (ii) directed observations of classroom situations, (iii) unique experiences inside and outside of education; and (iv) decision processes in the steps leading to employment. These omissions are characteristic of the common and limited perceptions of induction. But even with these omissions included, the induction concept has much greater and vital potential in the continuing growth experience of teachers.

Beyond the introduction to a position, there are the induction experiences of (i) receiving modified assignments within the position; (ii) transferring to different locations and responsibilities; (iii) adopting new curricular patterns, (iv) acquiring new instructional materials and equipment; and (v) changing a vast variety of school policies or societal expectations. Induction, then, constitutes all the activities and experiences appropriate to the new expectations and opportunities continuously confronting professionals in education. It includes all the conditions and processes by which individuals gain direction and encouragement through increased understanding. Induction is a continuous process, and as such becomes an extremely important developmental effort. In this context, induction is as important to the experienced teacher as it is to the beginner.

Renewal

The idea of renewal as merely beginning again is too limited to serve the concept of development. Much current work that is called development is an attempt to better motivate or renew on–going activities. To be sure, renewal can be a reinstatement of a former activity, but it is more progressive in nature when viewed as an extension or a reinvigoration of both purpose and process. Renewal as an extension of purpose relieves the constraints of being limited to earlier designs. The development of new designs opens the door for the development of new patterns of process. These earlier patterns can be utilized as referents that lead to creative planning and action. Professional renewal must be a genuine learning experience that results in more effective and efficient teaching.

Individuals usually have a number of responsibilities impinging upon them at one time. Learning to control and coordinate them is a developmental experience. The degree of attention allocated to any one or a combination of responsibilities will vary over a period of time and, thereby, challenges the ingenuity of the individuals involved. There are times when the individual must concentrate on one responsibility over an extended period of time. During that time, application of other abilities may remain dormant and unused. In due time, the action demands may shift back to the dormant areas of responsibility. This return may leave the individual with a sense of inadequacy in an area of former competence. Such instances must not be interpreted as deterioration but rather as an opportunity for renewal. Renewal is a reestablishment of earlier strengths. Renewal is also the reinvestigation of an improvement process in a previously progressing area of development. Renewal is, in fact, the complex of processes essential to continuing improvement of personal and professional qualities. Renewal of personal competence can lead to program vitality and a guarantee that improvement will be a continuing and individual realization. Successful professional renewal is dependent upon change, and change is an essential component of development.

Redirection

A simplistic perception of the term redirection is that it is an admission of an earlier error or weakness. The author finds such a myopic view inadequate and unacceptable. The more accurate meaning is that redirection is the assurance of human ingenuity being applied to the clarification of purpose, restructuring of strategies, and, especially, targeting the adjustment of human capabilities. In this view, personal vigor supports the continuing review of goals and objectives, cultivating the capacity for adaptation while using past performance as stepping stones to improvement.

Retrenchment of education personnel and programs due to varying societal factors can result in the obsolescence of particular skills or narrow certification constraints. An individual may have developed abilities, expertise, or competence beyond the task originally assigned. These added skills may be quite valuable to a district or educational enterprise. Redirection is a technique to meet the need for change by an individual to fit a mold that may be dictated by society. Redirection takes advantage of skills already possessed and moves an individual on to a new assignment or task.

Redirection, then, stands as the open pathway to the stimulation of excellence in association, authenticity in purpose and process, and recognition for expertise-based accomplishments. Redirection stimulates courage, vitalizes confidence in creative ability, and gives reassurance that improvement through development is the benchmark of excellence for education personnel and programs.

Development

The discussion of the meaning of induction indicated that much more was a matter of concern than the beginning of a new position. All of the areas in which induction activities are appropriate can be areas targeted for development. Induction is the beginning not only of the formal teaching commitment but also of each new evolvement in the teaching tasks. Development is continuous improvement which occurs via many avenues, including expansion, advancement, maturation, elaboration, conversion, evolvement, and progression. Each of these avenues traverses one or more of the components of induction, renewal, or redirection.

Each individual follows diverse paths as a means of increasing the quality of personal contributions to the improvement of student learning opportunities and educational outcomes. Renewal, as defined above, is a significant thrust that supports the goals of development. Renewal sets the stage for many induction activities. Induction and renewal efforts would result in partially realized outcomes if redirection did not exist as a definer of purpose and an evaluator of process. Redirection also stands by itself as a technique to retool a valuable human resource into a workable unit. It is the reinforcement and interaction of these three action thrusts — *induction*, *renewal*, and *redirection* that make *development* the appropriate designation of continuing improvement.

The title of this book uses the term *Teacher Development* and, thereby, infers that the content is applicable to the instructional staff in a school or school district. The entire book makes frequent references to teachers rather than school administrators, supervisors, and other specialized personnel. This directional emphasis is intentional because the major concern is for the teacher-learner interaction. The concepts of induction, renewal, and redirection, however, are equally valid applied to those who serve in administrative, supervisory, and other support capacities. It is hoped that all categories of professional educators will share in many developmental activities. The joint effort will reinforce mutuality of purpose and effort toward the desired outcomes of continuing and well-coordinated improvement in the educational programs.

Peter J. Burke

Part One
Getting a Start

Chapter 1

Teachers Are Learners

Teachers are required to show evidence of learning in order to gain legal entry into the teaching profession. A notion that still seems to prevail is that the primary requirement of the teacher is to have a sufficient amount of knowledge to pass on to the students. This leads to the simplistic conclusion that, if teachers have enough knowledge, they will be successful in directing the learning of others. It is imperative to look frankly at teaching as a profession to realize that simply knowing enough is inadequate. It is not difficult to view teachers in almost any setting and to discover that, even if many different people seem to have achieved the same level of learning, they still may behave quite differently as individuals. This should tell us clearly that the amount of learning is insufficient to predict success as a teacher. What you are and what you learn establishes only the beginning of the kind of a teacher that you will be. The individual needs to know what kind of a person he or she is and must relate that understanding to learning and to experience in order to chart a course for a teaching career.

Procedural skills must be mastered in order to enter the teaching profession and to stay in it with any degree of success. It is important to recognize that subject matter expertise is not the sole determinant of success in teaching. The next realization should be that procedural skills require appropriate application. Without appropriate application, procedural skills alone will not assure success any more than will amounts of learning when it is divorced from individual personal development. These are the basic requirements of those who would become teachers. The constant interchange of personal characteristics and knowledge with the procedural skills, along with the appropriate application of those skills, result in continuing demands for improvement upon the individual.

Each person who enters the teaching profession and hopes for a successful career in education must have a desire to meet the demands of performance. One of these demands is *constancy of purpose*. It is a simple and basic rule that a person must have a goal, and this goal, or purpose, must have some validity and staying power. This does not mean that purposes cannot change, but rather than stated goals become one of the first points of recognition as one seeks to attain a successful level of teaching.

A second demand placed upon the individual in the teaching situation is *alertness to opportunities*. These are the opportunities to scrutinize purposes and possibly to make adaptations. More important is the alertness to the opportunities for application of knowledge and procedural skills that will pave the way for effective learning not only on the part of the teacher but also on the part of those the teacher helps to learn.

A third demand for those who desire to perform well is that of *insight into the variability of setting*. The students who come into the classroom will not be uniform in nature, purpose, or ability. Their variations in response will require insight on the part of the teacher. It also is extremely important to attempt to understand the influential environments in which the teaching situation is located. Those who desire to perform well in teaching must be learners in the sense that the demands itemized here require continuous learning and application. Just as setting may change from location to location, so, too, may setting change in the same location year after year.

This chapter is organized so that each section is related to a specific chapter in the book. These chapters will be identified as the discussion of each of the ten sections is pursued. The areas identified in each section represent challenges. These challenges might be called significant concerns important to all teachers. They should be infused into the learning responsibilities of the teacher. The ten areas will be indicated only in general in the following discussion but will be referenced to specific chapters that follow in order to provide detailed help.

This book is for those in pursuit of a continuous, satisfactory, and stimulating career in teaching. If this motivation is lacking in the reader, the message of the book is not likely to achieve its intent. The problem of authors is the same as the problem of teachers: knowledge must possess both substance and quality. When these two are combined for people who have a serious intent to pursue success in their teaching career, the suggestions in the following chapters can be productive. This productivity will be enhanced by the challenge to self-development found in the specific aids following each section and by the parenthetical identification of the three components that serve as the basis of this book: induction, renewal and redirection.

Discovering Evolving Expectations

Expectations have been identified as being goals rather than constraints. It should be recognized that expectations have a way of evolving. To be sure, there are set expectations for everyone in the work-a-day world at any point in time, but these expectations may shift over time. In other words, a set of expectations encountered at the time of entering into an employment contract does not mean that those expectations will remain substantially the same throughout even one year let alone a teaching career. The teacher as a learner must learn to discover and to identify the expectations that are evolving. Most of them grow out of the assignment which was accepted at the time of entering into a contract with the school organization.

Chapter 2 will involve many angles of consideration for the expectations that evolve from an assignment experience at any point in the teaching career. There will be another approach to expectations in chapter 9 which deals with the management of expectations. It is well to recognize that individuals, entering into a teaching contract or accepting a teaching responsibility, have set many expectations for themselves. One of these is the identification of personal goals. A personal goal is an expectation that will guide and stimulate the direction of accomplishment. Each individual must learn that there must be a relationship between personal and institutional goals.

A written job or task description, if one existed at the time the teacher accepted responsibility, would involve certain general state-ments regarding expectations that the school organization was placing upon the individual. Some of these may not be the same as the personal goals which the teacher brought to the assignment. Here then, is a case of learning how to relate one's own goals to those of the institution. Clarification of the assignment characteristics cannot be accomplished in a one-page position or task description. The teacher must learn to deal with the various aspects of the expectations and be able to find ways of adapting personal goals to the institutional goals. The teacher must also find ways to develop to meet the challenge of existing expectations.

Many outside personal and cultural traits and traditions are influential in the discovery of the expectations constantly arriving from over the educational horizon. These personal and cultural encumbrances are the ones that perhaps other people have established and are reluctant to give up. Often, it goes beyond reluctance in giving them up and extends to the point of trying to impose them upon others. Teacher effectiveness may be measured against these traditions. This means, then, that the definition of competence must have some careful consideration.

Competence is found in the task action rather than in the product. It is easy to say that the end-product is the total measure of competence, but this begs the important consideration of process in teaching. It is insisted here that one of the areas of challenge and concern is the development of competence by teachers as learners to discover evolving expectations that can be experienced in specific situations. It calls for a high level of agility in accommodating and adapting to the expectations that grow out of a community and out of a job assignment. Understanding self and developing an ability to relate personal goals or expectations to the process of teaching is a key developmental stage in teaching.

Chapter 2 can help in developing a systematic procedure that is required to make personal goals compatible with the personal goals of others and with the institutional goals within which personal goals are sought to be realized. It means that, with the many origins of evolving expectations, each teacher is a learner who is compelled to identify the sources of assistance and to make creative use of them.

Many people both in the school organization and in the environmental area can render assistance in learning to make adaptations and in understanding and measuring expectations. But, here again, the teacher must learn that help makes a difference only when it is used. Chapter 2, 'You and Your Assignment', is specifically offered as a detailed way of structuring an assignment analysis so that a better understanding of evolving expectations can be a source of strength rather than a burden. Aids for self-development in this and subsequent chapters serve as a basis for information collection regarding professional development needs.

Working With Self and Others

Knowledge, experience, and the personal qualities of the individual must supplement that which is learned in order to produce an appropriate approach to continuous and successful teaching. Individuals must have a desire to analyze themselves and others with the intent of discovering what the working conditions are that make people mutually reinforcing as they go about their unique assignments in the teaching profession. A formalization of statements of working conditions often develops into school policy. Policies are the bonds of productive relationships among people when they are developed cooperatively by all those who are subjected to them. Management has often been characterized as structuring policy to the detriment of progress. Perhaps this idea of management involvement in policy imposition can be developed into a supportive role and seen as a goal rather than as a thwarting influence in a teaching career.

The amount of coordination implied in policy development is detailed in chapter 3. Coordinative policy development is seen as a positive factor in which sharing can become a resource to each individual involved in the teaching act. It means that teachers must continue learning about themselves and about others. In this area of study, self-accountability will again and again become the subject of concern and of challenge.

Accountability is not an imposed penalty. It is rather a reward when one looks positively upon the working relationships with others. With the amount of learning that is required to enter and to remain successfully in teaching, it is hoped that accountability will be looked upon as a challenge to continuous development and an assurance of competence in performance at all stages in the career. The teaching position is situationally subordinate. Creativity within a subordinate position transcends the ordinary concept of accountability and creates a promising alternative.

The individual's qualities and knowledge still must have some additives. These additives can come from the influence and support of other people for they are the expansions of individual uniqueness. Individual uniqueness is essential, but it must grow beyond its original boundaries; in this sense the teacher must always be a learner. The particular challenge or area of concern here is to find ways of working effectively with others. Relating to others successfully whether in team teaching or the development of policy can be labelled *coordination*. Chapter 3 will deal with the sources of coordination in substantial detail. You will discover that some of the greatest resources for coordination will be those with whom you work. There is no intent in chapter 3 to detract from the necessity of self-directedness. Self-direction can strengthen coordination and does not necessarily pull individuals away from the group purpose and group enterprise.

A recognizable truth, nonetheless, is that there may be some inherited management aversions that teachers bring into the profession. These are kinds of things that grow out of previous experience or out of the moods and expressions of others who may have some opposition to what might be called management. Chapter 3 deals with problems of this type and hopefully, some therapy for the individual with management aversions is available. Teacher creativity in working toward goals is stressed.

Expectations for teachers present more positive stimulation than constraints. Yet people often feel burdened with the expectations not only that they place upon themselves but also by those that are placed upon them by others. Look upon expectations as goals rather than constraints and chapter 3 can provide some substantial help. Eventually, the teacher will realize that coordination and expectations can be put together in the form of appropriate educational policy.

Imaging Your Teaching Career

Each individual perceives a reason for being. In a similar manner, individuals perceive differently the teaching career in which they are seeking opportunities for development of self and of the educational program. The reason for becoming a teacher grows out of the understanding of the teaching position and its related responsibilities — in other words, the expectations. It is well to be reminded again that each individual teacher should put him or herself up as an object of analysis and appraisal. This is a more productive subjugation than using one's self-appraisal as the norm for judging others. It means that the ability to adapt to expectations and to situations should be achieved as was outlined in the challenge of working with self and others within the framework of self-confident action outlined above.

The teacher as a learner must develop an ability to judge self. This judgment should be based upon an analysis that provides the kinds of information or data that can contribute to a valid self-appraisal. It might be well to refer to this as the 20-20 perception, in other words, the clearest possible view of one's self. A vision such as this constitutes the image of a teaching career. It is well to see one's self in the truest light so that the best in a teaching career can be achieved. The clear perceptions that the individual has of self and his or her work commitment must be freed from the area of cliches and stereotypes because these may inhibit the individual's capacity for progress. If one retains the cliches and stereotypes about people and about teaching, there is little hope for mastering the kinds of adaptations needed for directing the learning of others.

An assumption easily can be made that when the teacher has

completed all of the requirements for teaching and the certification has been granted, learning can be terminated. It is well to look upon certification only as a key to the opportunity for professional growth in the teaching position. It does not mean that the learning that has taken place is not valuable. It does mean, however, that it is necessary for each individual to be resourceful in finding ways of adapting to the many persons encountered in and around the classroom. Preparation to teach is one firm basis for self-confidence. Knowledge of omissions in preparation should lead to the development of continuous learning activities.

The privileges of learning and of helping others to learn are thrilling and stimulating parts of the teaching profession. Chapter 4 begins to develop these privileges into positive accounts of self-confidence. It is well to keep one's perceptions of self and of the teaching career in proper perspectives which can be preserved. Some people, while observing an individual, do not gain insights into the experience observed. The teacher must learn to master the communication media of those persons who observe and share experiences in the professional activities. Success is not a matter to be achieved according to a time-table set by the individual teacher, but rather success must come in its own time. Self-confidence is a firm base upon which a successful teaching career may be built.

Another way of expressing the development of success is in the thought that responsive accountability is productive and satisfactory. Steady progress is based upon responsive accountability. Accountability has a necessary component of self-analysis and the image of one's self in a career can supply the resources and adaptations required to be a continuing learner as a teacher. Chapter 4 will be helpful in charting the way to this self-confidence through appropriate self-analysis and self-appraisal techniques.

Discovering Educational Influences of Environment

Reference was made in a preceding section to the fact that expectations seem to change unceasingly in character and number. This discussion, which is expanded upon in chapter 2, focused primarily upon the individual teacher and the school assignment.

While some references were made to the fact that outside influences do get into the schoolroom, the emphasis was primarily upon revolving and evolving expectations as a part of the teaching responsibilities. It is well to look at another area of concern and

Figure 2:   Dynamics of the Teacher Career Cycle

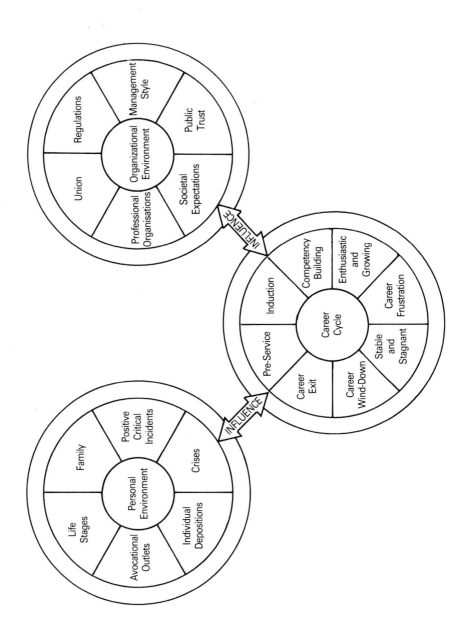

Source: FESSLER, R. 'A model for teacher professional
            growth and development', in Burke P. and
            Heideman R. (Eds.) *Career-Long Teacher
            Education.* Springfield, IL Charles C. Thomas, 1985.

challenge, namely, the influences and expectations that come from the people in the environment of the school. Much more specific detail will be presented in chapter 5, 'A Look Beyond the Classroom'. It is well to do some exploring of the kinds of environmental expectations and influences that come to the individual teacher as well as the school organization. The interrelatedness of environmental influences with a teacher's career are outlined in figure 2. This figure is described fully in another publication (Burke and Heideman, 1985) and will be used as a reference throughout this text.

The individual or the group of educators responsible for teaching at times may feel that the influences from the environment are more to be described as ambushes. Probably the impression of walking into an ambush is more a product of personal perception than it is the actual intent of others. There is no doubt that the people in the environment of the school do desire and intend to impress their wills upon the educational program and operation of the school. This more often is an outward act and seldom is one in which the surprise strategy is planned. It must be recognized in all fairness that just as teachers within the school vary in professional desire and intent so too do the people in the community have similar variations. These desires and intents which are directly related to education naturally become an influence to be reckoned with by those who are working on the school staff.

On the lighter side, it could be said that teaching never was designed for dull moments. Indeed, the students in the classroom, the peers in the school building, and the multitude of influences in the environment produce enough surprises in the teacher's day. At the same time, the teacher must be prepared for these various influences and learn how to deal with them so that the influences are managed rather than allowed to rage out-of-control. In this sense, the light must shine from the classroom just as those outside influences want their light to shine into the classroom. There is a mutuality of purpose here that must be recognized. This mutuality becomes a part of the challenge to the teacher.

Some objectivity is essential in viewing and analyzing influences from the community and in learning to distinguish between aggression, disregard, reconciliation, and possession. Such distinctions can help the teacher learn how to manage those influences which do come from the community. One of the important distinctions that must be made is recognizing the difference between the official and special interest arms of influence. There are legally constituted groups that have a right to contact and influence the school. It is also appropriate, although no legal power is involved, for people in the community either individually or in organized groups to seek to influence the shape of the educational program and the procedures by which it is carried out.

With the objectivity necessary in studying environmental influence and with the kinds of distinctions suggested, the time may come when people recognize that there are reasoners, adapters, conciliators and resolvers in that community who can be positive influences rather than deterrents to the educational program. Chapter 5, 'A Look Beyond the Classroom', gives much more assistance to the teacher making the transition from the classroom to the outside environment and back to the classroom. This chapter suggests a number of ways the teacher can discover and manage the influence efforts originating out of the environment of the school. The separate parts of the environment will be studied individually, and then as a composite to help teachers identify special needs.

Measuring Self to Expectations

The elements of influence, self-evaluation, and expectation have been suggested at several points in this chapter and will be treated throughout the book. In each reference, there has been the inference that the individual must assume the responsibility for learning how to deal with expectations and influences whether they originate within the self, within the school organization, or within the community.

The measuring of self to deal with these expectations and influences involves the concept of adequacy. Immediately, one must raise the question of adequacy for what. Here again the teacher needs to scrutinize personal and organizational goals and procedural arrangements in order to determine whether the expectations are such that they can be managed by the individual teacher or if help must be secured from others in dealing with those expectations and influences. One of the problems in the measuring of self is to determine priorities as one thinks about the influences that play upon the educational program and attempts to deal with them. The mere fact that an influence or expectation exists does not mean that there is a demand for automatic compliance. The individual teacher, in learning how to cope with all of these things, is also measuring self-competence in dealing with such phenomena.

Some thinking is needed in this area of challenge and concern, namely, that of measuring self against the expectations and to achieve a balance between independence and dependence. The concept of professionalism keys on independence of action and self-sufficiency. Too much independence might lead one to be arrogant and to ignore the proposed contacts, influences, and expectations that come to the teacher. On the other hand, too much dependence upon others or upon the school organization might result in a teacher performing in a perfunctory fashion. There must be a balance between aloneness and togetherness which are related to the matter of independence and dependence. There is no virtue in being alone unless the work of the moment can be done better in that way. Likewise, there is no need to postpone doing things until there is a conflict between the individual and others in the organization.

A part of the area of concern in managing influences and expectations is to learn how to scrutinize support facilities such as time availability, materials, and schedules. These are support facilities which can be turned into controls. Here again, the teacher has an area of concern and challenge in learning how to develop self to be equal to the demands of the position. There are conditions of self-reliance and there are limits of self-reliance. This is a part of the area of concern which will be discussed in much more detail in chapter 6, 'The Nature of Self-Sufficiency'. The mutualities of individualism and groupism are well worth scrutinizing in studying self as measured against the expectations and influences requiring attention.

Unique problems relate to success as well as to failure. Success may lead to an increase of expectations to unrealistic and unreasonable proportions. It may be thought that, if teachers are successful in one thing, others have a right to expect success in many things. Failure, on the other hand, gives no relief from attempted influences and expectations. In fact, failure often increases antagonistic attitudes toward the one who has failed. Here again is seen the challenge and area of concern related to self-sufficiency of the individual. Appropriate correlation of ability to expectations as a force to reduce failure is also addressed in chapter 6.

Balancing Independent and Cooperative Action

Individual teachers work in a group enterprise and, thus, must organize their operational procedures in relationship to others in the organization. This calls for decision as well as action on the part of each individual as a continuous learner. Teachers must have the independence to act decisively in the classroom, but their decisions must have the good of the entire educational enterprise in mind.

Success in the enterprise of teaching is a legitimate personal and professional goal. Success is learning and doing. Thus, the individual teacher-learner must find the opportunities for learning both as an individual and as a member of a group. It is probable that others can contribute to the success of the individual teacher. Self-management on the part of the teacher is one of the products of continuous learning but must include a willingness to accept and use the assistance of others. It is unreasonable to assume that any help offered or given by others constitutes an infringement upon individual prerogative or a detraction from the probable success in the teaching enterprise. Self-management in this sense includes the identification of the help that is needed and the use of the help that is available. This is a part of the process by which the individual must chart personal activities so that there can be product assurance.

The process of balancing independent and group efforts may be quite dependent upon coordination with others. This is the reason that frequent reference is made to the fact that a part of learning to be a good teacher and to be a continuous learner as a teacher depends upon the coordination with others who have similar, yet different, responsibilities. The individual, in this sense, can be a product of another person's effort. The ones that can best help the individual to succeed have made a contribution and the individual who received the help is the product of the efforts of someone else.

The products of teaching are direct results of the input of appropriate resources. Everything in the teaching realm must be ordered and sequenced with other activities that are involved in fulfilling the responsibilities of teaching. It is a continuous learning process that is required to keep influences and expectations in proper balance and to work them into a sequence that provides the individual sole and coordinated opportunities to work. Each teacher should recognize that others can contribute to his/her success and that the process of contributing may be satisfying. Contributing to others is better than attempting to solo one's way through the career of teaching.

The arrangement of the coordinated activities and the placement of things into proper time and sequence is a continuous responsibility both of purpose and of action. Setting priorities is another way of saying that everything has a time and a place in a sequence. There must be a choice from these priorities of what will be included in the activities of a particular moment and what will be excluded. This is a part of the balance between the independent/cooperative decision-making identified as an area of concern and challenge. Much more detailed treatment is provided and more specific suggestions with respect to the elements of success (which includes both the process and the product) are presented in chapter 7, 'Success: Process and Product'. These suggestions can help individuals see themselves in the ongoing activities of educational responsibilities and to achieve a balance in personal efforts along with the efforts of others.

Expecting the Unexpected

Expectations placed upon a teacher in a classroom are varied, numerous, and subject to change. There have been some discussions to the effect that expectations can come as a surprise and sometimes have different purposes which vary all the way from support to destruction. It is important to recognize this area of concern and challenge, namely, that expectations are always going to be showing up and it is well to be prepared to 'expect the unexpected' at most any time. Expecting the unexpected means developing one's capacity for anticipation. When situations are anticipated plans of action can be formulated to deal with circumstances as they arise.

Anticipation leads the individual to alertness to the kinds of demands that may be made at some future time. When the expectations become increasingly specific they begin to look more like routine demands, and, thus, become individualized. They present a new kind of problem for the individual teacher to manage. The increased specificity does mean that there is less and less freedom to deal with expectations than would be true were they generalized and yet identified with the current goals of action. Even the specificity of evolving expectations should be anticipated and reaction patterns planned for them.

Much of the determination of expectations is to be found in the perspectives of the individual. Past experiences affect the expectations as viewed by the individual. This reinforces the argument that personal characteristics are determinants of teaching performance and of success in fulfilling teaching responsibilities. With an alertness that comes from the anticipation indicated above, there are some productive results that should be sought. Specific problems can be identified and structured as a result of an analysis of the expectations that are directed toward the individual and toward the school.

One of the difficulties identified in structuring problems in teaching is the ever-changing nature of expectations. There is no way for anyone to maintain expectations in an absolute controlled manner throughout a day and certainly throughout a career. An increasing *variability* in meeting and managing the expectations that present themselves is involved. Changes and inconsistencies are part of any group endeavor. Variability is, in fact, a part of the challenge and should not be viewed as something impossible to deal with nor something that ought to be controlled by some other source. Variability includes a diversification of technique on the part of all of those who are involved in the educational process.

Diversification can strengthen process as long as all of those involved in the activity recognize and agree with the stated goals. It must be recognized here that there are a variety of people, both inside and outside of the school, who are directing expectations toward the school. These people often can develop some outstanding examples of peculiarity in their expectations and, unfortunately, they will continue to exist. These things have to be dealt with and become a part of the expectations that must be managed so that they do not stop the progress of the educational outputs. In contrast, inflexible people who refrain from unexpected patterns of behavior may, through their inflexibility, thwart the progressive action that is necessary to the continuous improvement of an educational process.

Expectations emanate from various sources which act independently and, therefore, are often not coordinated. It is to be expected, then, that the expectations themselves are not coordinated. Source coordination becomes a part of the individual teacher's work in conjunction with associates in the profession. Sources and expectations must be identified and molded into a manageable process before they can be managed. There are resources of rationality such as a commitment to reason, that can be tapped by the individual teacher in the process of learning how to manage the multitude of expectations that come from a multitude of sources. The resource of rationality must originate primarily in the individual teacher who then acts as its source to others. Chapter 8, 'Inherited Merry-go-rounds', is really an expected review of the unexpected impacts and opportunities that present themselves continuously to the teacher who is willing to keep on learning while fulfilling teaching responsibilities. Every teacher has the opportunity and the ability to become a self-fulfilling prophecy in their own development into a master teacher.

Systematizing Multi-task Controls

Expectations, goals, and instructional objectives are individual components which become completely intertwined in practice. There are expectations inferred in the position assignment itself. These are multiple in nature because each student in the class does something to the uniqueness of expectations placed upon the teacher. The goals of the school and the influence of the people in the community all become a part of the task-assignment for the teacher. Based on these goals and the uniqueness of the students, a teacher sets objectives for instruction. This is one of the many reasons why teachers are challenged by, and committed to, continuous learning and improvement.

A necessary task here is one of arranging these multiple expectations into a system that can be used to establish order in the multiple tracts that are suggested and imposed. Chapter 9 addresses this concern directly. The origins of expectations by nature lack any sort of a built-in coordination with each other. The teacher must discover and exercise the controls over the systematizing of the varied expectations that are placed upon the teaching situation.

The teacher is responsible primarily for establishing the coordination among the many expectations. It is important that the teacher accepts the responsibility of developing a professional mastery that can be used to establish coordination of effort and purpose. It may appear that the teacher is one against many. The appearance is more than just a vague notion — it is real. There are many origins, many people, and many expectations emanating from those origins. The teacher has the responsibility of developing and learning the systematic procedures for identifying, analyzing, relating, prioritizing, and expediting the activities that are generated by the expectations. These are the requisites of management skills needed to establish the systematic control and use of expectations.

The variability of expectations creates a kaleidoscopic effect that causes them to appear a little differently each time they occur. The reason for the difference may not be that the expectation has changed but rather that it occurs in a changing environment with changing personnel. There are some complicated situations that must be systematized and coordinated, and it takes deep insight on the part of the teacher to accomplish this. Such is the nature of the area of concern and challenge related to the multiplicity of the impacts experienced by teachers as they go about their professional activities, particularly in the classroom.

Systematic management is necessary for acceptable consequences to flow from this multiplicity of influences and expectations. Systematic management becomes one of the tools of the teacher and must be learned and mastered in order to keep the educational process on track. It is a matter of teachers learning to control and to cope with these expectations. Coping means coordination and management of the multiplicity of expectations, pressures, and influences experienced by the teacher. Chapter 9, 'Management of Expectations', offers many clues to the control potentials of the expectation parade. Take advantage of these clues and develop the individualized system that can bring about a coordination of effort in the face of the multiplicity of influences and expectations playing upon the teacher and the classroom.

Mastering Variability and Adaptation

The *variability* of expectations and influence has been emphasized at several points in this chapter and will continue to be emphasized in the chapters that follow. Variability is a simple indication that most things just will not stay as they are. As a matter of fact, it probably would be unfortunate if they did. There is a need, however, to design and master those procedures through which management can occur. There is no use trying to achieve this mastery over the expectations by deciding which ones can be discarded and which ones used. The only sure way of approaching them is through the process of role adaptation. Adaptation of personal goals to expectations within the environment is essential, and keeping the main objectives of teaching in mind while doing this is a necessity.

Even recognizing that things will not just stay as they are must be accompanied by an awareness that the individual teacher also does not remain the same. Each experience occurring in the classroom, with peers on the school staff, or with people in the community immediately sets in motion a growth pattern through a series of differentiating perceptions. The teacher must recognize the changing nature of everything in the environment as well as in the staff, and particularly the changing nature of self. This means that, if greater mastery can be achieved, learning must take place. It is impossible for the teacher to survive without establishing a study of self and environment as an approach to the control of things that affect teaching and learning in the classroom. A personal growth program for development as a teacher must flow from this study.

An easy concept to espouse is that the management of variabilities occurring must be characterized by equality and fixed treatment. This, however, may increase the inconsistencies in the situation. Strategies must evolve from the particular situation rather than follow a rigid pattern of treatment.

Adaptation, however, means that the ingredients of every current situation can be used in the next situation. Adaptation means that the individual takes what is and changes it so that it will apply to what is to be. Equal and fixed treatment would deny this type of variability and probably could result in nothing other than failure on the part of the teacher and of the educational outcomes anticipated. Relativity becomes important in determining the degree to which one move shall be made and the degree to which another move shall be initiated. The relative importance of the purpose and of the action and relative seriousness of the consequences of action or inaction, become the variables that must be studied in the teacher's mastery of the adaptation demands.

The personal competence of the teacher, while including some skills and characteristics beyond the systematizing of the control factors, must be characterized by a generous amount of compassion for others. This is the only way that coordination can become a cooperative enterprise and the only way that there can be mutual support and contributed help. Concern for and sensitivity to others becomes a part of the mastery that the teacher must achieve in order to be the controller of the adaptation process.

Variability has been referred to above as diversification. Diversification or diversity unmanaged can be disruptive to the teacher and the teaching process. But when the diversity is managed, it is a source of strength both to the teacher and to the processes of establishing and maintaining an improved outlook on educational programs. Variability is seen in this area of challenge and concern as being managed only through the processes of adaptation. The challenge to the teacher is to develop a 'Mastery of Adaptation,' which is the title of chapter 10. Chapter 10 can help each teacher cope with the adaptation demands, and this becomes a part of the basic contribution that the teacher makes to the educational process of continuous development.

Anticipating Professional Futures

Each individual involved in a teaching process is assumed to have an ambition to continue in teaching and to be successful in that effort. This means that the teacher as a learner must have as a goal a continuous development of self, organization, and the educational program. This is a part of anticipating the professional future. It is not to be accomplished alone but rather cooperatively as a part of the educational process and movement. Purposes held by individuals for the success of their future create a desire for professional growth on their part. The purpose itself is a stimulator as well as a director to the efforts that are put forth.

The ability possessed by an individual is essential as a support to the achievement of professional growth. The application of ability tends to sustain the vigor of the individual to continue as a learner and as an aggressive person in improving self as a part of the educational organization and facility. The awareness of ability and competence provides a pyramidal effect on future challenges. That is why the concept of continuous development is one that must characterize every teacher in the improvement process.

The awareness of the competence that brings this about or makes it possible is the pyramiding effect which has the achievement of one purpose as the source of the establishment of a new purpose. The new purpose in turn commands imagination and ability to do those things which will bring achievement to the new purpose and so the process continues. This is why *induction, renewal,* and *redirection* are seen as continuous development. Horizons do exist for each individual as they envision their professional future. Individuals must look beyond the horizons of future and define the problems that exist there. The problems that are encountered and developed are for solving. They are the elements which challenge the individual to seek improvements throughout the learning process for one's self within a group endeavor.

The hopes and ambitions that develop as one progresses in this effort to improve are for fulfillment. These hopes and ambitions, in turn, provide height to the pyramid upon which success is the apex. Accomplishment in this sense becomes a part of the reason for the vigor that goes into continuous development. Accomplishments are for sensing. Individuals have the right and the obligation to sense the things they achieve as a product of their own insights and efforts. The continuous development processes bring about the support for this concept of growth as a part of the professional future. Chapter 11 offers some highlights and spotlights on continuous professional improvement. The suggestions presented there constitute a summary of the specific areas of challenge and concern that have been outlined in the previous sections of this chapter.

Chapter Organization

The references made in each of the sections above indicate that each identification of an area of challenge and concern simply presented a brief introduction to a more detailed study of the chapters related to those sections. These have been indicated in each of the sections with suggestions as to how the detailed chapter can support those who are willing to recognize the identified area of challenge and concern. The challenges and areas of concern themselves will not disappear, of course, even with the mastery of the individual's ability to establish self-management controls over those things which constitute the concerns and the challenges. It would be unfortunate to lose even the desire to meet new problems and to resolve them simply because the ability has been developed to achieve the controls of the moment that are indicated as desirable. All of these areas of challenge and concern are applicable to career stages, thus the matter of continuous development is the element of the pyramid which brings each individual teacher to a higher level of desire and a higher level of career accomplishment.

The desire of the author is to help readers who are engaged in the induction, renewal, and redirection processes to see themselves as a library of resource material that can help in the mastery that brings about improvements in the individual and in the program. The Aids for Self Development at the end of many of the sections are offered as helps to the individual teachers to study themselves, using their own experience and learning as resources to perfect and polish their professional skills. These exercises may also serve as discussion topics for group review of the reading material.

This book can be helpful only to the extent that the individual wants to be helped. At numerous places in the text, you will find statements to the effect that help is not help until it is used. It is the hope of the author that the reader's use of the suggestions made in the various sections and chapters will provide the stimulation to (a) maintain and increase the probability of success in the induction process; (b) welcome the invigoration originating in the renewal process; and (c) recognize the benefits of adaptation in the redirection process. Recall now the summary suggestions in the Preface that *development* is the descriptive term for continuous improvement, which is dependent upon the three main action thrusts of *induction, renewal,* and *redirection*. These three terms (induction, renewal, and redirection) will appear parenthetically throughout the text as a reference for the actions described as continuous development toward improvement. The shifting sands of a teacher's environment should be continually in mind as one reads the following chapters, and reference to figure 2 regarding this environment can help to form a coordinated picture of continuous teacher development.

Chapter 2

You and Your Assignment

The way you see yourself is called self-perception. Self-perception exercises much influence over the way you do things. You may not be very aware of the fact that the picture of yourself that you hold in your mind is exercising much control over the way you behave. You have a perception of your teaching assignment and this perception will influence the way you fulfill the duties and expectations of your position.

One of the controls over your behaviors is in the selection and retention of certain life goals. You have chosen to be a teacher. How do you see yourself as a person when the picture in your mind puts you in the classroom? Perhaps you have never analyzed nor even been particularly aware of these self-perceptions as controls over your behaviors. It is good, then, for you to give some attention to self-analysis in order to find out what kind of person you are. The purpose of this book is to help you analyze the influences you yourself place upon your own progress in teaching so that you can maintain control over the processes of development. Success is not the automatic result of a degree, a certificate, or a contract. These only open the gates of opportunity. Success may be thwarted if you omit the privilege of analyzing. Analysis is your weapon for resolving the real and imagined barriers to your desired accomplishments and it is your vehicle in pursuit of effectiveness in teaching at any point in your career. This particular chapter is designed to help bring you and your assignment into a more rewarding relationship.

The desire to achieve at a high level and the desire to improve steadily in a chosen field of work is properly a part of your self-perceptions. Your perceptions of yourself and of your assignment may change with experience and, particularly, when you work with students and professional associates. Your choice now is whether you want to control your self-perceptions or whether you will permit others to impose their control. You may choose to let others maintain that control but your growth will be more stable if you chart your personal and professional development under your own primary direction. The impacts of others can be sources of stimulation (induction) without absorbing your self-will and self-direction. The thrills of expression and realization (renewal) as a creative person, however, may be lost when the control over self-perceptions is yielded to the dominance of others. The distance between self-determination and alter-dominance is an uncharted area that is well worth your scrutiny.

A bit of self-determination (redirection) at this point in your career may make you a self-stimulating and self-directing person who has mastered the ways of securing and using the help that others can give without letting these others control you. The important assumption is that some help, in fact much help, may be needed from other people. Such help most often comes from those who are called supervisors. The more meaningful supervision (development) will be that which *you* stimulate, invite, and direct for *yourself.* The development of teaching style, however, needs both the invited and the assigned types of supervision.

The accomplishment of a relationship with supervision of either type requires careful analysis of yourself as an initiator of opportunities. Chapter 3 will detail the first steps in becoming a self-directing teacher with a substantial improvement potential which includes the skills of relating with others in a coordinated manner. You may begin your self-analysis as some selected cultural handicaps are identified below.

Throwing Off Cultural Handicaps

The people who constitute your human professional environment may have fixed in your mind the idea that what always has been always has been because it should have been. There is nothing very unusual about people thinking that way. It is usually more comfortable to think in terms of staying as you are than to think in terms of ways of changing or improving. Perhaps that old notion of 'what has been is good simply because it has been' may reflect the extent to which a cultural status has been appropriated by people who lack the energy to remake themselves.

Some more serious and burdensome cultural inheritances nevertheless might engulf you. Some of these need-to-be-questioned ideas are:

1 *A Person Knows Herself/Himself Better Than Others Know Her/Him*

Proximity apparently is the reason why people think that the person knows herself/himself better than another who can observe her/him. Counselors, consultants, advisors, psychologists, and psychiatrists established careers on being able to make wise observations of other people. It seems, then, rather foolish to settle for the idea that nobody can help you because you know yourself better than any other person possibly can. You are your own best source of help, but this should not exclude the help that can be available from others.

2 *A Person is the Same Person in all Circumstances*

People get the notion that whatever makes them behave as they do in one situation is going to be there when they behave in another situation and, therefore, there will be a continuity of types of behaviors. As a matter of fact, it is fairly clear now that individuals behave differently, even almost as different persons, depending upon the group and the situation in which they find themselves. Unless individuals become aware of their own many-faceted being, they are unlikely to be able to maintain mastery over their own self-perception and, consequently, may behave the same way in all situations.

3 *A Person who Employs Introspection is Using Self-therapy*

People who believe that introspection is self-therapy may fail to question whether it simply identifies those things which can be an object of worship and, therefore, maintained, or which can be an object of concern and, therefore, corrected. Introspection is always a therapeutic experience. Introspection, however, is one facet of the analytic process. The individual must maintain a base of objectivity if introspection is to provide a measure of self-therapy and personal growth.

4 *A Person Cannot Trust Anybody*

Cynical people believe that Diogenes must have been right when he carried his lantern in the hopes of finding an honest person. It does seem to be rather cynical at this time when, even though the news media bring stories of malfeasance in life, many people place confidence in love as the greatest human trait. There can be no happiness in believing that fear and distrust march with you every step of the way. You may need to develop some means of knowing the benchmarks of trustworthy people but you need not deprive yourself of all possibilities of association and assistance simply because you stay on the alert.

5   A Person is Secure in Trusting Herself/Himself

This has come from a long line of poets, religionists, and people in the helping professions. Perhaps it has much truth in it so long as you define the range of things to which it is to be applied. You need to be true to the best part of yourself. The best approach, then, is through some rather thorough self-analysis in order to observe those best parts of yourself that are worthy of your self-devotion. Look around for a few other selves that may merit emulation. Then, you can be true to your evolving capacity to select the best of you and others.

A struggle may occur for improving self-perceptions in the complex of cultural trappings. There may be many influences in our environment which seem to work against the kinds of activities and kinds of attitudes necessary for the improvement of self-perceptions. Highly inflexible people would be happy to reduce all of life to a formula. This might be pleasing to those who desire to exercise control over others. Fear and the sense of insecurity lead many to accept subjection to others in the multi-faceted influences playing upon the individual in this complex society. Hopefully, you will choose the better course of rational determination of your personal and professional behaviors.

One of the aspects of winning the battle for improved self-perception is that of developing the ability to distinguish between reality and imagination. There are no specific tests from others that can be offered to you. The best way, even though it scarcely can be called a test, is that of talking to another person and reporting specifically some of the kinds of things that you see about yourself. A trusted colleague often will be able to detect whether your analysis is based upon reality or upon imagination. In this case, the supervision simply would be visiting with someone in whom you have confidence and having a free exchange of opinion about some of the things that you hold to be true.

6 *A Person is Burdened by the Natural Conflicts Existing in the Environment*

Natural conflicts such as male versus female, supervisor versus teacher, and parent versus school can be found. Too often people are not willing to analyze their conflict experiences in terms of whether the conflict is natural or contrived. The point here is that, if individuals are victims of a cultural cliche the mere fact of believing that the cultural conflict exists will cause them to behave as though it really does. This is an instance in which reality has been subjected to imagination. Analysis of the interaction between two or more people is the only basis for determining whether there is a natural or a manufactured conflict that grows out of a problem situation of the moment.

A general notion or assumption also exists that any constraint from an outside source tends to stifle freedom and creativity. Perhaps attention should be given here not to a question of whether the source is another person, or agency, but rather to a determination of whether it constitutes a safe-guard or a constraint. Here, again, a test of reality versus imagination is needed. This must be determined by your own judgment. Determine whether you feel that the suggestion of an expectation from another person, whether that person is a supervisor, a colleague, or a fellow teacher, might or might not make the difference to you. Remember, the constraint is the important thing to study.

7 *A Person must Recognize that 'Upward Mobility is Position-bound'*

In other words, if you strive to be better, if you strive to secure approbation, if you seek a status of prestige and recognition, you can do this only by getting a position that comes at higher prestige rating in the hierarchy of positions. Practically, the monetary advantage of position has been the basic ingredient in the concept of upward mobility. Recent success in negotiating teachers' salaries may challenge the whole idea of what constitutes upward mobility. There are some hopeful signs on the horizon such as the recent work in teacher career ladders. Some people believe that the upward mobile person is one who seeks to do better the assignment which she/he has accepted rather than simply to move up on the hierarchical position scale. Here, again, the tests of reality and imagination might clear up the handicap better than any other procedure.

Self-development is based on the premise that people will change if they see a need for change and if they have a major role in effecting any needed change. Sometimes it is helpful to have self-analysis and self-development structured in order to view one's self in an orderly way on the basis of information collected. Here is the first of a series of *Aids for Self-Development* activities in which you become the source for data to determine change. In each of the aids there are single and direct questions or statements which will elicit your response.

. . . .

Aids for Self-Development

1   Make a list of six personal characteristics possessed by you and that influence your performance as a teacher.
2   Use the list of personal characteristics, identified above, to determine:
    (a)   the characteristics that have the most and those that have the least influence on your performance;
    (b)   the characteristics that may appear positive and those that may appear negative to other people;
    (c)   the characteristics you developed by yourself;
    (d)   the characteristics that were developed with the help of others.
3   Identify the most serious personal problem you have had to resolve. List alternative solutions to the problem. Explain why you resolved the problem as you did.
4   Identify the most serious teaching problem you have had to resolve. List alternative solutions to this problem. Explain why you selected the solution you did.

. . . .

Management of Strengths and Deficiencies

Advice comes from many quarters indicating that each person should gain some skill in determining the existence of her/his own strengths and deficiencies. The question can be raised immediately, however, as to whether yours or another's strengths and deficiencies concern you most. The assumption made here is that your own should be your major concern. It is well to recognize, however, that in the casual conversations heard in most informal groups, it would seem to be the strength and deficiencies of others that get the most attention. This may or may not mean that the emphasis of importance or priority is based upon the others or self. It is well to be aware, however, that as you think of strengths and deficiencies you might analyze both those that may exist in you as well as those that may exist in others.

A proper question may be raised as to what business it is of yours when the strengths and deficiencies are in others. The converse query also may be raised as to what business it is of others when your strengths and deficiencies are involved. Others may be concerned with your strengths and deficiencies because that may be the very thing that makes their work easy or difficult and effective or ineffective. The extent to which you are concerned with your own contribution to a professional enterprise may determine the relationships of your own strengths or weaknesses to those of others. Since others may be affected by you, it is well to make an assessment occasionally as to how the strengths or deficiencies of others (induction) may be affecting your work.

Your strengths perhaps are not reinforcing others as much as they could if you are not permitting the interaction. Deficiencies may be overrated or cause a myopic view of your performance record. Regardless of the rationale arrived at in the determination of where the strengths and deficiencies lie, one must be realistic in recognizing that there are penalties both in success and in failure. There might be penalties at times which appear in the form of ridicule. Ridicule is a most unkind type of reaction for yourself or another person. Some penalties may involve a rational adjustment, imposed by one's self or another, which is directed by objectives that are not always apparent. One must learn not to be disheartened by the disparagements that arise from others as a result of one's own success. This is true in almost every area of life's activity. Those who can perform well often are perceived with envy by those who cannot perform well. Those who cannot perform well often are looked upon with disdain by those who can perform well.

The above types of negative procedures, reactions, or treatments are non-productive and not representative of the kinds of things expected of you as a member of a group that has accepted a common objective, namely, the education of youth. Probably the best therapy for getting over the habitual ways of acting that people have developed over time, is that of learning (renewal) to share mutually. It is recognized at the same time that sharing is a delicate maneuver in the relationship of people. There is such a thin line between support, protection, discipline, and abuse. Good intentions may be misread by the receiver of a kind act. A friendly offer of a professional book or of an instructional strategy could be resented by a peer who wrongly thinks your offer is to shore-up a weakness. Protectiveness even may be a most wholesomely motivated action on the part of one person and yet be misinterpreted by the receiver of that action. Offers of assistance must be accompanied by a tactful approach.

People who are dissatisfied with their interactions with others may seek some basic means of discipline — anything from ignoring a person to an outright attack and abuse. It is hoped that an understanding of the way that groups work together and of how they can reinforce each other may substitute (redirection) for some of the more negative types of observable interactions that exist in many of life's enterprises. Perhaps the greatest skill that can be developed by any individual who is working in a group, is that of intelligent compromise and purposeful adaptation. Compromise is seen by some as a weak action and an adaptation as an attempt to steal an idea or procedure from someone else. This need not be the only interpretation of what these words indicate. A compromise does mean that two or more people may have to make some adjustments and adaptations of the purposes and procedures as well as the ways of estimating whether their goals have been attained. When this is accomplished, the individual and group establish a base for seeking and finding mutually acceptable goals and procedures for achieving them. For many people the development of the skills of compromise and adaptation may be the re-shaping of one's own assumptions and beliefs. The people who chose to live by their own assumptions without ever having challenged them, may be the ones who are standing in the way of compromise and adaptation. Certainly, these interactions have an influence on all parties involved. These experiences will discourage some and stimulate others.

The least helpful of all of the ways of dealing with this problem of relative strengths and deficiencies is the temptation to find a solution through concealment. In other words, the bright students in the class have demonstrated sometimes that rather than be called 'the brain' they choose intentionally to do poor work that will cause them to get somewhat less than the top grade. This is unique not only for the students. Teachers and administrative officers sometimes seek to conceal the things that they are doing which they know to be successful but want to avoid jibes that might come from some of their colleagues. Here, again, the best therapy for this kind of a temptation is in self and project analysis (development). It must be recognized, however, that having gone through the trouble of analyzing one's own purposes, actions, and outcomes, there must be a description offered to someone as to what the analysis has developed. This other person becomes a referent point or reference judge for determining the status of one's own activities. The determination of this status may be enhanced by comparison with the person who is evaluating the analysis. Let it, at least, resolve itself into the simple rule that, if it is worth analyzing and describing, you must have someone listen to you after you have completed these two activities. At the same time, you must recognize that, if it is good for you to have someone to tell, you inherit an obligation as a member of a group enterprise to listen to someone who may want to tell things to you. This might be helpful to you and most assuredly would be helpful to them.

These *Aids for Self-Development* should help you to list suggestions that will give you assistance in deciding how to handle the strengths and weaknesses in yourself and others.

. . . .

Aids for Self-Development

1   Identify a teaching situation that you have experienced as being difficult.
   (a)   What strengths did you bring to this situation?
   (b)   What were your weaknesses in this situation?
   (c)   Who in your circle of acquaintance (students, teachers, principals, friends, etc.) recognized your strengths and/or weaknesses and reported their observation to you?
   (d)   What assistance did you need?
   (e)   What helped ease your induction to change in this situation?
2   Identify a situation where one of your colleagues admitted failure in a teaching unit.
   (a)   What strengths did this colleague have?
   (b)   What weaknesses did this colleague have?
   (c)   How did you help this colleague identify strengths and weaknesses?
   (d)   Did your comments help renew confidence and mastery for this colleague?
3   Identify a situation where a peer gave you some constructive criticism regarding your teaching.
   (a)   Describe how you reacted to this criticism and/or suggestion.
   (b)   How would you constructively criticize a peer in a similar situation?
   (c)   How were you able to redirect your teaching?
4   Identify a classroom situation that involves a problem with one

student. Describe your personal strengths in resolving this problem
with:

(a)   other students;

(b)   parents;

(c)   administration;

(d)   teaching peers;

(e)   the student.

5   Select three friends and see if they are in agreement with your
estimates of yourself and your relationship with others.

6   Review your own analysis and establish four or five personal
guidelines which seem logical for you to follow.

. . . .

Self-Improvement Is Not a Ritual

The complex nature of each individual demands unique strategies for
each person's self-improvement. Some strategies may approach commonality but they must not be sought in a ritualized way. There is a
much more creative and positive way to work. The individual ought
not to misinterpret the purpose of advice and the widely accepted
approaches to improvement but it is essential that ready-made procedures be adopted only by rational choice. The most important personal
obligation is that you make a choice of your particular way for
improvement.

A new type of working relationship is emerging (induction)
between fellow-workers as well as between those in different levels of
authority. This is the concept of 'quality circles'. Respect for associates
displaces fear of superiors or others who may perform at levels different
from those of your own. This respect, as a displacement of fear, makes
it possible for more creativity to be developed in one's self-improvement (renewal) efforts as well as in using the help offered by
others. There can be nothing ritualistic in relationships if individuals
identify the purposes and accept the changes that have occurred in the
relationships among people in group enterprises. These changes in the
relationships in the organizational effort, however, are not an invitation
to irresponsible action. It is wise for individuals to sharpen their
definitions of the nature and limits of authority and autonomy. It is also
wise to think carefully about the relationship between authority and
autonomy.

It is well to speculate on what would happen if autonomy should become the ritualistic control that was true in times past when authority was the only means of the management of an enterprise involving people of professional stature. A part of the reason for this change in the concept of authority is the recognition that the greatest authority is not position-bound at all but rather is a by-product of success in the individual's responsibilities. Those persons who have proven in the past that they can perform tasks effectively are those who can help others. They are persons who will be attributed by others with the kinds of abilities that make for success. The concept of leadership has changed in a similar manner. Leadership now is the characteristic (redirection) of persons who demonstrate by performance the ability to solve problems, to anticipate needs, and to recognize the resources available in their colleagues.

Each person has a certain amount of uniqueness. Your uniqueness may catapult you and your work situation into a contrast with others of a different uniqueness. This does not necessarily mean that one is wrong and the other right. It does mean that you have an opportunity to observe the uniqueness of another person but not necessarily to *adopt* as opposed to *adapt* those uniquenesses to some of your own. This is the break away from the ritualistic concept of self-development that existed for so many years past. We are beginning to recognize that being different is not being wrong, but neither is it being absolutely right. So deeply imbedded is this concept that you have to be different from the crowd that it gets misinterpreted to mean that unless you are different you cannot be right. Some, but not all of the differences among people need to be harmonized. Many of them can exist in harmonious relationships and still remain unique. The most important thing is not to look at the process by which the uniquenesses occur but to the purposes for which they exist.

Much more harmony exists among the ultimate goals, or even among the intermediate objectives of the members of a group, than differences in the ways they go about achieving those objectives and goals. It does mean that someone, you or the other person, must have not only the capacity but also the willingness to mediate when the objectives seem to indicate that the uniquenesses are in conflict. Here again it is not necessary to go into a ritualistic procedure in order to have objectives and goals duplicated between all members of the group enterprise. The main thing is to mediate to the extent that, so long as a common objective is held fairly constant, people are free to exercise their own creative ways to achieve those objectives.

Thus the old concepts no longer prove to be adequate. These

concepts that used to say 'do as you are told,' 'go to a group briefing,' or 'read a professional publication,' alone could not change you or others. The old concepts invariably resulted in conflict in process as well as purpose. This then is the break away from the ritualism of the type cited above.

You have personal responsibilities to establish mutually rewarding relationships between you and your work environment. A part of your work environment includes those other people who also have the task of achieving harmony between them and their environment which includes you. Analysis, a study of discrepancies, a seeking of alternative ways of doing things, and objective judgments are not ritualistic behaviors. They are the creative evidences of the break away from ritualism. You really are on your own and you can achieve self-development only if you choose to develop. If you choose to develop, you cannot turn the process over to someone else. You can seek and get much help from others, but in the end it is a personalized effort on your part.

These *Aids for Self-Development* will help you analyze yourself as an improvement potential. That is, in your role as a teacher, you should be able to identify activities that have the potential to lead you to improvement.

. . . .

Aids for Self-Development

1 List specific examples of induction activities you have experienced as a teacher in each of the following categories:
   (a) as a person (for example, 'I put pep into lessons');
   (b) as a professional (for example, 'I speak at faculty meetings');
   (c) as a planner (for example, 'I try new teaching methods');
   (d) as a communicator (for example, 'I listen to what other teachers say');
   (e) as an evaluator (for example, 'I ask students to evaluate my work');
   (f) others (list).
2 Determine whether your experience with each of the activities above has been frequent or infrequent. If infrequent, is there potential for development?
3 Outline a development plan to support the activities you have selected in number 1 above.

4 Discuss your professional development plan with selected colleagues and see if some of them have the same needs as you. Make plans for redirection or renewal based on these discussions.

. . . .

Help Is Where *You* Find It

The invitation, as suggested above, is recognition that others possess resources that can be of help to you. Such help probably becomes available more from the way you invite it (induction) than from the other person's skill in sharing. Many people are sincere in wanting to help others. There are, at the same time, people who love to meddle into other people's business without having a clear intention to be either helpful or harmful.

The individual needs to keep aware of these extremes but needs also to develop and maintain an awareness (renewal) that some offers of help are in good faith. Any other conclusion about the offers of assistance would tend to deprive the individual of much help that perhaps has led to a level of success that already has been achieved. The necessity is to develop skill in the resistance of generating suspicion in the mind, when an offer for help is volunteered. Perhaps it does not have to be voluntary. Even when help is requested, sometimes it is easy to become suspicious of that person who attempts to help.

Some of the types of help to recognize (redirection) are:

1 Friendly commendation from someone who has observed us in action.
2 An enquiry about how things are going.
3 A direct suggestion as to what might be an easier or more effective way of accomplishing a task.
4 An invitation to compare what another person is doing and to see if the success of one is equal to, better than, or poorer than that of another.
5 The 'here's how I do it' type of offer, in which a person is simply saying, 'here's the way I do it, would you react to it?'

The above suggestions on how to recognize the forms of available help, and they can be only a few of the many different ways that help could be available, may depend more upon the receiver's attitude than upon the quality of help being offered. In such cases the receiver's attitude (the receiver is you) and how the receiver accepts the offers of help become very important determiners of the quality of that help. A positive suggestion cannot be accepted in a negative way without having suffered some loss of quality. As you deal with those people who are available or even who offer help, it is important to be able to ask questions in order to clarify not only their intent but, more importantly, the substance of their suggestions. The teacher needs, then, to develop the skill of asking discovery-type questions rather than rapping-type questions. This is renewal.

Discovery-type questioning is for the intention of understanding. Rapping-type questions are for the purpose of subduing those who have approached you either by an offer of help or by asking to interact with you about your professional work. When something new has been suggested to you, try it. You do not have to adopt the entire suggestion but rather to try some part of it, thus seeing whether you like the idea. When you have made such a try, go back to the person who made the offer of help and report what you see as your success or failure in using the suggestions made by that person. Then, jointly ask 'why?' It is just as important to know why it was successful as to know why it was a failure. These are some of the ways in which you can find help. It takes active interest and effort on your part if you are going to accept the help that is so easily identifiable and accessible. This is redirection.

These *Aids for Self-Development* are to assist you in identifying sources of help and analyzing your responses to suggestions from others.

. . . .

Aids for Self-Development

1   Summarize a recent suggestion for development you received from a colleague in each of the listed areas:
    (a)   teaching techniques;
    (b)   classroom management;
    (c)   curricular planning;
    (d)   instructional supervision;
    (e)   peer influence;
    (f)   teachers association activities;
    (g)   others (list).
2   For each suggestion listed above, how was your action related to the suggestion or recommendation? Classify your reactions as induction, renewal, or redirection.
3   Describe those situations in which you were able to develop a better way than that suggested.

4 Start a notebook of these suggestions. Indicate who made them, and your reaction to them.
5 Make it a point to interact with those individuals whose names continually recur in your notebook as giving beneficial suggestions to you. Share your experience of improvements with these people.

. . . .

Making Your Supervisor Effective

References to the sources of help in your teaching activity, as indicated earlier in the chapter, have avoided labeling the supervisor or the administrator as either a chief source or the best source. The most important posture that you can take is to avoid the notion that the teacher-supervisor relationship is a contest. It is not a contest. If it is one, however, you need to raise the question as to whether you or the supervisor made it that way. In all probability, if you turn back to the last section on 'Help is Where *You* Find It', you will realize that your supervisor, by whatever title, is there as the most easily accessible person in the whole school organization who can offer concrete assistance to you or can become that other person who would be valuable in listening to you about your self-analysis.

The availability of a supervisor is something that the school has provided for you. The supervisor is not there just for purposes of organizational control. You must remember that, if you have some sensitivity as to your relationships with the supervisor, it may be equally true that the supervisor has some sensitivity about relationships with you. The influence of this relationship is depicted in figure 2 in the organizational environment under management style. Supervisors are often responsible for where an individual is in their career cycle.

There is always the uncertainty of the experienced person who associates with the less experienced person in determining whether a contact would create tension or assistance. So the supervisor perhaps is waiting for an appropriate opportunity to do for you what supervisors can do. The way that you go about using (induction) the help of the supervisors may be the one major factor that causes supervisors to work harder for you than they would have done had you not initiated the contacts. These contacts are not those in which you have to flatter the persons in the next level of the hierarchy in order to win brownie points for yourself. This might be the most disgusting opener for the supervisors that you possibly could devise. Why not be matter-of-fact about the job that you have to do (renewal) and the job that the school must have wanted you to do when they accepted you as a member of the staff?

The ease of interaction between you and the supervisors probably is more dependent upon the way you behave than upon the way the supervisors behave. Remember that mutual satisfaction on the part of two people, peers or otherwise, is more than the sum of two individuals' satisfactions taken separately and independently (redirection). Teaming, even if there are two members to the team, has many merits to be considered and, perhaps, adopted.

These *Aids for Self-Development* will help you make an analysis of your approach to a supervisor. They should help you think through what you want to talk about with your supervisor.

. . . .

Aids for Self-Development

1 State whether you feel the responsibilities listed below belong to you as a teacher alone, to your supervisor alone, or to both you and your supervisor jointly:
   (a) development of the goals of education;
   (b) statement of the objectives of an instructional unit;
   (c) preparation of instructional materials;
   (d) selection of evaluation criteria for teaching;
   (e) determining professional development needs;
   (f) final evaluative report on teaching;
   (g) others.
2 List the ways a supervisor can be a resource person for developing those responsibilities that you have identified as yours alone.
3 Identify ways you can have influence on the renewal or redirection of those things that are the sole responsibility of your supervisor.
4 Discuss your responses to number 2 and number 3 with your supervisor. Be frank about your own reactions and recognize that your perceptions may be improved.
5 Plan a schedule for joint evaluation with your supervisor for a list of interests and issues that may emerge and for which you will seek the counsel of the supervisor.

. . . .

Inputs, Throughputs, and Outputs

The center heading indicated above includes some of the words that seem to be appearing increasingly in the professional literature of recent years. It is important that you develop some sort of a definition of terms so that, when you see the word input, you see something besides a child being fed into a machine called the school. The word input includes all of the preconditions necessary for you to interact successfully with all aspects of your assignment.

What are the conditions that make it possible for teachers to do what they have been trained to do to help students learn? What are the conditions that make it possible for students to learn what they are capable of learning? Is success in the total enterprise attributed to the arrangements for the activities of both the students and the teachers in what is called *throughput*? The *throughput* or *process* of education includes all of the activities that are occurring during the teaching-learning events. These are the things that the teacher and the student do as they use the inputs to seek the goals which have been agreed upon as a proper purpose of the school. When that has been done, you have the term output, which means goal accomplishment. The output is the determination of whether the support facilities have been wisely utilized, whether learning in all of its many aspects has been accomplished.

A clear vision of the dependent inter-relationships of *input, throughput*, and *output* can lead you to a state of objectivity in your perceptions of you and your assignment. Objectivity will help you to establish good working relationships with your professional colleagues, your students and the laymen in your school environment. It all adds up to freedom to be creative — creative (development) with the help that is made available to you at the hands of many other people, as well as the abilities and ingenuities that you bring to the task of teaching. Freedom to be creative means that you must be self-confident.

The Next Step

Many teachers seem to feel that their preparation for teaching has been completed whenever they have completed the courses required in the major content field or when the specific methods courses have been taken. This is a case of over-confidence which needs to be modified somewhat so that the realistic confidence in one's own personal-professional preparation can substitute for the closed-mind approach to the viewing of one's own preparation. Considerable attention will be given to the necessity for viewing the things that other teachers do and the ways that they do them when they get into an employment or clinical situation. The assumption that the latest word from the campus is the most correct often creates a dysfunctional relationship between a teacher and teaching peers in the local school assignment. Attempts will be made to establish a procedure of analysis that will help to put your own preparation and the products of other people's preparation into a proper perspective. Some emphasis will be given to the fact that every problem that can develop in a school system and in a teacher's classroom does not have a ready reference as though in a card file to a certain page in a textbook so that the remedy may be found easily. Some people appear to think that the solution to major and minor teaching problems is about like looking up the proper name of a physical difficulty in the home-doctoring book which has a specific treatment for every malady.

The approach of this book is in the direction of increased self-analysis in an environment of interactive people. A base will be sought for achieving individual development in an ever-improving group enterprise. The initial support for that base is identified in the goal-coordinated relationships. Chapter 3 'Sources of Coordination', will present many specific concerns in the development of coordination and the individual's contribution to that achievement.

Sources of Coordination

Teaching is a group enterprise. Teacher–pupil, teacher–teacher, teacher–administrator, teacher–supervisor, and teacher–parent are but a few of the connections that indicate continuous interaction and involvement. Each interaction has a unique contribution to the educative process, and the uniqueness of one should mesh positively with the uniqueness of another. This meshing is a process of coordination. Strength and effectiveness of individuals are enhanced by the relating or coordinating of each individual in a systematic group activity for every stage of staff development.

The word *coordination* stimulates a great variety of images in the minds of people. Some of these images come from the direct experience of working in a group with a common purpose or in a group of individuals each of whom has a purpose wholly unrelated to the others. The purpose in either instance might have been the same, but the way that individuals go about their specific tasks could vary widely. *Coordination*, then, is the action of bringing together diverse actions to a common purpose.

A distinction between the motives of actions and the observed overt behaviors of colleagues is often difficult to make. Regardless of any bias based on previous experiences, it is helpful and necessary to develop an understanding of a person's relationship to people. The next step is to direct, or coordinate those relationships to work toward the common purpose. In its most negative view, this coordination may be the personal loss of freedom to be a self-directed person. In its most positive sense, it is the rewarding synchronization of human and material resources that leads to self-realization in goal achievement.

Management is a primary source of coordination. You are managing when you walk into your schoolroom with full responsibility to summon your students to the building, to your room, and to control them in terms of learning activities. Without institutional management, however, the teacher would have to buy, deliver, and distribute needed supplies. Without organizational management, the teacher would be engineer and building custodian as in the early days of the one-room school. Many of the support services that are taken for granted now were not always available in what might be called the pre-management era of public education in this country. The presence of support services relieves the teacher of many management tasks and thus releases more time for teaching. This freedom is nurtured by the coordination of space, materials, and persons involved in the total school operation. This coordination constitutes a positive influence from the organizational environment of a teacher's career as depicted in figure 2.

There is an important discriminating responsibility as individuals think together about this business of working in a coordinated group. This is the determination of whether what they think and what they see are real or imagined influences and controls. Most of the stereotyped concepts of influence by others involve a great amount of control. Indeed, control is essential to coordination but much of coordination may be in the teacher's own hands, who then would be the one exercising the control. Think, for instance, how free the teachers are of influence by others at the school building or school system levels when they close the classroom doors and begin to teach. Aside from some coordination requirements such as change of class periods, rest breaks, mid-morning milk services, etc., there is only limited control exercised over teachers in the classrooms.

Consider whether concerns about regulations, particularly if the teachers feel some antipathy towards the existence of constraints at all, are attitudinal fixations as opposed to externalized influences. These attitudes, represented in figure 2 as the personal environment category of Individual Dispositions, can find expression in many ways. It is well to consider whether internalized control means that the control originates only within the individual (personal), whether it originates within the building or within a school department (organizational), or whether it originates in other environmental expectations. Perhaps it originates by some other choice which makes it internalized only because the teacher chooses it and not because it has a unique control dimension.

Consider externalism as being those influences and controls which come from outside the building or from outside the school system. The impositions made by a legislature when laws are passed might be considered an externalized control (Societal Expectations). Yet there is no reason why the people of a community cannot use their legislative bodies to set up the limits within which the internalized controls at the local level may take place and achieve proper purposes. Again, the positive way of thinking is the more helpful one as responsibilities for coordination are considered. Pass over the psychopathic cases both on the part of the school administrative and supervisory staffs as well as the psychopathic reaction of those who are in positions subjected to constraints. Such cases deal in an area that is not rewarding for teachers and it also deals with a small percentage of the total professional population.

Concentrate on the two-way potentials to be found in coordination and living successfully with group-normed guidelines. In many ways group norms provide an enhanced freedom of choice, for the teacher, for the school staff, and for the school system. The enhanced freedom of choice arises from the fact that the rules of the game are known and the total system personnel are protected against the unfair impositions of those who would control for wrong purposes. A clique within a school staff that wished to impose its will upon an entire faculty is just as much an undesirable constraint facet of school operation as is a psychopathic administrator, supervisor, department head, or group leader. In this sense of enhanced freedom of choice, there is reciprocity. In other words, if the teachers can receive the guiding dictum and find ways of living with it rewardingly, they will find in turn that service and support advantages come as a result and in terms of reciprocity. These are the balanced benefits that can come from the two-way potentials in a proper view of coordination.

Another source of coordination is the process of progressively constructed relationships. This means that, if the kind of freedom exists within internal and external influences as indicated above, the construction or reconstruction of relationships can be like a learning experience. Consider five major contributors to the processes of progressively constructed or reconstructed relationships which are listed here. Each will receive some discussion in later sections of the chapter. They are as follows:

1   Relating to shared responsibilities.
2   Describing unique contributions to outcomes.
3   Reviewing the variety of acceptances.
4   Revising plans.
5   Enjoying realizations.

Watch for the concepts as they occur and recur in the discussions which follow. Many different words will be used to add meaning to these contributors as the concepts continue to expand. Continuous development through *induction,* *renewal,* and *redirection* will gain added depth. These terms will appear parenthetically throughout the next sections to relate the discussion to the main theme of development.

Rationale as a Source of Coordination

The archaic notion that administration and management exist as a strategy only to control others has been dissipated in many organizational efforts. It takes some rugged objectivity to dispense with the old notion that a word such as management stimulates in order to achieve some of the newer elements of a rationale by which intra-group relationships can be seen as mutually beneficial. Rationale, then, is the underlying reasons or principles for actions.

The strategies of control used in schools were resisted through many decades primarily because no one bothered to attempt an understanding of what constituted the rationale of coordination in the first place. Smilarly warped assumptions developed about the term *teaching.* Teaching can be looked upon as the efforts of one person to maintain control over others (learners). The orderly view of learning strategies becomes the rationale for the management of a classroom. Those who fail to scrutinize the rationale may oversimplify the processes of coordination and become dissident individuals. It is clear that co-ordination does include controls, but only those controls which have a workable rationale. Even when the rationale exists, there needs to be a periodic review to see whether the goals of the organization and the environment in which it seeks to achieve these goals have changed enough so that a new or modified (redirection) rationale might be advisable. When there is no rationale at all, the influence or control practices need to be brought under critical review as to whether they should continue to exist. Often it may be simply the fact that no one ever bothered to scrutinize the rationale; therefore, none existed. If a rationale for coordination can be developed and is found to be satisfactory, there is no reason why this cannot constitute a clarification of the role of control in group action.

The question properly can be raised as to whose responsibility it is to initiate a clarification of what constitutes coordination in order that a rationale can be identified and appraised. Generally, the responsibility is posited in the administrative or supervisory offices. Often, however, the administrator or supervisor is unable to determine in a unilateral manner whether the existing controls tend to handicap or to stimulate those whom they are designed to influence. In this case it is much wiser that the responsibility for initiating clarification (induction) be taken by the subordinate-in this case the teacher. The teacher, in order to fulfill such a responsibility, must have some skill in the analysis of coordinative activities.

The responsibility for clarification at this point has been dealt with only in terms of those who should initiate such clarification. The most rewarding action would be in the development of a relationship among administrators, supervisors, and teachers. A systematic procedure might be developed for bringing the appropriate mechanisms and their rationales under scrutiny with some degree of regularity and without embarrassment or fear of penalty to anyone. One of the characteristics of personality that has made it difficult for anyone to initiate clarification activities is the fact that there has been a lack of mutuality in determining procedures. As indicated above, the most rewarding approach would be a mutually accepted responsibility for clarification. It means that such mutuality, because of our current pattern of interrelationships, would require a mutuality of rejection that coordinative controls have only one source.

One way to move beyond the purely academic type of approach to this clarification is to go directly to a discussion of the tasks to be performed by all members of the organization. This means that the coordination activities or behaviors can have meaningfulness for task accomplishment by individuals in organized groups. Moving to the task oriented type of consideration of the effect of coordinated mechanisms would reduce the all-or-nothing over-simplification to a minimum. The possibility of more task-centered consideration might encourage more creative strategies (development) for influencing people to make palatable contributions to group purposes. View this as an extension of the preceding chapter dealing with 'You and Your Assignment'.

The resolution of highly personal and emotional charged consideration of controls must be dispelled through a series of positive activities leading to joint planning (redirection) designed to achieve joint controlling with effective coordination. The people environment of this day, however, tends to fractionalize staffs to a certain extent. In other words, teachers negotiate for what they need and the administrative and supervisory personnel tend to negotiate separately. Perhaps in due time maturity will occur in the negotiations process and less effort can be wasted on one trying to out-do the other.

Increased objectivity in the analysis of coordination may lead to a consideration of whether the so-called constraints of organization offer a control that is less, equal to, or more satisfactory than control by peer group agents. When a school staff delegates to an agent, or to a small group of teachers, the negotiations of those conditions which are deemed to be essential in carrying on the teaching act most effectively, there is the possibility that individuals may or may not agree with those who are taking over this function. An unorganized group of teachers may include dominant personalities that tend to take over the decision functions for a majority of the teachers. When this occurs, there has been peer control to a greater extent perhaps than that which administrators and supervisors exercise. Here again, there is no reason to assume that it is wrong for one teacher to attempt to exercise leadership over peer teachers, but it is wrong to assume that there is no need to analyze the activities and impacts of such teachers with respect to the essentials of coordination.

The rationale for coordination is highly important and a scrutiny of the process perhaps may be the greatest therapy for relieving frustration. A thorough knowledge of the analysis process is an essential skill in coordination. Individual members of a teaching staff probably have no choice as to whether there will be controls exercised. This does not mean that individuals are being done wrong but rather that they are operating in a group in which some degree of orderliness seems to be demanded of all personnel. An extended imagination can see the school with no controls as somewhat of a fenceless jungle.

For example, teachers tend to look upon the equipment in their own classroom as belonging to that classroom and to being somewhat exclusive with respect to their control. *Midnight requisitioning* means that a peer simply walks into the room, takes a globe, a map, a set of books, or removes some piece of equipment that perhaps was heavily depended upon by the teacher. This is the kind of a fenceless jungle that one could live in without protection of privacy or without rationale for coordinative activities. Rationally, however, it must be said that the fenceless jungle, as well as unreasoned control, give little choice of preferences since both are highly objectionable. A sensible control, with the rationale known, gives the individual the greatest freedom and opportunity to go about the chosen tasks.

The *Aids for Self-Development* given below are designed to help identify the sources of coordination in your teaching experience. They will identify their origins and reveal a rationale that sustains them.

. . . .

Aids for Self-Development

1 Identify one rule which affects intra-group relationships initiated by:
    (a) the board of education;
    (b) a statute;
    (c) the faculty;
    (d) yourself;
    (e) the administration;
    (f) the state department of education.
2 Make a list of other rules and identify the initiator(s).
3 Identify influences other than rules that you have experienced in relation to:
    (a) administration;
    (b) curriculum development;
    (c) instruction;
    (d) supervision;
    (e) evaluation;
    (f) extra-curricular activities;
    (g) other professional tasks (name)
4 List alternatives to these influences that are related tc your role expectations.
5 Using the categories from figure 2, list in two parallel columns the influences that:
    (a) facilitate your teaching activity; and
    (b) interrupt or thwart your teaching plans.
    After each item in each list, identify the source of influence in parenthesis.
6 Ask a colleague to use this approach for the purpose of comparison with your findings.
7 Make a list of things that will help you understand your role more fully. Periodically check back over your record of progress and extend your list.

. . . .

Security as a Source of Coordination

The theme of the preceding section dealt with the fact that roles, rules, and regulations could be put into harmony and could exist in a mutually helpful fashion. The understanding of your own role as well as the role of your associates, particularly the role of your supervising staff, gives you a sense of security in knowing not only the source of the expectations directed toward you but also much about their nature.

Responsibilities for the commitments which are made are not generalized types of things. They are specific, in fact, just as specific as the expectations that are placed upon individuals. When pondering the nature of responsibilities to one's self, to the school organization, and to professional colleagues, it is well to think of these in terms of expectations that each has for herself/himself as well as those that each has for others. It becomes particularly important to the sense of security as one looks at self in association with the others of the school organization. Knowing the role of the supervisor, however, does not suffice in so far as determining the supervisory expectations that are placed upon the teacher. One of the tasks found in the role of the supervisor is to communicate the expectations (induction) that are designated for each assignment. These cannot come only from the professional preparation programs. Adaptations (redirection) must be made to the local system and to the local people. These expectations and their adaptations must be known and understood at the time of initiating any new or revised assignment.

A great sense of independence or autonomy (renewal) may be felt in declaring one's own competence to determine personal expectations. This constitutes *security* in one's position. It is well to keep in mind those areas in which expectations are self-determined. Individuals, however, probably do not know the limits of such areas until they know the limits of autonomy that are granted in the particular assignment assumed in the contractual relations with the school district. Much self-determination perhaps would be granted by school policies but to experience self-determined expectations, purely for the purpose of experiencing the process, is not the kind of rationale that will make one an effective member of a professional group. It is not necessary to sacrifice, however, all of your prerogatives of self-determination. It is an individual's responsibility to find out the balance that can be achieved between the imposed expectations and the self-determined ones.

The early stages of a teaching position (induction) seem to stimulate the development of some expectations that are wholly unrealistic. They may be unrealistic from the standpoint of the volume of work that would be involved. They may be unrealistic from the standpoint of support facilities that can be made available by your professional associates and by the school district. It is well to inject into the dream department a certain scrutiny which will help to differentiate the illusions and improbabilities from the practical realities of self and other person expectations that you may wish to assume. As a volume of expectations is accumulated in any particular position, there will be times when some sort of a sanctuary from the pressure of the tasks that crowd in upon the daily tasks must be sought.

One of the persisting problems both for the beginning and the experienced teachers is to face unresolved problems (redirection) without hiding behind a presumed expertise that grew out of special-ized training at an institution of higher learning. This is why reference is made occasionally to the unneeded sanctuary of credentialism. The fact of having had courses, just as the fact of formal preparation for teaching, does not guarantee a readiness to meet every type of problem. Self-analysis, in fact, becomes an important skill and it reflects the realities of the hopes that people have for themselves. It is well to review one's own credentials or competencies to see if they need to be strengthened (renewed) from time to time but never assuming that credentials constitute the proof of worth. Continuous development is essential.

The above statements suggest that there are varying levels of self-satisfaction. Recognize the fact that, in some areas of work, the highest level of satisfaction can be realized because of a competency in the skills and knowledges required for that particular task. Keep these experiences in a proper balance by not assuming that great strength in one area will guarantee recognized strength in all other tasks that become a part of the expectations in an employment position. The fact of varying levels of self-satisfaction is no signal at all that one should view any segment as a weakness. Rather, it signifies that one person can have highs and lows in expertise. There can be high self-satisfaction in the high levels of expertise as well as in the ability to recognize those instance in which there is a need to seek out and use the expertise of others.

A supervisor also has varying levels of self-satisfaction in meeting the supervisory tasks. One supervisor might excel particularly in the area of audio-visual applications to the instructional strategy. Another may have high expertise in the area of measurement. It is not to be expected that each one can master all of the major tasks imposed upon a supervisor and at the same level of expertise. There is no cure but there are some helps that can be offered (renewal) to the ups and downs of the experiences based upon these varying levels of expertise and varying levels of self-satisfaction with work tasks.

Develop a confidence in yourself and your supervisors even though all may exhibit these varying types of reaction patterns which are not to be viewed as weaknesses. It means that, as you go about observing yourself and analyzing the relationship between you and your supervisors, you develop (redirection) certain self-monitoring skills. High among these skills would be that of appraising the identities of your areas of high expertise. It is well at the same time to develop the skills of observing where you have low expertise and to view, without alarm, the fact that you may be doing an ordinary or less than ordinary job in some areas. You may have some future work to do (renewal) in order to improve your professional services.

These *Aids for Self-Development* are to identify expectations that you place upon yourself, some that are placed upon you by teachers, and some placed upon you by administrative and supervisory staff.

. . . .

Aids for Self-Development

1 Describe a performance expectation you have for yourself in an administrative task (for example, 'keeping attendance records').
2 Write a performance expectation that you think other teachers have for you in the area of curriculum development.
3 Ask students to write a performance expectation that they have for you in instruction.
4 Write what you think is a parental performance expectation for you in the area of performance evaluation.
5 Write what you think is a performance expectation of administrators for you in the area of supervision.
6 Explore other expectations and indicate the persons you believe to be the initiator(s) of each.
7 Design several professional development activities that will increase your efficiency in the performance of each expectation you have identified.

. . . .

Policy as a Source of Coordination

Policy is a good means of keeping the way ahead clear of those hazards encountered as conflicts with interests that are antagonistic to your own as a professional. When policy is not established you operate on the basis of expediency. Seldom does activity based upon expediency result in a high level of consistency of behavior or of coordination.

Policy is a general statement that gives direction to action. It is well to identify the general statements that are designed to give direction to your action (induction). The purpose of policy ideally is to provide assurance that the talents of people in pursuit of organizational goals will result in self as well as organizational satisfaction in accomplishments. There are occasions when policies seem to be antagonistic to each other. When these inconsistencies are observed and if they impinge upon the behaviors of individual choice, it is well to go to the sources of policy-making and indicate the nature of the puzzlement resulting from the lack of clarity or of consistency between two or more policies.

Policies give direction to action and in this sense the process is regulatory in nature. The people in the community expect the board of education to express community policy with appropriate action. The board, in turn, commissions the superintendent to act for it in carrying out the policies adopted. The direction of action really follows the hierarchical lines of the organization. This does not mean that, at a given point in the hierarchy, the teacher acts improperly in seeking clarification when there are conflicts or inconsistencies. The immediate supervisor probably is the one most responsible for monitoring the implementation of policies so far as individual teachers are concerned. The immediate supervisor is a logical source of clarification. It is not necessary to follow the hierarchical line to the origin of a policy in order to seek a clarification and possibly to initiate new policy statements (redirection) which can iron out the conflicts or inconsistencies that may have developed.

The allocation of enforcement tasks does not exempt teachers from receiving such a delegation. Many of the policies have to do with students and their parents. Such policies become a director of action for individual teachers as they go about their professional duties. Each individual is an important link in the chain of policy implementation. Each individual can become a facilitator of a policy, an advocate of a new policy, a changer of old ones, or an escapee from responsibility by saying unkind things about those who made the policy in the first place. It is well to remember that those who made the policies may have made them at different points in time and with different kinds of pressures from different kinds of problems.

Somewhere along the line of professional experience one will experience some of the hang-ups of non-direction. This means that people who are in a position to establish, implement, and monitor them, may prefer to operate by the decisions of expediency of the moment. There is little that one can do about it if the supervisor or the people in the community want to keep it this way. One can be very frank in reporting, however, that the frequent variations of directions which may come in the form of rules and regulations or specific requests of performances make one a less efficient person in directing the activities of instruction — the basic purpose as a teacher.

A proper approach is to ask the supervisor, principal, or super-intendent for the statement of operating policies for the district. Study these, ask questions about them, and, particularly, seek information (induction) as to the interpretation by others as to what directions they see the policy suggesting. In this way one may become an important figure in eliminating the non-directiveness in a complex organization. There are certain needs that must be fulfilled. Teachers want the respect of the people in the community, and the administrative officers in the school system. They may not know what particular kinds of need deficiencies and satisfactions an individual might have. Many of these can be revealed in a discussion of policies and the actions that they infer. Talk about the policies and make them clear in your own mind as to what kind of directions they are suggesting for professional behaviors.

These *Aids for Self-Development* are to help you determine if regulations are consistent with developed policy.

. . . .

Aids for Self-Development

1   Identify a regulation which is most important to you in each of the following areas:
(a)   attendance;
(b)   grading;
(c)   supervision;
(d)   teacher in-service;
(e)   audio-visual;
(f)   budget;
(g)   field trip.

2   Add regulations from other areas. Separate the regulations into those that are acceptable to you, and those that are unacceptable to you.

3   Determine whether each regulation you have listed is consistent with stated school board policy. If it is not, explain why not.

4   If there is need to redirect yourself concerning regulations you have identified, outline a professional development activity that will facilitate the change.

5   Ascertain whether your school system has a procedure for analyzing and changing policy.
   (a)   If a policy exists, select a 'minor' change you would like made and test the procedure.
   (b)   If a policy does not exist, visit with your administrator to determine if such a procedure could be developed. Move slowly.

. . . .

Teaming as a Source of Coordination

The preceding section gave substantial emphasis to the necessity for policies and regulations in order to produce a smoothly operating group in an organizational setting. Earlier in the chapter there were some discussions of the problems of controls and how to deal with them. We turn now to another type and a much more voluntary aspect of the matter of interacting with colleagues.

Each person wants to have the feeling of an identifiable part in the action of the organization. This desire for identity requires no apology. Each person may react differently to the amount of satisfaction that comes with identity. Perhaps an even more fundamental urge on the part of all individuals working in a group situation is that of having a sense of belonging to the group. This is a matter of more than identity because identity is an individualized type of awareness. Belongingness means that the individual is recognized as an integral part of the group that constitutes the professional staff of the school. Often there develops a kind of tension between the maintenance of identity and the achievement of a sense of belonging. Individuals place priorities upon one or the other and perhaps no one can keep them in complete balance. The successful struggle is consummated when the individual can achieve both identity as an individual in the group and the sense of belonging to the group and its purposes.

Individuals can experience a sense of identity and belongingness while being quite aware that each one has unique competencies. If each member of the group can see values in the expertise possessed by herself/himself and others, it is possible to find a rationale for the resolution for what might be called equal shares. The concept of equal shares, however, gets generalized when it should be held more specific. If one person, for instance, has recognized expertise far above that of other colleagues and the group is confronted with a decision or some planning in the area of that competence, it seems foolish that all members of the group should claim equal shares in the influence over others as a decision of planning proceeds. Each one has to be a party to guaranteeing to colleagues the recognition of an equal or unusual competence and, at that point, to graduate the sharing of controls and influences according to the contribution that can be made.

Many occasions arise when equal sharing can be generalized for the entire group. The biggest problem is to have this concept of general sharing with unequal bases of contribution carried through all interacting activities of the group. A test of unequal competence and equal sharing well might be found in what can be called the initiation-to-completion process of whatever activities may be at hand. Again, if one person has exceptional competence in the task at hand or in the skills required for that task, that person probably can move from initiation to completion in record time. On the other hand, a person of little competence in an area of low expertise, will find the gap between the initiation and completion too great to be acceptable.

The discussion about equal sharing may be viewed now in a somewhat different way. The person with high competence should feel called upon to offer more than an equal share of ideas, effort, leadership, and implementation than those who have less competence. It is to be hoped that in this process a person of high competence will not lose caste in the group because of the envy of those who have low competence in this particular area. There are many things that can be shared other than the expertise or competence as used in the illustrations here. All can share in achieving the commonality of the acceptance of the goals of the organization. All can share in contributing to the development of policy and controlling regulations which will help them to operate as effective individuals and as a group.

Review your own aspirations to see whether priorities with respect to identity and belongingness support or thwart (renewal) the skills of self-appraisal of competence and the appraisal of the competence of others. Some persons, who have not found success in gaining their identity and sense of belongingness, tend to give up and go into what might be called a posture of martyrdom. Some want to make this martyrdom well observed by others. Others tend to express their satisfaction with martyrdom in terms of silence and withdrawal. None of these are to be recommended. The best cures for martyrdom are found in vigorous action of the types that are discussed earlier in this section.

Some behavioral goals within a school seem to draw people to them as a rewarding and fast way to achieve whatever it is that they want in the group enterprise and in the teaching assignment. If it is power, then, in all probability, the magnet that draws them to a particular activity will be the opportunity to exercise personal control over others. If they can reason out of the endemic urge to achieve power, they can choose ways (redirection) of making their own special competencies serve not only the purposes of their own in the classroom but the purposes of their colleagues and of the school as an organized unit. The key to the solution of the problems of satisfaction of aspiration, avoidance of martyrdom, and the proper pursuit of power is to be found in the interaction between yourself and your colleagues.

These *Aids for Self-Development* are structured so you can list things that you have found in your school experience that give you a sense of identity in the group. You can also identify the special competencies which you feel that you have and which you feel that your colleagues have.

. . . .

Aids for Self-Development

1 Name four things in your school experience that give you a sense of identity. (For example, 'I suggested a new attendance procedure'.) These are your *identity indicators*.
2 List competencies for each of the identity indicators you named above. (For example, 'I have the ability to organize'.)
3 Determine the competencies of your colleagues that would complement the identity indicators you named above. (For example, 'Ms. B. has ability in supervision'.)
4 Identify times where you are a *contributor* of expertise to your group.
5 Identify times when you are a *consumer* of the expertise of others in your group.
6 Choose appropriate self and colleague competencies that will harmonize the expertise of both and increase *group identity*.

. . . .

Synthesis of Goal and Process as a Source of Coordination

The utility of goals is to give direction rather than to provide a prescription for achieving them. Process is much more individualized than goals in a group activity in which the responsibility is to take the pupils to the desired goals as established by the school. Sometimes, teachers feel that they have not had an opportunity to participate in the setting of those institutional goals. This often is true. Governmental bodies have implemented a goal-setting prerogative, and they have a legal right to do so if they choose. It does not mean that the goals established by a legislature are as good or better than the school-determined ones but it does mean that the right to determine goals must be recognized. The local board of education also may engage in goal setting and it must be recognized that the board is operating within its legal rights. Both the legislatures and the school boards, however, are inclined to accept input from professional or special interest groups. This is an appropriate direction to be moving and should be given careful thought by professional groups as to how to cooperate in that enterprise.

A carefully designed process of goal setting must exist. If the idea of goal setting is accepted, (and it will be encouraged in this book) then, each teacher and each group of teachers, in fact all members of the educational profession, must accept some responsibility individually for determining a somewhat uniform process for goal setting. The uniformity itself need not be rigid, but it needs to result in an orderly exchange of ideas among those concerned. It would be worth your while to find out just who made the existing policies and what was the process by which they were developed. Study your role as it really is or as you would like it to be in the process of goal setting for the educational enterprise.

One of the goals that might be developed from the process which you would help to create might be the goal of the goal-process determination itself. Think for a moment of the possibility that, in determining the kind of process to use, the importance of setting a goal for process determination is to secure as broad an input from all professional workers as is possible. Your own contributions can be a matter of rewarding self-realization if you share in the processes of goal setting and in contributing to a philosophy that results in the goals of process determination. Bringing together as many diverse organizational thoughts as are implied here, calls for a synthesis of the thinking of many people, many special interests, and many persons of diverse individual purposes. It will require, as does any synthesizing activity, fertile imagination.

Try in your imagination to think the thoughts of some of the students with whom you will have to deal. Try to imagine how you think they may think you are thinking. This is the kind of imagination that might bring on a synthesis of action (renewal) that would be good for the process of goal setting and for the goals of process determination. As you work along in this type of activity be certain that you keep an active respect for alternatives. The people who thwart group action more than anyone else are those who have only one way, and one way does not leave room for the accommodation of alternatives which represent the basic conditions of coordination. The essence of survival is found in the strategy of your ability to locate imaginative alternatives (redirection) and your ability to do some transacting of compromise with others who have alternatives in mind. This kind of process is available to rational people only. When people have closed their minds to alternatives or when they have chosen only one way of going, they have lost the rationality that makes it possible to do the sort of goal setting and goal-process determination required in coordinated effort.

These *Aids for Self-Development* will identify goals which you observe, as well as some of the processes which may or may not be in agreement with the achievement of those goals.

. . . .

Aids for Self-Development

1 State four goals you observe at the present time. (For example, 'An integrated career education program.')
2 Look at each goal and identify the process to reach the goal. Write down the steps in this process.
3 Identify the cases in which the goal and process have not merged and have generated antagonisms.
4 State a professional development activity that is possible to improve the merger of goal and process.

. . . .

Creative Subordination as a Source of Coordination

The central concern in this chapter is *coordination*. It has been looked at from a number of angles, most of which were intended to be of the positive type. Among the aspects of coordination, however, it is well to accept certain realities and recognize that it has not been void of some negative inferences. The cultural imposition for many people is that a state of mind has been created in which the organizational structure is designed to put people in a straightjacket and thus achieve coordination.

Normally the culture would indicate that the boss is above you and heads the hierarchy of controls in the bureaucratic system. Many observing people realize that the most underestimated boss in the system is the subordinate. At the present time, many of the chief administrators in school systems are feeling the whiplash of organized subordinates. In this sense, being a subordinate does not create the dominance that subordinates may imagine. If you listen to the talk of your colleagues, particularly those who are very conscientious about teaching the students assigned to them, you may find that the most over-estimated and underrated boss is your own subordinate, namely the student. Students are beginning to organize and to demand some of the rights from teachers that teachers are requiring from the upper echelons of the school organization. Whether or not it is a matter of control for personal purposes, it is a subject for appraisal.

The 'bossism' that is found in the subordinate may be simply the gentle expectation that the subordinate places upon the superordinate. In other words, you may feel that your students have confidence in you and, consequently, expect much of you. They are the ones who keep you working late at night rather than some remote power figure in the bureaucratic design. Somehow there is a challenge in the bossism that students impose upon teachers by way of confidence and expectations in the teachers' abilities to help them. A clue could be taken by the teachers at this point from the students and they might make their own subordination to administrators and supervisors more creative. By allocating respect, confidence, and higher expectations in the administrative superordinates, you might get them to feel (induction) that their bosses have subtly imposed many extra hours upon them and yet meet it with enthusiasm.

Creative subordination produces few victims of weariness and restlessness. Weariness and restlessness often comes from that state of mind which dictates that management and superordinates are proper targets of destruction. The lack of power to destroy them or the choice of martyrdom as a means of living with them, often does result in weariness and restlessness on the job. One of the creative things that can go with subordination is to identify with the successes and failures of an enterprise. For too long, teachers solely have been blamed for educational failures. Assurance of relief from blame can be gained now from the fact that those assessing the accountability of the schools are looking to many of the support facilities, and certainly to the unique contributions that can be made by support personnel such as administrators and supervisors.

Your analysis of the reasons for success or failure may bring into the action, in a creative way, other people who can help to identify the causes of success or failure and in the process may find themselves as responsible as you. Here again is a suggestion that is not one to be used in reprisals and general accusations but rather to be used as a creative act (redirection) of a subordinate. Within the ranks of peers, there will be differences of opinions and even opponents of specific decisions and actions. With the traditional view of the relationships between super-ordinates and subordinates, in other words, administrators, super-visors, and teachers, there are points of differences and sometimes each is considered the opponent of the other. Here, again, is the importance of the state of mind that makes it possible to view an opponent as likely to be loyal as to be disloyal. In other words, to signify the right of those who differ with you probably will strengthen your own right to differ with them and display, again, a mark of creativity on the part of peer or subordinate.

Demonstrate the fact that you are an intelligent person and that you are able to accept an institutional purpose in a group without either destroying or being destroyed by those who come up with some different notions in the way things are to be done. In all probability, the state of mind referred to at the beginning of this section can be cured primarily by your own realistic observance of the kinds of reactions that characterize you. To the extent that you can do this, you will find introspection an excellent self-therapy. Try to discover the extent to which, when you walk down the hall in your school, you affect every person you meet. Think back over each day for a while and consider the kinds of response that you gave to the students, to your colleagues, or to your supervisors. Sometimes you may recall that there had been a point of differences. Could you and the person(s) involved talk in terms of alternatives? Were you or were you not a person who could identify the extent to which you had personal responsibilities in affecting the output of the other? Increased contact is a great part of the therapy. But contact, in itself, is no good unless you are able to achieve positive results in a creative and interactive way.

These *Aids for Self-Development* will assist you to look at yourself as a subordinate to others and as a person who has subordinates sitting in the classroom.

. . . .

Aids for Self-Development

1   Identify examples of creative suggestions you have made or can make based upon your induction in each of these areas:

(a) curriculum;
(b) budgeting;
(c) scheduling;
(d) instruction;
(e) extra-curricular;
(f) grading;
(g) special education;
(h) policy implementation;
(i) needs assessment;
(j) competency testing.

2 Select those suggestions from item number 1 that you would change, or redirect, if you could relive this encounter. Describe this redirection.

3 Check your perceptions, identified in number 2, with at least one superordinate, one peer, and one subordinate.

4 Determine your follow-up in terms of professional development activities based upon your discussion.

. . . .

Accountability as a Source of Coordination

This is the age of *accountability*. One can scarcely pick up a professional or organizational magazine of any type without finding some attention given to the topic of employee accountability. It has not been limited to those employed in educational institutions but has been extended to management in business, industry, and government. Accountability is the word because people seem to want to know whether they are getting their money's worth.

How can the teacher or anyone working in the school organization harmonize the desired professional freedom with the accountability demands that are placed upon them? Turn back to some of the earlier sections in this chapter, particularly the one dealing with participation in determining the goals of process determination. Certainly this is a point at which the professional workers can join patrons in many interests of life. This is occurring more often and is increasing in the amount of success that is generated in the discussion of school issues. This is a much more rewarding direction for the teacher and supervisor to move than it is to reduce the teaching action to the level of quackery in order to detour the accountability demands. Quackery used here means that one can easily confuse the non-educator as to the kinds of accomplishments that are identified. It is easy to put on a show of what one is doing while, in the process, concealing the results that should be forthcoming in terms of student development and learning.

The accountability that is conceived here is one of open and free interchange between the teacher and all others who have expressed an interest in the school organization and its outcomes. This is more productive than one in which accountability is viewed as a competition between the non-educators and the educators with the educators resorting to a type of quackery in order to confuse the group that otherwise you could not subdue.

One of the things that will stimulate the harmonizing of freedom and accountability in an environment of accountability demands is to be a contributor of much accurate information. Auditing the process of teaching as well as the outcomes of the teaching-learning effort might do much to put at ease the minds of those who are demanding accountability. The notion that you can use standardized tests as a simple measurement of all of the outcomes of the school has been indicated time and time again as being inadequate. You as a teacher can find many types of information which you could collect, organize, and release, that would give much better light to the specifics of the progress of the school. Taking the information that you as a teacher individually can develop and release, there is some guarantee of insurance in the fact that you then can help the public as well as your colleagues to develop the criteria that will permit a wiser interpretation (redirection) of the information which you have accumulated.

A teacher can start out with a job description and performance expectations that was the basis for the employment in the first place. Earlier in the chapter there was some discussion of the importance of having a clear understanding (induction) with the administrators and supervisors of the school system as to what were the performance expectations. These can be kept in mind not just at the beginning of the school year, but throughout the school year as a continuing assessment on the part of the teacher.

One of the more important guards to set up at the outset is to take the position that you would like to have these sorts of conferences at some time other than at the end of the term or at the end of a period for which accountability seems to be levied. This is called on-the-way conferencing, and ought to be available to you on a weekly, bi-weekly, or daily basis if you feel that you are needing it. In all probability, your initiating this sort of conferencing about the data collected by you, the criteria based upon your job description, and the performance expectations might lead to a creative relationship between you and your supervisor. This would establish you very early in the accountability system as being a person who knows how to get knowledge and as a person who is knowledgeable. Perhaps this in itself would establish a stature that builds confidence in you on the part of your colleagues, administrators, and supervisors, as well as the lay people in a community.

Think of the personal rewards that come from not sitting back and waiting for accountability to strike you but rather of moving out aggressively in fulfilling an accountability program of your own initiative. The rewards can come in the form of frequent *advice* in gaining someone who will become an *advocate* on your behalf and certainly for those who admire your objectivity and ability to analyze your own professional activities. *Approbation*, then is due to you. So the Triple-A Accountability for you to remember is *Advice*, *Advocacy*, and *Approbation*. The Triple-As are as essential to coordination as they are to accountability because accountability leads to a mutuality of interaction in a context of common purpose. An understanding of the power and utility found in the sources of coordination will assist you greatly as you analyze your new assignment.

A Look Ahead

The chapter opened with the thought that coordination is a descriptive term for the satisfying and productive interaction of people. An educational program would not exist without the coordinated activities of people whose contributions are mutually reinforcing. Reference was made many times in the chapter to the benefits accruing to each individual as the realization of personal contributions were sensed and acknowledged.

Coordination, then, contributes to successful group action and stimulates the individual to strive continuously to maintain and increase personal and unique resources to the tasks assignment and total educational program commitment of the school.

The result of experiencing efective coordination gives support to the evolving and developing self-respect and self-confidence of the individual teachers. Coordination of program activities and individual self-confidence are reciprocating in effect. More specific treatment, then, will be given to self-confidence in the next chapter (chapter 4), 'Bases for Self-Confidence'. As you study the specifics of that chapter, relate to the analyses of coordination found in this chapter, 'Sources of Coordination'.

Part Two
Settling In

Bases For Self-Confidence

Lack of confidence in one's self is among the major ways of inducing failure. Lack of confidence is easily observed. Usually, lack of confidence in self generates a sense of insecurity and even a failure which becomes evident in the frequent hesitation in the way one behaves. Lack of confidence is but one step from under-confidence and either state is a handicap. Possession of confidence on the other hand makes it possible to perform in a manner by which training and experience build capability. Individuals can undermine their own contributions by feeling less than capable of performing the tasks at hand. Lack of capability may or may not exist, but to create it as a result of lack of confidence or under-confidence is most unfortunate. It is essential, therefore, for all teachers to develop a secure basis of self-confidence about their profession.

The person with a wholesome amount of self-confidence is easy to observe. There is a firm pace that supports rational action in almost every endeavor confronted. One of the first assurances that self-confidence is possessed appears in people doing the things that they know how to do. Pre-service programs help in knowing what and how to teach but the desire to perform effectively must come from within the individual throughout the teaching career.

Accumulated knowledge and experience usually follows a line of action guided primarily by the individual's life and vocational purposes. This accumulated knowledge and experience should help a person to make adaptations of the things known to newly-assigned or assumed tasks. The deliberative adaptation (redirection) of what is known to new tasks is the best evidence of creative flexibility. Individuals really learn from doing. As individuals learn not only to do better what they are prepared to do they also learn that adaptations to new situations are dependent upon their creative ability. Extending the years of teaching experience with this outlook on self provides the opportunities for continuous development.

The major concern of this chapter is with the review and analysis of the things that build self-confidence throughout a teaching career. At the outset, it is well to give some consideration to the fact that over-confidence may invite errors and eventual failure. Over-confidence tends to blind the individual to the exclusive results of personal effort and blurs the awareness of many influencing factors playing upon the processes by which purposes are realized. The process is not good or bad within itself but good or bad because of the results produced. When an individual has over-confidence to the point of being blinded to results, there is almost certainly a failure in a competent control of the tasks at hand. This may also result in a failure to achieve group coordination as discussed in the preceding chapter.

Many people of low self-confidence view the rules imposed by others as requiring absolute conformity stronger than a self-imposed rule. The deliberative adaptation mentioned above would indicate that any situation needs to be evaluated in order to realize the wise and rewarding use of abilities. The weakness of the individual in seeking and holding to an imposed rule may be stronger than the free choice of action which each person should be competent to make. This weakness, for instance, becomes dramatic for the ultra-conforming teacher who works under an administrative directive to keep students in the classroom until a specified dismissal time. The absolute observance of the directive is both foolish and futile if a student wielded a knife in a threatening manner. This is an example of conflicting influence from the two environmental spheres given in figure 2.

The tendency to substitute a rule or regulation for deliberative thinking is characteristic of a person with a closed mind. The person with the open mind is the one who can weigh all the elements of a situation and bring a deliberate choice to the selection of behaviors. The person with a closed mind is prone to consider that the total situation is under control and, therefore, little consideration need be given to what others might say, do, or think.

An important first consideration in the matter of selecting the bases of self-confidence is to realize the substance of pride. Pride is strongly influenced by the personal image of how people think others see them. This personal image is also a strong influence in the choice of behaviors as people go about their work. The substance of pride becomes the guide to determining successful task activities. The discussions which follow will make frequent reference to the self-image and the importance it plays in the guiding of behavior so that self-confidence may be developed with ease and effectiveness.

The discussion of the bases of self-confidence will be organized into several categories. The category identifications are found in headings of the succeeding sections of the chapter. Each heading will indicate an important aspect in the development of self-confidence.

Colleagues and Me

The career cycle depicted in figure 2 shows several different facets of a teacher's career. You may see yourself occupying one facet, and feel close to others you see in the same position. You may have less of an affinity for those in other facets. The preceding chapter, 'Sources of Coordination', indicated that many of those sources are to be found in professional associates. The message is that people can learn from colleagues, particularly those who work in similar responsibilities. As individuals view colleagues, they will find that there is a selectivity in likes and dislikes. It might be rewarding to question just why an individual likes one and dislikes the other. There is always the possibility that individuals are being their own mirrors. In other words, if you dislike a person, it may be because of likeness to you. This does not mean, however, that the disliked person has any less concern with your work nor any less capability to offer you encouragement and assistance by way of help and support than the ones whom you like.

A determination needs to be made early in your experience as to whether you think you can be objective in the observation of your colleagues and in your associations with them. This determination needs to be reviewed frequently during the entire teaching career. Your judgment constitutes an interpretation of how you see your role in a group such as your school faculty. Your responses to your colleagues will be apparent in the pattern of communication that you establish with them. You communicate sometimes with words and sometimes with actions. The means of communication may determine the interpretation that others place upon it. Be selective and evaluative of your own procedures of interpretation and communication as you relate to your colleagues.

Being admired, respected, and wanted by colleagues is exciting, but such responses do not come about automatically. They come about, usually, because of the efforts of both parties. Colleagues or peers influence each other whether they are aware of it or not. The mere fact of making judgments about colleagues (induction) means that those persons have exercised enough influence to assure an awareness of them. Some of your colleagues are considered as being significant to your purposes and others are not. The degree of significance, however, does not measure the amount of influence each person has on you. The person whom you consider to be non-significant in your professional and personal life may be influencing you more than some whom you consider significant. Those who are significant you may wish to emulate, but those who are non-significant you might attempt to avoid emulating. In either instance, you have been influenced by a peer.

An awareness of this kind of behavior gives you knowledge that supports security. Security comes from the fact that you are discovering the kinds of influences to which you are susceptible. This gives you a base for profitable and pleasurable personal and professional interactions with those with whom you work.

As you establish relationships with colleagues, you soon find that the element of prestige is a powerful one. Prestige is mostly the image that you hold of yourself with respect to how other people see you. If you see them viewing you as a significant person, a person with whom they are happy to associate, a person whom they respect, you get a reinforcement simply because your sense of prestige has been supported. As these experiences in reinforcement grow, you will be developing an awareness of compatibilities that you have with some or all of your colleagues.

The achievement of compatability is desirable whether it is with those you consider significant or those who are non-significant in your professional life. There are different kinds of compatibilities. It is not just a matter of being able to converse pleasantly or to enter into social interaction, but rather to interact with respect to teaching methods, curriculum content, and institutional purposes. Compatibility can be established even among those who do not agree on some issues. The compatibility resides in the fact that a respect for the judgment of the other is mutual. There are many opportunities to establish these compatibilities (redirection) and to experience the respect of your peers. The approval of your peers will be a powerful influence in the pattern of your professional behavior as you continue in your teaching situation or as you go to some other assignment.

The *Aids for Self-Development* that follow are to help you to be a careful and purposeful observer as a member of a teaching staff. It will point out resources and influences that may be found in your colleagues and help you control and shape these to improve your experience.

Aids for Self-Development

1 Describe a type of observation that you would like each of the following persons to make of you:
  (a) central office administrators;
  (b) building principal;
  (c) classroom teacher;
  (d) pupils;
  (e) supervisor;
  (f) support personnel.
2 Rank order the observations from above in the order of most significant to least significant in influence upon you.
3 Describe an observation that you have made, or would like to make, of each of the following persons:
  (a) central office administrators;
  (b) building principal;
  (c) classroom teacher;
  (d) pupils;
  (e) supervisor;
  (f) support personnel.
4 Rank order your observations in the order of most significant to least significant in influence upon you.
5 Compare your ranking from numbers 2 and 4 above, and identify the most and least influential colleagues in your situation.
6 Determine induction or renewal activities that will create a more useful resource from those colleagues who were found to be least influential.

Analyzing Contradiction

The choice of a profession is a deliberative act. A few people drift into a profession but most people assess the potentials of that profession, the requirements of preparation, and the promise of satisfaction in the production work of a future. The student entering the program of preparation for teaching (induction) normally does so with high professional hopes for teaching as a career. The professional hopes at this point are not and need not be separated from personal ambitions about what to do with life. The experienced teacher has motivations similar to those entering the preparation programs. Teaching experience (renewal) opens new vistas of opportunity and new horizons of professional challenge (redirection).

This is a good time to look at the preparation program in teacher education and to explore the possibility that its design and procedures might produce contradictions by selective emphases or omissions. The same type of contradiction might exist in advanced academic experiences where continuing teaching progress leads to modified or completely different responsibilities (renewal). One of the first contracts between the student and the academic program is with the college or university bulletin. It is here that a description of the requirements and extended opportunities of the program are found. The understanding of the major program requirements might change as a teaching career progresses (induction).

The bulletin often does not reveal the fact that there are alternatives in academic programs. The easy conclusion is that the prescriptions of a university bulletin indicate those emphases which later are translated into the categories of major task obligations in the employment situation. It is important not to build the idea that the unique selection of requirements in any one institution is better or worse than those in others. There is a rationale behind each of them. The important point for the teacher is that of viewing these as possibilities, each of which has strong promises for supporting successful teaching careers. In this way, the teacher approaches the first teaching task or a modified assignment, not with the idea of being constrained by the importance of bulletin descriptions and, therefore, by inflexible rules, but rather as a place where one can select from many alternatives in teaching strategies. The choice of strategies from many alternatives (renewal) is the best guarantee of success.

The early contacts with college and university programs often create an awareness that there are certain course-professor territorial imperatives that require attention. The enthusiasm which professors may have for their own particular contributions to the total teacher education program often may cause an over-estimated evaluation. Extravagant claims of superiority for a particular course may do injustice to other courses or other aspects of the program. Few teacher education programs survive unscathed in an environment less than free of some disciplinary areas being declared as superior in intellectual stature. Too often there has been an assumption that the academic demands are more substantive intellectually than are the courses or subjects commonly referred to as pedagogy.

Many history-based notions exist about the relative importance of selected aspects of the educational program. Some disciplines believe that learning for learning's sake is sufficient justification for a devotion to their courses. The teacher in preparation, however, already has made the choice of not only learning for learning's sake but also of learning to help others learn for learning's sake. This makes the learning for learning's sake quickly identified with the status of a vocational pursuit. But what is wrong about referring to a course as having a practical value in support of one's desires to make a living? It is consistent with the desire that one may have to remain an intellectually alert and continuously learning individual. Thus, *redirection* gives *potency* to the academic process of continuous career development.

The history of the relationships between intellectual and menial activities have tended to create at least two worlds for those in the teaching profession. It is unfortunate that in a democratic society and in the intellectual field the idea is perpetuated that some things are better than others because of their being intellectual versus menial in nature. The purpose of earning a living is not something that needs an apology. It may be that in past centuries becoming an intellectual was achieving status in which a person would have relief from the necessity of having to do those things which constitute the economic support for life. Some of these campus-based concepts may be contradictions in a tactful manner while evaluating the value of all points of view. This will help in the clarification of some unnecessarily blurred concepts.

History records another misfortune in the dichotomy of theory and practice. There is continuously the expressed feeling that the person in a field teaching position is a practitioner and has no time for theory. Yet, the very basis of academic programs is in theory. Theory, in that sense, leads to good practice. It is unfortunate that the teacher must move from an environment on a campus to an environment in the field and feel that perhaps an apology is necessary for having been on campus because of this antipathy for what the practitioner usually refers to as purely theoretical experiences.

The academic programs should bring theory to the support of good practice. The teacher, at whatever stage of experience, must weigh this seeming conflict and be able to see the relationship between the campus contribution, personal ability, and the school environment in which the teaching experiences are attained. The campus-field suspicion, then, probably will continue through the period of clinical experiences and internships and into the early years of teaching. Gradually, as one matures in the profession, there is a probability that the field and the campus can be seen as complementary rather than antagonistic to each other. Experienced teachers can help their younger colleagues (induction) to reduce the unproductive concepts of campus and field diversities.

Another possible misinterpretation may grow out of the academic program which seldom is given much attention; yet, it may be a potent influence on each teacher. This misinterpretation is that of having been in the early twenties. There is a tendency to draw a quick and unfounded conclusion that anyone who is ten years older certainly is in a rut if not actually posing with one foot in the grave. This makes a rather difficult relationship between the beginning teacher and those more experienced ones in the employment situation. Yet, seldom have beginning teachers or experienced teachers taken the time to analyze the influence of moving from a uniform to a mixed age group. This move requires reinterpretations or re-evaluations (redirection) of assumptions that may have evolved unsuspectingly.

One of the elements of stress between the beginning and the experienced is that of the newer ones so recently from the college experience assuming that the best knowledge is printed in a book. An experienced person is quick to state that there are two major sources for trying to decide what is the best way (renewal) to proceed in the practice of teaching. One is to see what the book says and the other is to analyze one's own experience and the experience of colleagues. This difference in authority source makes a point of stress between the beginning and the experienced teachers in the school. One way to analyze the difference in a teaching staff is to use the career cycle in figure 2. Other ways should also be determined to do this analysis.

The *Aids for Self-Development* that follow are structured to help you as an individual to analyze some of the beliefs that you have that may stem from your preparation programs. The analysis should help you make judgments regarding your purposes, procedures, and goals in the profession.

. . . .

Aids for Self-Development

1   A belief is a statement that you hold to be true. The situations or concepts listed below are suggestions for you to state a belief (something that you think is true) about each area:
    (a)   teacher pre-service education;
    (b)   teaching the same grade or subject over and over;
    (c)   teacher lounge talk;
    (d)   teacher in-service meeting;
    (e)   asking other teachers for help;

(f)   asking the principal for help;
(g)   interaction with colleagues outside the school;
(h)   the esteem of teachers in the community;
(i)   pride in the teaching profession;
(j)   educational theory and teaching practice;
(k)   others.

2   For each statement of belief you have written, determine the source of that belief. Did it originate in the campus segment of preparation, during your clinical experience, during the induction phase, after entry to the profession, outside of your profession activities, or in some other place?

3   Identify the beliefs that have been a positive growth influence upon you and those that have been negative.

4   Choose a course of action regarding each belief — whether to retain the belief, modify or redirect it, or change it completely — and the approach you will take to modify or change.

5   Begin the steps in your plan to redirect or renew your beliefs.

. . . .

Ego Status and Certification

A transitional point in the teacher-preparation program is that of being certified by the preparing institution to receive a license from the proper state agency. The teaching certificate or license constitutes the legal right to practice in the profession. The fact that such a certificate is held means that a school district is eligible to employ this individual as a teacher and to pay a salary from the district funds. The renewed and upgraded certificate has similar implications for experienced teachers.

Teachers should review their perceived privileges and responsibilities associated with certification. It has meanings beyond the legal right to enter into employment as a teacher in a public school. The certification requirements often are seen as standards for teaching performance. The term may indicate to some that the requirements are unchallengeable guarantees that the teacher is qualified to fulfill the obligations of a defined teaching position. The certificate indeed is the state's best method of assuring parents that students in the schools are to learn under the direction of a qualified teacher. It is well to recognize, however, that no set of standards for certification can account for the myriad abilities and skills that a teacher must exhibit in order to be a good teacher. The standards constitute primarily the minimum of assurance that the licensed person is qualified to preside in the classroom. Teachers are in continued and progressing awareness of the need to update and expand (renewal) the academic preparation for the expanding responsibilities of teaching.

Other terms exist in the vocabulary of certification that give the notion that the academic program is a complete assurance of professional excellence. Beyond the term 'standard of certification' there is the term 'accredited institution'. There are several agencies that provide accreditation. The American one is the National Council for the Accreditation of Teacher Education (NCATE). Many of the state educational agencies likewise enter into a study of each teacher preparing institution and put it on an approved or an accredited list. The standards used either by NCATE or by the state are not antagonistic in nature. They are mutually supportive but each one requires somewhat different kinds of information about the teacher education institution and program, and yet, even though differing, are gathered and interpreted in terms of the same basic goals, namely, the assurance that the graduates are prepared to teach. Similar status reviews are made of the graduate program opportunities of those finding study needed beyond the initial requirements needed.

The standards of certification and of accreditation have a certain national significance. Many of the states have reciprocal agreements that make it possible for the person licensed in one state to be automatically licensed in another state if the individual so applies. This type of cooperation increases the mobility of those who enter the profession. It does not signify any greater assurance of excellence and neither does it imply that the states entering into reciprocity are better states insofar as teacher certification is concerned.

The standards of certification and accreditation generally relate to the structure found in most college and university bulletins, namely, that there are three identifiable areas in the programs of preparation. The areas are (i) the general studies; (ii) the specialization of fields of concentration; and (iii) the pedagogical studies. There are few elements in the standards of teacher education institutions. The standards indicate that the three areas are important in the preparation of teachers and that, in order to become licensed, there must be evidence of credit earned in each of these areas.

It must be remembered, however, that no one has implied in any of the documents — such as bulletins or standards of certification and accreditation — that the requirements in terms of credits and course patterns assure life-long proficiency in teaching performance. Some states and some institutions are moving in the direction of performance criteria rather than course credit criteria as a basis for certification. Generally, at the present time, it is taken for granted that there are relationships between the patterns of requirement and the probability of good teaching performance.

Another easily acquired conflict in the early views of certification is that the license presumes a right to expect employment. It is well to recognize that one may hold a certificate, yet there may be no place that wants the particular abilities represented in the preparation program and within the certification limits. Persons who receive teaching licenses, on the other hand, may find a place to teach but can not be sure that their particular abilities will fit expectations and requirements of the position accepted for employment.

Recognition of the preparation for teaching and the licensing privileges do not guarantee excellence in performance and do not guarantee a continuing high level of performance. This is what is re-ferred to as the maintenance shock. It comes as a shock to some people to find out that, after having completed four or five years of college level preparation and having received a certificate from an accrediting agency, there is still a need to keep on studying (renewal) in order that the skills already developed may adapt to the changing demands of schools.

Self-confidence is supported by taking a rational view toward certification, accreditation, and employment privileges. Over-con-fidence can be replaced by a confidence related to the probability that one has in performing the assigned tasks well. It comes, then, to the simple conclusion that the proof of qualification is in the quality of the output. At this point, it is well to raise the question as to who will judge the output quality. The answer to this is that the teacher is the first and best judge but there are many others standing by who will impose judgments upon teachers and their work. Give thought to these kinds of things as you move through your continuing teaching experiences. Induction, renewal, and redirection merge into a rewarding support system for a continuing record of development and recognized accom-plishment.

The *Aids for Self-Development* below are structured to help you look at teaching from the point of initial certification up to your current position and beyond.

. . . .

Aids for Self-Development

1   Describe your attitude regarding your competence and abilities to teach when you were first granted certification.

2 Describe how this attitude changed, if indeed it did, upon your initial teaching experience.

3 From your current position, which of the above two descriptions are closest to the way you feel now? Is your current attitude about your competence and ability likely to change? How might it change, or, if not, why not?

4 Outline your feeling about teacher as a profession, and identify ways to improve your feeling and to improve the status of the profession.

5 Work toward the improvement you have outlined with your colleagues.

. . . .

Awareness of Expectations

Assignment descriptions and expectations placed upon the teacher are among the first and most helpful (induction) of the elements in establishing self-confidence. Prior to or accompanying the assignment description will be conversations about the nature of the position. Many schools do not have specific written job or assignment descriptions which constitute the basic list of expectations placed upon the teacher. The best that can be hoped for in such situations is to ask the right questions at the time of the assignment. A tactful approach is wise as questions are asked of the administration since it might be concluded that you are more concerned about protecting yourself than determining whether it is an assignment in which your capabilities are appropriate to the tasks. This is one of the interpretations that the administration may develop from too hard and early questioning by the teacher.

The point of view or attitude that is exhibited at all times and probably that administrators would appreciate is the fact that you are only seeking the assurance of your competence by permitting yourself to accept types of assignments for which you feel prepared and capable. No matter how carefully you study the assignment descriptions and question the administrators about expectations being placed upon you, there will be many unexpected demands that you discover after you begin the assignment. It is important at this point not to assume that all of the expectations should have been cataloged by the administration. It is utterly impossible for any person to tell you all of the things that might be expected, particularly since many of them might not yet be known. The reason for this is that many of the expectations placed upon the teacher come from students, fellow teachers, administrative and supervisory personnel, school board members, and people in the community.

Expectations stated to you after your assignment begins may come as a surprise but do not interpret that as information withheld at the time of the assignment. Many of these come up because of an observation of the situation and your part in it at that particular time. One of the kinds of queries that you can make to protect yourself against too many expectations or too many unexpected ones, is to ask about the time available (renewal) for planning.

If you have time to plan your work, certainly you can meet each day with more self-confidence. This is far superior to walking into the school situation each morning wondering what surprise will be sprung that day. The probability of surprises cannot be eliminated completely but you can, by teaching each day in terms of your plans for the next one, reduce the number of surprises that might confront you. As you gain assurance that you know what is expected, you have time to plan for it and you gain the capability of making instant adaptations (redirection) to new problems. These warnings are offered for the purpose of reducing the probability of any psychoses with respect to having been dealt with unjustly during the assignment actions. As you move through the days of your experience with the poise that goes with the sense of being competent enough to perform the expectation of your role, you can begin analyzing how you are doing by watching the reactions of others.

The first reactions to watch will be those of the students. It will not be long until you know whether they like to work with you, whether they like to take your suggestions, whether they are making a game of challenging you, or whether they are happy because you are doing the teaching. You also can watch the reactions of your fellow teachers, particularly those who have similar assignments to your own. Watch also particularly the reactions of the administrative and supervisory staff. It is easy to read the attitude of another person in terms of friendly interactions or those intended to communicate references to impending criticism. If you can gain some experience and competence in detecting and interpreting the reactions of others, you are in a good position to begin resolving the expectation conflicts (redirection) that may confront you.

Expectation conflicts appear in terms of different people wanting you to do different things. There are often conflicts between the expectations of students and parents. There are conflicts in expectations between teachers and the parents of the children who come to your classes. There are conflicts of expectations between administrative staff, school board members, and special interest groups in the community. There is no use wishing that these conflicts of expectations would go away because people and communities are made that way. People have a right to pursue their own interests and the teacher must develop the skills of relating the proper expectations of the particular assignments to the interests of others. The fact that the teacher is a professional means that the teacher, better than anyone else, can read the proper role to be followed in helping people in the community achieve the hopes of education for their children.

Many non-teaching expectations are placed upon teachers. Historically, this was a serious problem but in recent years teachers have had less constraints placed upon them by way of their personal behaviors. There are, however, some expectations such as participating in activities which are termed non-teaching and even non-school in nature. The people of the community like to feel that their teachers are a part of the community. Teachers can manage their own problems of teaching much better if they generate that feeling on the part of the lay people of the community and that they too feel a part of the community.

The initial days, weeks, and months of the assignment provide opportunities for updating (redirection) the description of expectations for each position. As you analyze yourself, your assignments, and the kinds of problems and successes that you have, it might be well to offer to the administrative and supervisory staff your suggestions with respect to what might have better described your tasks at the time of assignment.

The next *Aids for Self-Development* are to help you summarize the variations between your actual assignment, its formal description, and what you think it ought to be.

. . . .

Aids for Self-Development

1   Describe your actual assignment in terms of:
   (a)   curriculum;
   (b)   administration;
   (c)   teaching;
   (d)   extra-curricular;
   (e)   routine duties;
   (f)   community service;
   (g)   other.
2   Separate the formal description of your assignment (if one exists)

into the components listed above and compare this description to your own.

3   Update, or create, your assignment description to reflect the best possible combinations of duties as listed in number above.

4   Devise a strategy to renew your assignment to reflect the components you designed in number 3 above.

. . . .

Anticipating Success

The suggestions made in the previous section of this chapter were focused upon the problem of surveying the bases of self-confidence. There have been numerous suggestions as to what might be done to build self-confidence as well as indications of why it is worth the building. Turn now to the idea of how you can reinforce your sense of self-confidence by anticipating some of the things that may be observable on the way to success. You have the basic control in your own hands over whether you will succeed or fail, and the suggestions here with respect to self-confidence consider only the probability of success.

A first observation to make in this anticipation is that of whether you are finding personal satisfaction in the assignment you have accepted. Nothing can be more distressing than to hate your work when you know you have a long time left in which you are supposed to be doing it. It is important, then, that you achieve recognition for the personal satisfactions which you experience in your professional opportunities and obligations in a particular teaching assignment.

Note the things that people say — not only what they say, but how they say it. Both are important. If people are offering words of commendation, do not succumb to the current cynicism of viewing unsolicited commendation as a threat of some future expectations. It is just as well to throw aside such crass views of the interrelationships of people. If you expect it, it is almost certain to happen. If you do not expect it, then perhaps you increase the chances that the art of commendation might survive. People may offer congratulations, suggestions of help, suggestions of sympathy even when sympathizing with an error creditable entirely to you. It means that they are supporting you as a person and believe you will be successful.

Watching the way people act and listening to what they say are very important. The ways people act may be one of the overt signs that you can discover whether you are getting off to a good start (induction) or continuing a long pattern of success (renewal). If people invite you to join in a committee or in other activities, it is an expression of confidence in you. It is an expression that they believe you have something to offer. You well may read this as an act of support. Observe also not only what you like about the actions of others but what annoys you and in what ways you annoy others. It is easy to become impatient with something that you wish would go away. It is another thing, however, to permit it to become overriding with respect to your own conduct. It is all right to be annoyed but it is not all right to let this become the dominating influence in your professional activities or in your social interactions. The frequency of contacts with your colleague group and your non-colleague group may be one of the best ways to establish balance with respect to what bothers you and what you do that bothers others. The frequency of contact either will build a base for better interactions or give you the opportunity to know why you may avoid contacts at some future time.

An excellent way in which you can get a preview of your future success is to be thoroughly frank with yourself in your self-initiated measures of outcomes. Be honest with yourself about how much the students are learning under your direction. At this point, you do not have to share the results of the measures with others but, if there is someone in whom you have confidence and would like to get their reaction, share the information with them. One of the helps in sharing information of this type is to get some appraisal or reaction as to whether you used the right kind of measure to judge the outcomes of your work. There are so many outcomes to almost every teaching act and the totality of them cannot be measured in any one brief or even comprehensive instrument. Your day-to-day recordings of your observations, the student's reactions, and your reactions to the students may constitute some of the measures of the outcomes of your work. Beyond these are the overt commendations that might come from school administrators and supervisors. Parents often are gracious in making overt commendations to teachers as they see and hear from their students what they have done in school.

The following *Aids for Self-Development* are to help you study your successes as a teacher. Be thoroughly frank with yourself in this self-initiated measure in order to develop an accurate review of your successes.

Aids for Self-Development

1 Record both the tangible and non-tangible evidences of your successes in the profession to date in two separate columns. Use the self-assessment sources listed below to state your evidence:
   (a) pupil rapport;
   (b) pupil learning;
   (c) colleague relationships;
   (d) principal relationships;
   (e) parental relationships;
   (f) community relationships;
   (g) supervisory relationships;
   (h) planning lessons;
   (i) facilitating learning;
   (j) communicating.
2 Review the data you have recorded above and appraise how you look to yourself as a teacher.
3 Save these responses and, keeping the self-assessment categories in mind, review your successes again at a future date. Since self-assessment is a continuous process you should compare your responses from one time to the next.
4 Share your responses with someone else to get reactions as to what renewal activities might help you gain the success you want.
5 Refine your data collection sources and techniques to redirect your self-analysis in the most productive manner for your future success.

Confidence with Modesty

The sections in this chapter have sought to analyze the bases of self-confidence. It was indicated at the outset that one of the major elements in self-confidence is that of self-image. Look back now to many of the suggestions in this chapter to see how many of them provided you the opportunity to check the image that you have of yourself. It is important to recognize that the development of self-confidence must provide a self-image which involves the absence of the sense of being threatened by something that you cannot see, cannot hear, or cannot control. The feeling of being threatened often is associated with a lack of self-confidence and would give you a self-image that is not pleasant to view. If there are feelings of being threatened, use these suggestions in seeking the means of removing them.

Just as important as freeing yourself of feeling threatened is to remove the facades which you build up around yourself. This means that an individual can have an over-accentuated formality or serious-ness as a means of covering the sense of being threatened. This facade so often leads to an interpretation on the part of others that here is a person who is either very insecure or who really does not know the job. You want neither of these things to burden your probability of success. Watch yourself then, in case you find some of these facades being used as a cover-up for some of your insecurities or incapabilities and set about removing them.

Try to be a person who is capable of trusting other people — their intents as well as their actions — and in becoming a person who is worthy of the trust of others. Trusting and trustworthiness may be among the unused resources that can be found in your school situation and particularly among your colleagues. Be the kind of person to them that you would like to have them be to you.

References were made previously to the matter of being adaptive. There will always be such requirements even though you have a job description and a stated list of expectations at the beginning of each new or modified assignment. There always may be changes in terms of how your behaviors will be affected. It is not enough to say that you are going to resist anything that was not in your original list of expecta-tions. It could be that your up-dating (redirection) of those expectations may have brought about some changes of facility and purpose not only for yourself but also for others. You want others to be tolerant of what you initiate and you in turn must be tolerant of those things which are initiated by others.

The use of the terms *significant* and *non-significant* others in a previous section leads to the suggestion now that you continually must appraise your perception of what is significant and what is not. In other words, you can determine what is important apart from those which only seem important but really are not. You must seek to improve your views of reality. Reality will be not only with respect to your own capacities but the realities demanded in your work situation. This includes not only the purposes and the expectations, but also the per-sonalities of those with whom and for whom you work. Involved in all of these things, the building of self-confidence can give you visions of the kind of future that you see in the teaching profession. If you begin to deviate into possible other kinds of work (induction) within the profession, this is not to be a source of apology but rather a matter of gratefulness for your objectivity in viewing yourself and your professional opportunities.

The teaching experiences will make you aware of the great task of managing multiple loyalties. Are you more loyal to yourself, to your organized teaching group, to your employers, to an idea that you have adopted as a guiding principle, or other targets? Managing these does not mean that you have to go to a single loyalty but rather to bring the multiple ones into wise priority insofar as your professional responsibilities are concerned.

The term *responsibility* should command your respect. Respect for your responsibility can be that responsibility which results after you have initiated the management of multiple expectations and multiple loyalties. If all of these things proceed well and you have been able to make a self-assessment, then you have achieved what many people seek throughout life, namely, constructive humility and wholesome self-confidence. These will serve you well as you become involved in activities beyond the classroom.

A Look Beyond

Self-confidence is generated by a continuing awareness of personal abilities and strengths. The action targets must be identified whether they are located within or outside the school. The recognition of personal adequacy is limited unless the abilities of individuals are tested in the arena of assigned or assumed responsibilities. The assignment within the school organization was the subject of analysis in chapter 2. The effectiveness of an individual is affected by the interrelating skills of all participants in group action. This was the focus of chapter 3 and it was identified as coordination. But there is a world beyond the classroom and the school. Skill in relating to the people in that world is extremely important to the success of the educational enterprise. Chapter 5, 'A Look Beyond The Classroom', presents many aspects of the responsibilities generated by people and forces in the school's environment.

Chapter 5

A Look Beyond the Classroom

Surveying one's environment in approaching an assignment may reveal some strengths and weaknesses of a teacher. These strengths and weaknesses, at the same time, are the beginning of an identification of the kind of help that is needed from others. Because of the importance of a unique personal outlook, it is essential that supervisors be looked upon as persons who can be of assistance. Their assistance, however, is not likely to be helpful unless the individual's own analysis of perceptions can give leads to the kinds of things that need to be straightened out in the outlook about schools and teachers.

The two spheres of influence in every teacher's environment are depicted in figure 2. These spheres contain examples that can be used as a beginning in the determination of perceptions. Things or images both inside and outside the classroom are a part of the environment that teachers must recognize for their influence on teaching and they must then identify means of using what they have found out to improve their status as teachers.

Here again what teachers see inside and outside the classroom may be a good clue as to what kind of help is needed from the supervisory assistance made available. Supervisors can help both with the identification and development of strategies to work with personalized influences from the environment. Teachers must work to implicate supervisors in their efforts to improve.

You can be stimulated by supervisors and by the opportunities to know what are the hopes, aspirations, and purposes of the people that make up the environment of the school. You should also see your opportunity and responsibility for assisting in the development of the communication capacity and facilities of the young people who come into your classroom. In that way, you can have a sense of contribution in anticipating your opportunities to direct the education of youth. This becomes a type of obligation that you accept and the acceptance of this obligation gives you a sense of belongingness, not only to the school but to the community that has created and supported the establishment and maintenance of that school.

Your first step is to analyze your personal and organizational environment to determine what things impact upon your teaching. The remaining sections of this chapter may give you some help in identifying those things which should be subjected to analysis and some ways that the analysis might take place.

Your Classroom Is No Lonely Place

The literature in education often carries reference to the fact or to the possibility that the classroom is an extremely lonely place for the teacher. This is a false assumption and is detrimental to the thinking about the opportunities that a teacher has in the classroom. Even though you can seemingly close out all the rest of the world, much of the world has already gotten into your classroom and you would not want to close out that part of it.

You have an assigned population in your classroom. It is difficult to say whether this be ten, twenty-five, thirty, fifty, or more students that you see in a day's time. Your assignment may depend upon the kinds of arrangements negotiated between the teachers' organizations and the administration of the school. At any rate, you have a group of students and these students bring to you a great variety of backgrounds, outlooks, manners of expression, and educational needs. You have in your classroom not only students but materials and equipment. These materials and equipment require adaptations (redirection) to the kind of instruction that you direct for the learners who come to your classroom.

Loneliness is not cured purely by having people around but by having also things that can stimulate and challenge you to use them to best advantage. There also are comings and goings in your classroom — sometimes perhaps more than you will want. But loneliness has no place in a classroom where students are coming and going as well as teachers, service personnel, supervisors, administrators, parents, and visitors. Many of these make frequent in-roads into the unique space called your classroom. All of these comings and goings perhaps present you with some unique kinds of challenges that give you no time to think about being in a world alone.

Great variety exists among the students. Their appearances, their attitudes, their wants, their rejections, their communication deviations, and many other identities of the differences that confront you among the teaching responsibilities of your classroom. Your responsibilities as a teacher include a great variety of activities on your part. You must make assignments, offer explanations, do much listening, make suggestions, give directions, appraise the students' work, report the results of learning efforts, and reinforce student self-esteem. All of these things will keep you busy and can be a source of excitement to you and most assuredly, all of these activities leave you little time to ponder about the classroom as a lonely place.

You have a structure for the future of your classroom and your school through planning, arranging, managing, producing, and involving many other people in the activities associated with teaching. It is to be hoped that you take time occasionally to review a resource (renewal) for your own excitement and devotion to excellence in teaching. All of these things are in every day's work. There is little time to be lonely in the classroom unless one chooses to avoid the excitements of teaching. You should make an occasional analysis of your daily activities and find ways of establishing priorities and of strengthening the things that you choose to do.

These *Aids for Self-Development* are designed to help you identify the resources available to you to make your classroom an 'alive' classroom.

....

Aids for Self-Development

1   One method to create an 'alive' classroom is to adapt and use certain resources available to you. Select a *resource* from the first column, and an *adaptation focus* from the second column and define a stategy to use the resource in some activity concerning the focus you have selected.

Resource	*Adaptation Focus*
students	planning
materials	arranging
equipment	managing
administrators	producing
parents	involving
guests	
teachers	
supervisors	

2   Identify strategies and activities for as many different pairs of resources and adaptation foci that you can match.
3   Induct or redirect your adaptation of resources into one or more of the following duties of teaching:
    (a)   explaining;
    (b)   assigning;
    (c)   listening;
    (d)   suggesting;
    (e)   appraising;
    (f)   reporting;
    (g)   reinforcing;
    (h)   other.
4   Design renewal activities to help you and your colleagues find more resource adaptations and incorporate them into use.

....

There Is An Outside

The introductory paragraphs in this chapter made reference to the existence of influence items both inside and outside the environment of the classroom. The preceding section gave primary attention to the inside of the classroom. It is well, at the same time, to give some thought to the nature of that outside world that envelops your school and classroom.

People in the community serve as school board members. Each teacher may have experienced some association with that board of education when entering into a contract for teaching service. School board members may be looked upon by teachers as outsiders but the outsiders with inside controls. Many of the regulations under which the classroom operates find their sources and certainly the approvals in this lay board of education. One might raise the question as to why should non-professional educators have so much control over the things that are done in the school by professional educators. It is the way that governmental services have been established. The same thing is true for all other public, social, and governmental services. The people who create regulations assume the obligation and privileges of regulating. It is to be hoped that these regulations do not deter the application of professional skills to the purposes for which they have been put under contract. When the regulations do seem to thwart your efforts as a teacher, they should be analyzed and discussed with your supervisor.

There are channels of communication by which you can ask for reasons and through which you can offer suggestions (induction) for the regulatory arrangements which gives you the best opportunity to perform your teaching service.

Another group important to your task as a teacher is composed of outsiders and they are, of course, parents. These parents entrust their children to you as a teacher because they want their children to get the benefits of an education. These parents do not have inside controls as do the members of the board of education. The parents, however, do have inside influence. This can be exercised first of all in the attitudes of the students that they send to the classroom. And much more directly, they can influence what you do through the personal requests that they make to you or to your administrators and supervisors who are responsible for designing the educational program.

That great outside also contains identifiable groups that can be called special interest groups. These special interest groups can have educational purposes. When patriotic organizations offer prizes for certain types of essays or artwork or for public speaking or musical presentations, they are expressing their special interest through the educational processes of the school. There are health groups that constitute a special interest in that they focus upon some of the aspects of health development or correction. Very often, these special interest groups in the area of health want to achieve their purposes through the cooperation of the schools. Thus, within your community and in that outside world, there are people who do have specialized interest and who work hard to realize success in that particular field of interest.

Organizations within the community also might be called competitors of the school. Competition here is not referred to as something that intends to put the school down but rather organizations that have a program that also is interested in the education of youth. There may be public agencies, there may be non–public agencies, or there may be public and non–public agencies that seek to use the avenue of the school for their own particular activities and purposes. These are identified only at this point as a part of that outside world that influences the classroom. A number of these will be discussed in greater detail later in this chapter.

One of the very important things to see in the world outside of your classroom is the ever lengthening arm of government. As federal assistance became more prominent in sponsoring educational programs that seem good for the nation as a whole, there have been increasing controls placed upon the local school district. You find soon in your teaching experience that some of these guidelines or regulations that accompany federal dollars will be presenting themselves (induction) to you and occupying a great deal of your time in order to comply. Local districts want the additional funds and teachers can gain from the kinds of services and materials that come from those federal dollars. It must be recognized, then, that some of these obligations for observing guidelines and regulations as well as for reporting the outcomes become a part of the obligation inherent in the receipt of federal funds.

The state government likewise has tremendous controls over what is done at the local educational level. Usually these contacts come through the State Educational Agency. But it must be recognized that there are increasing legislative, executive, and judicial impacts upon the things that schools and the teachers do in their classrooms. The outside supporters want a rationalization that leaves you not an antagonist to the impact but rather a partner to the development of those kinds of contacts from the govermental agencies that can support rather than thwart the kinds of things that you see as important to the teaching act.

The *Aids for Self-Development* that follow give you the opportunity to scan your environment for possible sources of influence.

. . . .

Aids for Self-Development

1 Select the outside sources from the list below that you see as a possible influence on your teaching:

(a)	parents;	(j)	service clubs;
(b)	school boards;	(k)	federal government;
(c)	teacher associations;	(l)	SEA (State Education Agency);
(d)	scout troops;	(m)	city recreation;
(e)	church groups;	(n)	parks department;
(f)	city officials;	(o)	sports;
(g)	police;	(p)	leisure activities;
(h)	fire department;	(q)	right-wing groups;
(i)	private tutors;	(r)	night life.

2 List any other sources of influence you have experienced in your environment.

3 For each of the sources you have selected as influential, write a statement that summarizes your perception of the relationship that source has with your classroom.

4 Describe the impact of each environmental source on your instruction. Identify ways to renew positive influences and redirect negative influences.

5   Check how the influences you have identified impact upon your
    status as a teacher using the teacher career cycle in figure 2.

....

Competing and Thwarting Interests

Reference was made in the previous section to the fact that the world
outside your classroom has the potential for many competing agencies
and services. Competing is not used in the sense of being an opposition
to education in the school but rather that it claims the attention,
interest, and money of people which otherwise might be concentrated
upon the school.

Perhaps it is well that there are competitive agencies or at least
agencies that have the competitive potential. They may be supportive
or they may not be. That depends upon the kinds of programs
sponsored and the aspirations of the people in control. An example of
those competitive agencies and services within the community is the
churches. This does not mean that the churches are aiming to take over
the responsibilities of your classroom but rather that they do sponsor
teaching that has an impact upon the students who come to your
classroom. Churches have long held that values are taught to those who
come to the church service. These values are brought into the classroom and either reinforce or perhaps compete with the value system
sponsored by the school. One of the things soon to be observed is that
the teachings of different churches are not uniform with respect to
values and personal behaviors. It means that you may have students in
your classroom who have had widely varied instruction in the churches, and yet you are expected somehow to reinforce those as individuals as well as with total groups of students. There are, of course,
church related schools that are in a sense competing for the available
students in the community. These schools likewise are beginning to
compete with the public schools for some of the funds and services
made available by both the federal and state governments. Here again it
does not mean that they are in any way violating a proper function of
the church when these kinds of activities are sponsored as educational
opportunities for the children of their particular religious group. There
are independent private schools in many communities and these also
tend to compete for pupils and services that otherwise might be
concentrated upon the public school.

Other types of competitive interests and agencies within the
community are the library, the art center, the theater, and facilities such

as a zoo. Here again, they can be reinforcing but they also can go an independent route which brings students into your classroom with a wide variety of interests and backgrounds that may challenge you to handle as a group in your classroom. The YMCA, YWCA, the Red Cross, and the scouts, likewise, are, in a way, competitive educational agencies within the community. Some of the services offered by these agencies can be reinforcing to what you would like to teach in the school if, perhaps you have the time.

A need exists for observing the great variety of student interests and habits that grow out of these other educative agencies in the community. There are also educative and competitive agencies such as television, movies, and, adult 'recreation'. The existence of facilities within a community established for adults do not only come to the attention of the younger people and they know too that they are barred from whatever the services may be in those kinds of agencies. Even though they are barred from many of the adult types of so-called educative influences, their fact of being barred tends to give them information that may be difficult for the teacher to handle in the classroom.

At the same time, many agencies within the community have direct and intended supportive potential. The competitive ones indicated above might or might not be supportive and they might or might not thwart the purposes and goals of your classroom. Among those who are organized to be supportive or to have the supportive potential are organizations such as parent teacher organizations, the band mothers, the educational societies and organizations of retired persons, and many others that have had and still do have and intend to have a part in influencing the educative experiences of the students. Many times these types of agencies can offer support (renewal) in the total education program that the school and the teachers would not have time to develop and to manage. There are many agencies within a community that offer organizational awards of various types. Fellowships and scholarships are awards that tend to enhance the desire of students to do well in school.

Recognition is given to many types of educative influence offered by organizations that do not have direct responsibilities for education but they do allocate part of their attention, talent, and funds to supporting some types of specialized educational opportunities. The police and fire departments of the community are such examples of agencies supportive of the educational service. The police and fire department personnel are available to come to the school by invitation and to offer direct instruction about many aspects of personal and public life. In this sense, the classroom is strengthened (redirection) by the supportive agencies to be found in the community. There are many natural resources that are available as field experiences for the students who might go under the sponsorship of the school and the teacher or who might go under the sponsorship of those employed to manage the natural resource agency. School forests are good illustrations of the type of natural resource that are made available as an integral part of the classroom experience.

Many agencies will provide information on request. This can be true of health organizations, industrial organizations, business organizations, and a host of others. The information made available on request often is of a type that perhaps the school could not secure from the regular suppliers of school instructional materials. It is helpful, then, to have these made available in the community. The field trip availability is almost unlimited. It is true, of course, that there are certain regulations that the school itself must establish in order to guarantee the health and safety of the students who take the field trips. The industry sponsored materials have for a long time been one of the rich sources of instructional materials. There are agencies that can make these materials available in direct form or through reference to the industrial organization for the unique types of materials that have been developed through the industry.

The various agencies in a community that can have this supportive potential have perhaps been instrumental in the rebirth of what is identified as community education. There is much more direct effort now to organize (induction) all of the educative resources in a community and to get them coordinated as a total educational program. This is a way to retain the vigor of those competitive agencies in the community and yet to make good use of the educational potential which they possess. The main thing in community education is to organize the community in a way that a common purpose can be achieved in the total education of the youth of that community while serving the needs of the adults. This rebirth of community education has gained enough attention that materials regarding it in great detail are available through governmental agencies. The State Education Agency or universities are leading the movement in most states. The federal government is supplying much of the funds required for that program.

The next *Aids for Self-Development* list some outside resources for you to judge the common characteristics and how they may be of use to you.

Aids for Self-Development

1 From the list of sources given below, select those that have a declared interest in the school and also those that need the attention of the school:

(a)	church groups;	(m)	police;
(b)	libraries;	(n)	agency awards;
(c)	art center;	(o)	educational societies (PDK, PLT, etc.);
(d)	theatre;	(p)	adult entertainment;
(e)	zoo;	(q)	fire department;
(f)	YWCA/YMCA;	(r)	real estate concerns;
(g)	Red Cross;	(s)	school forest;
(h)	scouts;	(t)	health agencies;
(i)	television;	(u)	industrial organizations;
(j)	movies;	(v)	business concerns;
(k)	PTA/PTO;	(w)	medical facilities;
(l)	band parents;	(x)	field trips.

2 Add other sources that you feel have some impact on your particular teaching situation.

3 From the list you have generated of interested sources, choose those you feel are supportive of education. Also, identify those that you feel are non-supportive of education.

4 Determine induction or renewal activities for those supportive sources. Develop a plan for your own use.

5 Determine redirective activities for those non-supportive sources. Work with your colleagues to change or redirect attitudes and ideas.

The Outside Can Get Inside

A reference was made earlier in the chapter to the fact that the students bring to the classroom much of the outside world. Each student is an official, if not an intentional interpreter of the kinds of things that are to be learned in the home and in the neighborhood. Each student, then, is a composite of many unique bits of that outside world.

The opportunity to learn from others as well as to be self-instructed is always a potential in an individual. Learning is occurring most of the time. Much of it is outside and is not as well organized as that to be found in the classroom. This is where the teacher's unique contribution comes into the education scene. No teacher, however, can afford to overlook the fact that much of the outside is coming into the classroom each day and in many different ways. Two students might have what appears to be a common experience in the home and in the neighborhood but each one may have a learner output that is quite different. This presents a unique problem to the teacher who must handle all of these interests at the same time, and, if possible, to use them as reinforcements (redirection) for the learning that is to be done in the school.

Each student is a liaison between those in the school and those outside. The student probably keeps the parents fairly well informed as to the kinds of things that are occurring in the classroom. The response of the parents to the reports that students bring home may return them to the classroom with an attitude that will reinforce the learning or that will obstruct the efforts at teaching. Perhaps the school has not been alert to the fact that since students are liaison agents between the school and the home particularly, instruction needs to be given to the student on how to report the educative experiences that occur in the classroom. At the same time, some effort should be made by school officials to help parents to interpret to the teachers the kinds of things that they think are being learned in the home. Working together they may be able to diagnose the kind of educational experiences that the students are getting and if possible, to arrange (redirection) them in such a way that they are reinforcing rather than conflicting.

The outside also gets into the classroom through the policies established by the school board. The school board is the official representative of the citizens of the community and school district. There is continuous input to the board of education from lay people in the community who want to influence the pattern and direction of the educational opportunities of the children. It is the responsibility of the school administrators to keep teachers informed (induction) about the kinds of policies adopted by the board and the reasons for such policy adoptions. In this way, teachers can relieve themselves of the burden of feeling put upon since it is the school board's prerogative to establish operational policy. When those policies interfere with the teacher's work in the classroom, the teacher should report to the supervisor or administrator (renewal) with the analysis of how the policies affect the teaching effort in the classroom. School administrators are the chief communicators for the inside to the outside interests. Administrators, however, need to be well informed as to what all the impacts are that teachers are realizing in the classroom and this requires some careful analyses and description to the administrators so that the communications can be effective.

Other ways that the outside gets to the inside of the school is through many governmental agencies. Most people are aware that the legislators are passing laws almost continuously which directly affect or indirectly influence the educational program in the school. Here, again, there needs to be input into the legislative process from those who are responsible for carrying out the educational program. At the very least, teachers must be informed as to what the legislative enactments are and should be able to depend upon supervisors and administrators as the accurate sources (induction) of information about legislation.

The governmental executive offices at the state level particularly have great influence upon the kind of programs that go on in the classroom. The State Education Agencies are executive departments of the state government and as such carry much power over the design and execution of the education programs in the individual schools.

The judicial branch of government in recent years has been much more active in decisions which influence not only through the society in which the school exists but also through the instructional program itself. This can reach into the pattern of content that appears in text and reference material as well as in the kind of facilities that are made available for the educative process. It is not only the state government legislative, executive, and judicial branches that influence education but also the federal government. It is well to think again of the many different ways in which the educative process is controlled in the classroom. Here, again, it is well to keep up a continuing analysis (induction) so that you can be able not only to understand these influences that get into your classroom but also understand how to change (redirection) those influences that fail to be supportive of what you feel to be the best interest of the educational opportunities of the students.

Another way that the outside gets to the inside of the classroom is through textbooks and libraries. The textbooks are written by people perhaps that you do not know and have never seen. At the same time, those who write the textbooks may never have visited your classroom and do not know the specifics of the needs which you feel would be most appropiate for your students. Libraries are rich sources of learning materials and are filled with materials that come from those who are not on your immediate professional staff. This means that many of the ideas, the processes, and the outcomes are determined by those who are outside your classroom.

The television, the radio, the telephone, microcomputers, and many forms of newsprint other than text and reference books have a great influence on the educative process in the classroom. Many classrooms are supplied with audio-visual equipment linking television, radio, telephone, and computer communications to the classroom. At the same time, many classrooms make use of various forms of newsprint. This means that, whenever these do come into your classroom, the outside is there working beside you. Your obligation and opportunity is to identify all of the things that are from the outside, to establish the priorities as to which would be most important for your classroom activities, and to see that it gets into your classroom in a manner that becomes an educative experience for the students under your direction. The outsider is not an intruder. The outsider is not something to be eliminated. The important thing is to make the right kind of use of and to give proper emphasis (redirection) to those things that are getting in from the outside and becoming a part of the educative process. The teacher needs to develop the skills for analyzing these many impacts upon teaching and upon the learning of the students.

These *Aids for Self-Development* are to help you identify and work with the influences that outside sources bring to bear on your teaching.

....

Aids for Self-Development

1 Identify an outside influence on your instruction that comes to your classroom from each of the following sources:
   (a) students;   (h) federal legislation;
   (b) parents;   (i) judicial decisions;
   (c) citizens;   (j) administration;
   (d) textbooks;   (k) PTA/PTO;
   (e) television;   (l) civic groups;
   (f) school board;   (m) negotiations;
   (g) SEA (State Education Agency); (n) audio-visual materials.
2 Determine the nature of impact of each influence on your teaching and on the learning of your students. Categorize the influences as personal or organizational within the categories given in figure 2.
3 Select those influence sources that you have found to have an important impact on your instruction and rank them in a priority of most important to least important.
4 Those influences that rate a high priority from you should have a modification (induction, renewal, or redirection) plan designed. Identify the necessary modifications and take the first step in your design.

....

Systems Within Systems

The term *system* has been in use for a long time and has had many different kinds of applications. Usually, it is related to a successful operation for some specific purpose. A simple definition of a system can be that it is a plan by which chosen goals are achieved through the coordination of involved persons, places, and things.

The fact of required coordination assumes that there has to be some knowledgeable management involved. This does not mean that an administrator is essential but certainly an administrator can be helpful. It does mean that all people involved must be aware of the purpose and of the many components that might be involved in any particular activity. An individual seldom can be the only component because a purpose almost always involves other people, material, space, time, and other aspects of a total operation in the classroom.

Systems can be inflexible or they can be flexible. The fact that one system works successfully does not infer that it must always be used without change. Differing people are involved at different times with differing kinds of purpose and material. All of this means that a system in itself must be scrutinized and the plan be changed (redirection) according to the purposes and the components available at that particular time. It is to be hoped that systems can be flexible enough that intelligent adaptations can be made quickly in order to continue the achievement of goals which have been chosen by those involved. Look in simpler terms upon the smallest system as the classroom. Within that classroom you have a plan. The plan involves others on the staff. It involves supervisors and administrators. You have major responsibility for making the adaptations of the system within that classroom which will lead to achievement of the purposes for which the classroom is established and for which you were chosen to preside as the teacher.

The largest of the systems can be envisioned as the federal government. References have been made earlier to the fact that the present federal government is becoming more and more a major component in the design and support of an educational system at the local level. This obviously will involve the classroom. It is important that you know (induction) what the federal plan is and what freedom of adaptations and adjustments you have in working as a component within that federal system. The same can be said for the state agencies which also constitute important components in your small system, namely your classroom. The school district likewise is a system which is much closer to you and perhaps with much more ease of awareness since you are in constant contact with it.

Many in-between systems between the smallest, namely your classroom, and the federal government as your largest system exist. The state and the district have been mentioned. You can identify other in-between systems such as the state or city health department, the police system, the fire protection system, the library system, the many systems identified as social and civic clubs as well as many others. All of these organizations have a plan of action. It is well to be aware that there are so many systems operating and, while they are not necessarily dependent upon each other, there are influences that can be identified. Certainly, the more imminent systems in your awareness would be those that call for the essential coordination within your classroom, within your school building, and within your school district. Coordination is not a matter of once a year action but a matter of continuous attention (renewal) to the relatedness of all of the parts of the systems called local schools.

Occasionally, some contesting systems exist that will be prominent in your awareness. An instance of this is the case of negotiations between the professional organization or association and the board of education. These may or may not be contesting systems but, at some point, probably they can be considered in conflict. When agreements have been made by all parties involved, coordination has been reestablished (redirection) and the systems rather than being competing or contesting can be supporting of each other. One of the systems in many school buildings is the two-way intercom system which can interrupt the classroom at anytime or by which the teacher can interrupt the office. It is important that the intercom system be planned in such a way that a minimum of frustration is experienced by those whose time is interrupted by the word over the loud speaker which usually begins 'May I interrupt?'. Obviously, by the time the short query is completed, the interruption has been complete too. This is an example of why attention should be given to the systems that operate near us so that we can keep them in a supporting rather than in an obstructive relationship.

Knowledge about what systems are and how each of them operates is the basis for your input into the design or planning of the changes in those systems. It is not a matter simply of taking the posture that you do not want to be bothered because you are going to be bothered. The main thing is that when bothered, you go about discovering, in an intelligent way, what there is in the system that might be changed and adapted (redirection) to what might be more appropriate to your way of seeing the coordination with other people and other elements in the total system.

Some people have a feeling that a system is something to be fought. It is best to give up the idea that a system, just because it is a system, must be destroyed. There can be differences with *the* system but that does not invalidate system as a plan of action. There need to be several plans of action. Input into those plans must be based upon the understanding of what a system is and why it must be put in good workable condition.

The following Aids for Self-Development are to help you sort out pertinent information regarding the interrelated systems within which you work.

....

Aids for Self-Development

1   Examples of different national, state, and local systems are listed below. For each system listed, identify a source of information that you have concerning that system:

Federal	*State*	*Local*
executive system (ED)	state teacher agency	city council
judicial system	state education agency	board committees
legislative system	legislature	union organization

2   Now, identify a source of persuasion, or communication, that is available to you for each system given above.
3   Outline how you can initiate change in each system through your available sources of persuasion.
4   Follow through on your outline and become a change agent for the improvement of a system within which you are working.

....

Taxpayer-Voter Possessiveness

Most people are quite aware that their environment is filled with people who seem to assume that they have certain prerogatives of control over others or at least over the situations in which they exist. Democracy was built on the idea that the citizen has a part in determining the ways that all shall be governed. In a large sense, the world can note that democracy has worked quite well. There is no doubt, however, that from time to time some people take excessive advantage over the fact that they are in a position in which they can affect the systems by which people seek to live together. The concept of democracy should not be lost but it needs to be re-evaluated from time to time to make sure that it has not been used by those who are willing to abuse the privileges which it makes available.

Increasing inclinations by legislative representatives at both state and federal levels to exercise controls over people and the things that they hope to do are observable. This increased use of public controls stimulates many citizens to gain some reassurance that the democracy they thought they possessed has not been lost. In order to reassure themselves, individuals may seek increased participation in citizens' activities. This often leads to some excesses on the part of the governed as well as of the governing group. This may be felt in the classroom by the kinds of controls that are established, not necessarily by school officials, but by citizens who are acting through their legal governmental agencies. There is a persisting acculturational residue which indicates that the 'voice of the people is the voice of God' and 'whoever pays the fiddler calls the tune'. These are ideas that have been stated through most of the decades of the existence of our government and many people tend to act upon them.

Certainly, their ideas are in part right but, when taken too literally, can be nothing other than an over-controlled exercise by some one person or a group of persons. These should be labelled as platitudes that have proved helpful from time to time in clarifying governmental relationships to the people. They do not, however, constitute an edict by which a way of behaving in this society can be determined. As people seek to gain the reassurance of the privileges of citizenship, they often turn to that public agency which has the easiest access.

The school gets nominated in the number one position from the standpoint of easy access. It is much more so than the formal agencies of government and certainly more so than the agencies that are set up independent of government. The people feel that the schools are theirs and their ownership entitles them to some privileges of influence and control that easily could be excessive from the standpoint of the wise operation of the school.

Educators in many ways have encouraged people to have an over confidence in what an education can do. The school has been inclined over many decades to indicate that whatever is needed in a democratic society the schools can supply. Many educators now are beginning to regret the fact that they did not use greater discrimination in setting the limits of the expectations that could be placed upon the products of schools. A review is needed, again, for instance, on the matter of values and whether the schools can satisfactorily provide values education for the people in a society that has such wide range of values which are often in conflict. Anyway, the question needs to be raised as to whether the school has the capacity to do all of the values teaching by itself.

In addition to the notions that have been built into our culture and in addition to the easy access that the schools provide to its public, many in that public look upon the schools as the most convenient scapegoat or as an excuse for other social agencies. Churches often have been critical of the schools because they do not teach values of the type and to the extent that they want. They likewise may point to the schools as being organizations that cause people to ignore the importance of the religious concepts that they espouse. There are other social agencies, such as health organizations, that may use the schools as a scapegoat for some of the things that perhaps they should have been doing themselves. For this reason, the revived (redirection) concept of community education can be very helpful.

Community education, as mentioned earlier, could be quite essential to the achievement of a coordination of all of the educative agencies and influences within a community. Such a coordination does not come about by chance but must be planned (induction) and nurtured. This perhaps will help as much as anything else to clear up the unwise and undue possessiveness that seems to be characteristic of schools in many communities. It must be recognized, nonetheless, that even the employees of a public agency should be available to some type of responsiveness from those in the community who support the educational enterprise. After all, it is their children that are coming to the school for the benefits of an education and they have the right to be interested and to exercise some influence over the patterns of education that may exist.

Political and social sub-systems that exist within the community often hold influential positions concerning school policy. The *Aids for Self-Development* given here are to help you identify these groups and their impact in order to work constructively toward planned change.

....

Aids for Self-Development

1 Identify an agency or organized group in your community that has a potential impact on your school in each of the listed areas:
   (a) social;
   (b) service;
   (c) legislative;

(d) judicial;
(e) educational;
(f) recreational.

2 Add other groups to your list, and determine whether the sphere of influence of each is administrative, instructional, fiscal, public relations, or some other area.

3 Rate the impact on you or on the school for each group as high, moderate, or low in influence.

4 Select the groups you have rated with a high influential impact. Rate their knowledge of educational purposes and practices within their sphere of influence. Is their knowledge high or low?

5 Refer again to figure 2. How do the influences you have listed impact upon your career status according to the facets of the career cycle?

....

Characteristics of Your 'Fishbowl'

The exploration in the classroom and in the classroom's environment presented in the earlier sections of this chapter may leave you feeling as though your classroom is far from being a personal responsibility but rather is a 'fishbowl' with you in it. It was not the intent of the earlier discussions to make the environment a frightening place. Rather it was to recognize that the environment has many different components that must be dealt with by you in the process of teaching.

The classroom is a fishbowl in the sense that many people are interested in what goes on there. The interest, however, can be supportive as well as annoying. The important thing is to recognize the nature of teaching responsibility and relationships to the rest of the school and to the entire community. These relationships, well understood, may become a part of the strategies which are used in teaching to reinforce the things that the teacher can control within the classroom. It must be remembered that many people are in the kind of work that probably also could be called a 'fishbowl'. Certainly, any public employee is under constant review by those citizens of the community who select and who support the many services that a public wants. It is quite possible that the teacher, then, becomes one of the viewers of other people's 'fishbowls'.

The teacher must be quite aware of the fact that there are many 'fishbowls' down the halls — not the least of which may be the administrative and supervisory offices. It is easy to develop the notion that being in a 'fishbowl' means 'big brother' is looking at you all the time. The inference associated with 'big brother' is that there are those who are snooping and for some purpose other than the one that you appreciate. Of course a 'big brother' can be watching any of us all the time. But there is no need to develop a psychosis and assume that everyone is watching for a chance to pounce upon the teacher either because of displeasure with what is being done or as a means of achieving ego-satisfaction.

Many people may be viewing the school fishbowl only through the eyes and ears of others. Reference was made earlier to the fact that the students are the liaison agents between the school and the home and many other facets of the community. What the students experienced and reported become the things that many people who receive the reports are inclined to believe. Here is your opportunity to exercise some influence upon those eyes and ears of the others who depend upon the students as the reporting agent. There is nothing wrong in helping students to understand why things are organized and presented as they are in your classroom. This, in turn, will help to give a more accurate report to the people who are willing and anxious to hear. This is not a form of snooping and need not become laden with threats against the students for reporting things to parents and friends outside the school.

Analyze your own perspectives with respect to your place in the school and in the community and try not to let those perspectives blind you to the friendly and interested others in the school and in the community. People may be observing your fishbowl for the primary reason of hoping to find a way to be of assistance to you. There are many fine people in the school and in the community who may seek the opportunity to do just that. It might be wise for you to give some careful thought to the ways in which you facilitate a complete viewing (renewal) which they could have and use as a basis for better under-standing of the educative process. Exhibits of student work either in the hall outside your classroom, the bulletin boards in your classroom, or in the store window downtown provide easy opportunity for others to view the output of the students you are teaching. There are many ways that the things you want to have viewed in your classroom can be presented and made available to the public. The important thing is that you take the initiative and provide ways of making this communication effective.

Study the advantages of being viewed. It gives you a sense of being understood and this, in turn, makes you a better member of the professional team of associates in your school. The advantage of being viewed is that, when you want to get some help from others, they may have a better understanding of the reason you want that help and be better helpers as a result of it. The direction suggested here is that you work toward an openness in your classroom in every respect.

One of the problems of moving toward the so-called open classroom is that many people fail to understand what was to be gained by it. It is one thing to talk about the school without walls and another thing to get people to believe that it would not be one continuous pattern of interruption among students and teachers within the school. If there are concepts of education invisible to other professionals and to lay people who are sending their children to your school and to your classroom they should be displayed. The openness of viewing (induction) can reduce suspicion and it can encourage support and respect for you and for the educational program.

Many reactions to classroom activities exist, and there are many purposes for these reactions. The next *Aids for Self-Development* are to help you choose the observers of your classroom activities who are important to your work.

....

Aids for Self-Development

1 Choose the persons or groups that you feel are direct or indirect observers of your classroom activities:
   (a)   students;
   (b)   parents;
   (c)   other teachers;
   (d)   principals;
   (e)   supervisors;
   (f)   board members;
   (g)   press;
   (h)   union officials.
2 Add other observers to the above list, and for each one listed, identify the purpose of the observer.
3 Identify methods that you might use to facilitate the observations of those persons or groups that you deem to be important to your work.
4 Determine ways to solicit the reaction of the important persons or groups that will facilitate your work.

....

Diplomacy Is Your Vehicle

References have been made in the previous sections of this chapter as well as in the earlier chapters of the book to many opportunities for interaction with other people. The interaction to be successful and positive must be a truly shared type of experience. Sharing goals with others is most important if you are to be understood as a teacher in your school. Sharing goals gives other people an opportunity to work in parallel and in support with you, even if their own immediate objectives and goals differ. Goals are not something that can be forced upon others anymore than leadership or respect can be forced upon others. It is a matter of achieving a common understanding and, in that way, the sharing represents an interactive experience. It is always helpful not only to share goals with others but also to seek knowledge about the goals of others. It gives several bases for gaining (renewal) additional information as goals and processes are reviewed. It also opens the gates for cooperative action with those others.

The sharing of goals requires that someone initiates an open communication of some kind. It is not safe to assume that one knows the goals of others because the assumption might be more a reflection of one's own perspectives than an objective observation of their goals. Communication, then, becomes one of the greatest of the strategies of diplomacy-providing. Communications must be open and represent an interactive experience. There are times when people exchange, through the communication process, information about their goals and their purposes and their own effort.

At times, communication exchange may seem to be the source of distress. It is natural that people do not agree on all points but it can be natural for each one involved in a divergence or in a difference to remain calm and objective in the face of those opinions and perspectives. The display of anger does not invite a continuation of an interactive process. Neither does it prevent those persons who would impose their own ideas upon others from being rejected.

Involvement becomes a most important activity or purpose for you as well as for the others in your environment. Substantial gains can be made by inviting involvement (induction) of the students in your classroom. This might help them to gain a sense of belonging to your class group as well as feel that they have some part in making the decisions as to how the individual and group action shall proceed. Here again, if this type of diplomatic initiative brings about the supportive attitude through involvement, the teaching and learning tasks will be easier and more effective.

Reference was made earlier to the fact that an expression of appreciation to those who have been cooperative or helpful or simply showing an awareness of what they are doing brings about a closer relationship between those persons and yourself. Your expression of appreciation of others may stimulate creative action on their part as well as identify more and better opportunities for being cooperative in the total teaching responsibilities. If involvement, appreciation, and confidence are a part of the interactive experiences in your classroom and in your school and comunity, you have a basis to plan, to evaluate, and to work together. In this way, involvement can be most satisfactory and the evaluative process which becomes a part or the result of planning as well as an introduction to planning (redirection) can be a rewarding experience. Objectivity in studying perspectives that each one has in relation to the target for planning and evaluating becomes one of the essential elements of the activity.

An expression of appreciation and involvement in the sequence of planning-evaluating-cooperative planning tends to preserve the self-respect of others. It is most important that you can maintain your own self-respect and, just as you value yours, you may be sure that others value theirs. The part of diplomacy that is based upon the respect for individuals and the task at hand becomes one of the ways of preserving self-respect and of operating together. Diplomacy is seeing together; not deceiving each other. Diplomacy becomes one of the ways that you can harness that environment as a part of your team for the teaching of the students in your classroom.

Back to Self

This chapter began with a reference to the earlier discussion of the phenomena within your own classroom and extended beyond your classroom to the great outside. It is time now to put those two concepts together, namely, the importance of the inside of your classroom and the importance of the outside of your classroom, and do some viewing of yourself as a basis for stimulating a creative type of teaching and an educative experience in your classroom. Chapter 6 will deal with 'The Nature of Self-Sufficiency'. It will discuss in some detail what is lost if you do not make use of the many and potent helpful aspects of your school and community.

Chapter 6

The Nature of Self-sufficiency

An earlier chapter took a careful look at the inside of the classroom. Yet another chapter looked through the classroom window to that great outside which constitutes the environment of the school. Whether looking inside the classroom or looking at the outside of the classroom, many people were seen. Some of these people had many expectations to place upon the teacher. Many, however, saw opportunities to support the teacher and, of course, many simply went about their own business paying no attention to the school. The important thing is to be aware of what is inside and what is outside the classroom.

The purpose of this chapter is to take a look not inside nor outside the classroom but rather into a teacher's mind. Look now at the kinds of values that one has which caused that person to establish a certain pattern of viewing and of relating to others. The idea of self-sufficiency is the central point here. It is an attempt to explore the extent to which one seeks to be an independent and self-sufficient person without looking into the potential of the strength that one might gain from others. Many people have an inclination to believe that their success depends upon the number of things that they can do by themselves without the assistance of others. Still others can view themselves as finding self-sufficiency not in isolation but rather in the association with others who would join in tasks which are a common responsibility.

Polar regions of sufficiency can be identified in this matter of self-sufficiency. At one pole, there is the view of the complete dependency. In this case, self-sufficiency seems to disappear in the usual sense of the word. This type seeks an opportunity to avoid decisions and to avoid independent action because they prefer to be dependent upon the decisions and the directions of others. The other polar region is that of complete self-sufficiency in which people who can help are rejected. The important thing is to seek a balance between dependency and self-sufficiency as defined here. Nothing is to be gained by seeking the means by which individuals can locate themselves at one pole or the other. A balance gives an opportunity for providing the experiences of self-sufficiency while at the same time enjoying the dependency that can be allocated in others. A balance can be sought, not so much in terms of how the individual feels about it, but rather by what the task at hand demands by way of self-sufficiency and dependency. Certainly there is no use either to seek the poles of martyrdom or arrogance. A balance does not require either of these. In all probability an inclination either toward martyrdom or arrogance will only destroy the potential balance that might be achieved between the worthy aspects of dependency and self-sufficiency.

The deprivation of associating with others is not a normal state of individualism. Individualism can occur in a group enterprise while sharing expertise with colleagues as one goes about the common and individual tasks. Analysis seems to be the best way to achieve a base for decisions about one's self and the relationship with others in the educational enterprise.

Self-Sufficiency May Shut Out Others

The opening section of this chapter indicates that individuals probably have considerable latitude of choice in determining an attitude toward self-sufficiency and dependency. If their attitudes are not compatible with any particular person's way of thinking, they might have to take advantage of their own individual expertise exclusively. In this case, they lose the benefits of cooperation with others and, in that sense, lose the benefits of other's expertise as it applies to the personal and the common tasks in the process of education.

An easily claimed attitude is that goals are personal property. It probably can do only a disservice to the individual and certainly to the people to be served in the school when this particular attitude towards goals is taken. The goals cannot be personal property so long as they affect the students in the classroom, the associates in the school, and particularly those people in the community who establish and support the total school opportunities. The overriding goal which cannot be personal property is that of the goal of education and of the particular school system. These must be used as the reference-point for the determination of individual goals and purposes which can be individualized but must still be in harmony with the goals of the total organization. The individualism preferred by the teacher is often identified as academic freedom. The term is meaningful primarily to those who seek the sense of being self-sufficient.

Weaknesses can be found in the usual concepts of self-sufficiency. It is well to include these in the analysis of the particular stance that each one is to take. As a classroom teacher, it is almost certain that self-sufficiency does not include things such as:

1 The services that maintain the working condition. At the present time, janitorial and maintenance tasks as teacher responsibilities would be severely criticized by those who teach in the modern school facilities and expect to have all of the favorable working conditions resulting from services by others.

2 The supplies and materials that are required for the teaching act. Students must have adequate supplies and the teacher must have access to those supplies. Teachers do not see self-sufficiency carried to the extent that they would order their own supplies and materials, go to the stores to get them, and then bring them to the classroom where they will be consumed.

3 The concept of salary delivery. As teachers, it is expected that salary checks will be delivered ontime. Back of that there are tax collections that must be made in accounting of funds as required by law.

The three examples above are support facilities and do not represent the full state of self-sufficiency that is envisioned only with respect to a particular part of the activities in the classroom. Most people like to receive the acknowledgement and expressions of appreciation from others. The whole concept of self-sufficiency would perhaps deny that these are essential and yet, as sensitive individuals, most of us would receive them without there being any evidence of lack of self-sufficiency on our own part.

The idea of self-sufficiency is usually limited to classroom management and instructional procedures. Teachers perhaps want the self-sufficiency of determination in how the classroom will be managed and how the instructional procedures will be designed and pursued. Yet, at the same time, they are unable to claim full self-sufficiency in this since the management in the classroom might affect school property and neighboring classrooms as well as the imprints made upon the students. Even weaknesses, in a sense, are found in the concepts of full sufficiency in that concessions must be made to the demands of those served and under the conditions that the service is to be rendered.

No simple choice can be made between involvement or exclusion. It is a matter of seeing what kinds of things others might do for us and what individuals can do for others to make each of their own tasks more effective and, at the same time, serve the full purposes of the educational institution. It means that a certain amount of openness must exist in each classroom and in each school. Openness means approachability and the inclination to approach others. Openness is not a pursuit of the things that others might consider personal with respect to their professional activities. It means being acceptable and available and to find similar traits on the part of colleagues. People may cheat themselves more than others if they try to refuse this kind of openness in a group organization.

The *Aids for Self-Development* given here are designed to help you improve your relationships to self and others.

....

Aids for Self-Development

1   List, in three columns, the items below that are self-sufficient, those that are alter-sufficient (satisfied by others), and those that are cooperatively satisfied:
     (a)   knowledge of the community;
     (b)   knowledge of the school;
     (c)   understanding of the student;
     (d)   knowledge of the profession of teaching;
     (e)   classroom management techniques;
     (f)   instructional supplies selection;
     (g)   determining economic standard for self;
     (h)   determining professional standard for self;
     (i)   understanding institutional goals;
     (j)   understanding personal goals;
     (k)   understanding professional goals;
     (l)   transferring institutional goals to objectives, both personal and professional;
     (m) developing curriculum;
     (n)   determining institutional techniques;
     (o)   creating lesson plans;
2   Among the items you have selected as being self-satisfied, choose the three (3) that are most important to you. Design an induction method to include one of your colleagues in a cooperative relationship to satisfy these three.
3   Look at the items you have identified as being alter-sufficient and choose the three (3) that are most important to you. Describe a

renewal technique to involve yourself with the other(s) in a cooperative relationship for these three.

....

Self-Reliance in Group Activities

The concepts of self-sufficiency as presented in the preceding section are not indications that any individual has to give up all rights to self-satisfaction. There are many ways to achieving self-satisfaction and the one to be discussed in this section is that of self-reliance in the group situation. This is the sense in which individuals may achieve (induction) the fulfillment of those tasks which they have been assigned or which have been initiated on their part.

The important thing to recognize in a teaching situation is that there are few if any one-room schools left. This means that the teaching assignment takes place in a school that has multiple classrooms, a staff of teachers, and supervisory and administrative personnel. A group activity, if it is to be successful, must be coordinated in some manner. This does not have to be achieved through the dominance of any one person in the position of supervisor or administrator and neither does it have to be achieved through the controls of a professional organization of some type. The thing to be noted in group activity is that there is a differentiated nature to work loads. If a school is to achieve its full potential, any one person can not master all of the requisites of a full educational program. There are different grade levels to be taught, there are different students to be taught, and there are different subjects to be taught. This means that, in a differentiated situation of this type, individuals can develop (renewal) some expertise unique to their own work activity.

Achievement can give the sense of self-reliance because of the differentiated nature which provides that each one has a sense of a unique contribution to be made to the total organizational expectation. The differentiation usually is identified in job descriptions. The job description indicates the nature of the assignment and expectations (induction) that are placed upon each position and each individual in that position. The job description gives the first indication of the nature of the expectations and the responsibilities allocated to each individual who has accepted a teaching position.

The differentiation in staffing, however, is not a form of separatism. It is not a way of saying that each individual is independent of all other individuals. It is a way of saying that each individual can know what other individuals know about their assignments, and what their own contributions are to be as well as the contributions to be made by others on the school staff. The identification of the unique responsibilities of each individual provides an opportunity to find the individual's contribution in the context of group goals. The individual goals as indicated earlier must be in harmony with the group goals. Then the individual contribution will be realized as moving forward (redirection) the total obligations and the teacher will attain a sense of success or self-reliance in providing that particular assistance in the total group enterprise.

Teachers have several facets to their careers in addition to differentiated responsibilities. The career cycle pictured in figure 2 shows several potential career facets. Teachers residing in the different categories who have assigned tasks will, necessarily, perform the tasks with different levels of success or effectiveness.

An enigma can develop in the situation in which the individual succeeds and the group fails. The opposite likewise can be true in that the group might succeed even though an individual has failed in fulfilling his or her obligations. It is important to observe the extent to which the total group is able to fulfill its obligations through the well coordinated efforts of each individual on the staff. This does not mean that each individual has to subdue individualism in order to achieve what might be called *groupism*. It simply means that each individual is to make a unique contribution and, in that way, to participate in what can be identified as group success. The success of the group activities is readily observable and can be analyzed. At the same time the individuals within that group can have their own contributions made observable and measure contributions of assistance to the total group activity. In this sense, the individual never needs to be lost in a group activity. The individual need not be deprived of the sense of self-reliance simply because there are others sharing various obligations and responsibilities in the total educational activity. The individual contributions are not only observable but they are subject to a recognition on the part of others as a unique contribution to the total task.

The fact of recognizing the individual's contributions to the group success does not constitute a sharing of the individual performance in the sense that someone else is doing exactly the same thing or a lot of others are doing exactly the same thing. The contributions are individual contributions and are to be reviewed in that sense. The constraints imposed by the group are not constraints upon individual self-reliance but rather constraints upon individual failure to pursue goals and purposes that are in harmony with the total activity of the educational program. Since the contribution of individuals and of the group are observable and recognizable it is crucial to find some of the ways of knowing that you are doing the job.

One of the ways of knowing is to assess the outcomes of the classroom activities, primarily the learning on the part of the students as meeting the goals that have been established not only by the individual teacher but by the group. There are specific measures of what is learned as well as some ways of observing the how of the learning. The individual teacher is self-directive in the sense that classroom management does structure the way that the teaching and learning takes place. A part of knowing that you are doing the job is to make sure (i) that all of the activities in the classroom are well supported by the supplies and materials required; (ii) that the individual students relate to other students in the class; and (iii) that there is a sense of community observable. Sense of community in the classroom can be observed as the acceptance of the students that they have a common purpose, namely, to learn. It does not mean that they all have to learn the same thing.

Another way of knowing that you are doing your job is that you are self-reliant in accepting the differentiated assignment just as you make sure that there are variations in the expectations placed upon the students. This is necessary because few classrooms have ever existed in which all pupils learn exactly the same way and to the same purpose. The individualization, not only in teaching but in judging the extent to which the purposes of the classroom have been achieved, becomes a way of determining whether your own self-reliance has meshed well with the group activities. When you have achieved a sense of self-reliance in fulfilling the unique responsibilities that you accepted in your position assignment, you can be aware of a sense of pride in the fact that you have achieved your commitment in the classroom. Also, there is a pride in knowing that your contribution to the total group is just as important for you as a teacher as it is for any person in any work assignment or individual enterprise. The pride to which you are entitled can be a sense of self-reliance and you will find it highly stimulating to continue to produce well for the purposes of your classroom and of your school.

You, in the experimental realm of teaching, must be aware of operations and feelings in both yourself and others. The next *Aids for Self-Development* are to provide you with the opportunity to look at what you do, what others do, and how each of you contribute to the total school activity.

. . . .

Aids for Self-Development

1   Describe the development of a learning experience for your students that you have been concerned with recently.
    (a)   State how you sensed the need for development and how you interacted with a colleague about it.
    (b)   Identify how you responded to the need and how you shared your response with colleagues.
2   Describe an evaluation activity that has been successful in your classroom.
    (a)   Outline your creative thought in imagining the activity and any contribution of a colleague in making a decision regarding it.
    (b)   Record your steps in inventing the activity and the cooperation you received from colleagues.
3   Describe a professional development activity that has had great meaning to you.
    (a)   Determine how you concentrated on this activity and describe how a colleague showed a comprehension of it.
    (b)   State how you organized your part in this activity and how colleagues contributed in the practice of it.
4   Develop a general statement from the descriptions you have recorded above that summarizes the blending of personal and interpersonal components of your professional activities. Note how this blending is helpful to school operations.

. . . .

Failure Coverup May Be Your Downfall

The emphasis in the previous section was on self-reliance as a meritorious experience as individual assignments are pursued in the total group activity. Self-reliance is not always a virtue because it can be a burden if it is applied to the cover-up of failures. There are varied aspects to failure and they need to be analyzed carefully. Usually the failure in the classroom on the part of the teacher does seem to draw severe criticism from many quarters. Perhaps one reason for this is that the teacher has not shared enough information with supervisors, other teachers, students, and parents about the kinds of procedures to be used in the teaching-learning situation.

A failure can be attributed to many factors other than the teacher's expertise in teaching. Unfortunately, teachers have been given the blame almost exclusively for many of the failures that occur in the school. At the present time, the concern for the basics seems to be something that the teachers should not have let happen. There are many aspects to what is taught, to how it is taught, and to how what is taught is measured. Keep these things in mind as the possibilities of an occasional failure are considered. The failure can be not just the teacher's lack of expertise or misapplied procedures but could be the attitude that the parents instill in the children before they come to school. The students who come to school and dare the teacher to teach them certainly are putting an undue burden on the measure of success of the teaching effort. These things need to be recognized, discussed, and dealt with directly (redirection) as factors contributing to the success or failure of the teaching and learning effort in the classroom.

The variables that relate to success and failure need to be weighted in terms of the degree of influence that each one has upon the success or failure in the classroom. The appropriateness of teaching materials so often is not given the weight that it should have in judging the success or failure of learning activities. Scheduling of special activities usually is beyond control of the teacher and yet the scheduling practices may have much to do with the outcomes of student progress. Obligations that come from legislated acts and the expectations placed upon the classrooms by the federal and state grants that are designed to offer categorical help often disrupt the procedures in the classroom, sometimes to the extent that the basic goals are diverted and, consequently, the appearance of teacher failure is created. Here again, the main protection for a teacher is to develop the habit of analyzing (renewal) the kinds of things that affect each major learning thrust.

One of the aspects of failure that should be noted is what might be called *failure tolerance* not only of the teacher concerned but of all others involved in the school activities. This is particularly true for the supervisory and administrative staff members whose failure tolerance for someone else might be lower than is justifiable. Teachers can help to a considerable extent in this by initiating (induction) conversations with the supervisory staff with the intent of analyzing those variables which affect the success or failure of teaching and learning. It is well to recognize, however, that when a failure occurs and — regardless of the tolerance of all involved with the existence of failure — there is little hope to cover up the failure. There has been enough of this type of thing at the national, state, and municipal levels in activities other than education to indicate that such cover-ups seldom can be successful. Of course they can be concealed for a short period of time but what is to be gained by this, if, when revealed, there is an added burden of suspicion cast in the directions of the school and of the teacher. There is strength gained in diagnosing and reporting failures. There is no need to attempt a cover-up when the procedures are anticipated which control the relationship between students, superordinates, and subordinates.

The diagnosis of the goals and their relationship to the selection of teaching materials, the time commitment of teachers and students, and many other aspects of the total teaching responsibility need to be identified, described, and judged in terms of influence (induction) upon the learning activities. Reporting failures with the diagnosis of variables that may have been contributors is one of the best ways to secure help from the supervisory and administrative staffs. Immediately upon reporting to others, those others will recognize that as a teacher you are alert and trying to face the total task of teaching in a responsible way. The fact of diagnosing and reporting leads to the identification of sources of help. Suggestions can be forthcoming because there is a direction for them to be pointed.

The analyses which each teacher makes of successes and failures in the classroom can at the same time reveal the kind of help or changes (renewal) that need to be made. It is not enough simply to say, 'This effort failed and what should I do about it?'. Any supervisor needs help in trying to respond with the expertise that supervision possesses, namely, to be able to go to the resources that are needed in order to make the teacher's effort in the classroom a success. Once the analyses have been made and the sources of help have been identified remediation is immediately possible. A negative attitude toward remediation as the proof of failure is too common. That is not the most productive attitude to take. It is better to look upon the remediation of failing efforts as being developmental in nature. It is developmental in the sense that the correcting of an error or the adjusting from failure to success is a matter of moving ahead. Moving ahead is development.

One of the most rewarding ways to avoid failure or to deal with failure is to look at it in the context of experimentation. It is not wise to attempt to do something new in the classroom by way of an experimental effort without making certain that the supervisors are well-informed of what you intend to do and how you intend to do it. At the time that the experimental effort is described, there should be some indication of what is to be done in preparation. Here again, having a basis for analyses of this type makes the cover-up of failure unnecessary. It is better to determine the attitudes of self and of others towards the professional effort (induction) so that the entire effort can be looked upon in a professional manner and not as one that is demanding or inviting some type of reprisal. This approach to the possibility of failure in the classroom again comes back to what was stated earlier in this chapter, namely, that openness is one of the great strengths that a teacher can have in dealing with the teaching problem in the context of a school. Natural openness in a relationship with supervisors, peers, students, and parents is almost a sure way to provide a cushion for failing effort and to provide an improved productivity that grows out of the analyses of failure. It is well to recognize the elements of failure for what they are, namely, specific activities that did not achieve the goal intended.

These *Aids for Self-Development* are designed to help you determine the cause of failure and to find methods for correcting it.

. . . .

Aids for Self-Development

1   The activities listed below are representative of areas where teacher failure may be evident. List, in two columns, those areas you approach with confidence and those you approach with doubt:
  (a)   developing an intention to teach;
  (b)   determining an instructional technique;
  (c)   using the technique;
  (d)   analyzing your performance;
  (e)   identifying your own personal style;
  (f)   determining your commitment;
  (g)   analyzing your contribution;
  (h)   revising your technique;
  (i)   evaluating your performance;
  (j)   solidifying your perspective.
2   Using the same set of activities, make a two–column list of those you undertake with genuine sincerity and those you face in a superficial way.
3   Now use the list to create two columns of activities that regenerate you in your profession or that cause you to capitulate too easily.
4   Look at the overlap in the columns that signify a loss (doubt, superficiality, and capitulation) and identify development activities to keep you from failure by moving these into the gain column.

. . . .

Walking Alone May Be a Long, Lonely Walk

The emphasis has been continued throughout this chapter about openness as a way of achieving the goals that individuals set for themselves and of opening the door for a rewarding relationship with peers, supervisors, and administrators. Aloneness is not proof of self-sufficiency. Aloneness simply means that the individual chooses not to open the association with others whether it be with a teacher in the next classroom or with parents of the students.

Aloneness in the extreme brings on many of the personal difficulties that may lead to less than full success in the teaching-learning activities. Avoiding loneliness opens the way for the individual teacher to invite others to the choice of applauding or deprecating the things that are accomplished. It is better to have this openness that permits the choice of response which then may be known by the teacher involved. This is much better than to have people applauding or deprecating your work in the classroom without your knowing which way the sentiments have been recorded. Aloneness does for other people exactly what it does for the one choosing to be alone, namely, it generates speculative suspicions. When people do not know what the other wants to do or is doing, there is a little inclination to draw some conclusions about what the other person wants and does that may be far from accurate. Speculative suspicions are perhaps the most dangerous both to the persons harboring them and to the targets of them. It is well, then, to invite the openness that gives people a basis for making judgments about others as well as about themselves on the basis of something other than assumptions or speculations.

The relationships between people can be based upon openness and, therefore, upon fact. Much depends upon the capacity for communication. The interaction that has been described under the word *openness* throughout this chapter is perhaps best described as communication. The person walking alone may be talking to herself/himself but that is not communication. Communication is a two-way interaction and is most rewarding in the supporting relationships that can be easily available to most everyone involved in the teaching act. The interaction of communication (renewal) also supports self-esteem which is so important to the individual's sense of worthwhileness. Self-esteem cannot be experienced when walking alone. It requires referents as the basis for comparing. There are few established norms for judging the quality of teaching but there are many ways of comparing the effectiveness of one method or of one person with one group of students as opposed to others that can occur in the same school. Self-esteem can be achieved by the openness that makes it possible for individuals to compare themselves to others. In this way, individuals can make corrections (redirection) when that comparison is unfavorable or can experience self-esteem and self-reliance that comes from seeing one's self in a more favorable way.

Individuals desire security in their personal lives as well as their professional activities. Security usually is acquired through people, not through individual effort alone. Just as self-esteem is dependent upon reference so security is acquired through the efforts of others or the reassurances of others in the profession. It may be monetary or the goodwill that can be generated among colleagues. Rewards are based on the judgments of others. The individual can supply much meritorious data that can help in the judgments regarding rewards but the reward decision is made by someone else. Certainly, the more interaction that can occur between the individual teacher and those others who are making the judgments, the more it will facilitate a good and a favorable decision for the teacher involved.

The emphasis here on giving up the aloneness and going to groupness may worry some in that it may provide a little protective screen for the individual teacher. Selectivity of associates is a privilege of the teacher just as selectivity of the approach to analysis is the prerogative of the teacher. Selectivity is a protective screen that can give the sense of confidence in the fact that rewards, security, and self-esteem are not only entitled and entitled rightly but rather that they are a practical status to be sought.

The next *Aids for Self-Development* are to serve as a basis for analyzing your perceptions of your peers and colleagues and your relationship to them in the school organization.

....

Aids for Self-Development

1   Listed below are some of the key interactors of a school setting. You may wish to expand this list, or clarify it, to make it specific to your situation. Determine the significance (high or low) that interaction with each of these groups or people has to you:
    (a)   teachers;
    (b)   principals;
    (c)   parents;
    (d)   counselors;
    (e)   students;

(f)   central office;
(g)   custodians;
(h)   supervisors;
(i)   board members;
(j)   others.
2   Now analyze the frequency of contact you have with each group. Is it daily, weekly, monthly, or even less frequently?
3   Describe the mode of communication most often used with each group. Is it spoken, on the telephone, written, or second hand information?
4   Using your responses from numbers 2 and 3 above, determine the best vehicle and frequency of contact for you from each group. If the ideal differs from the actual, design methods to change this situation.

....

Adversity May Not Be Stalking You

The reader may assume that a negative perception of aloneness controlled the preceding section of this chapter. Such was not the intent but the concept should be carried at least one step further in an effort to see what analysis can do in helping individuals to direct their own activities in a positive relationship with others. A perception of adversity can vary with each individual. Any annoyance could be considered an adversity. There are some people who may get the idea that somebody and something is always lurking in the wings waiting to pounce upon them and their work. It is easy to confuse adversity with the difficulty of the task at hand. Some people may be inclined to base their judgments on a false pride, in doing things in what may be called *the tough way*. Some people believe apparently that, if the task is accomplished easily, it must not have been challenging to the expertise possessed. It is important to clear away this kind of false assumption through the analysis of self-work and relationships to others. It is possible that the enemy is in your own mind rather than stalking you from behind or from hidden areas.

One of the common ways to build up adversity is to take a somewhat unrealistic view of one's own capacity to accomplish things. If there is an over-estimation of self-worth, it is possible that achieving a goal or developing a set of perspectives on self-worth might create problems for the individual. Individuals need to think about the good fortunes that they have rather than the adversities that can be appearing before them or behind them. The good fortune, first of all, is the opportunity to be a professional and be challenged by the work at hand, by analysis of ourselves and our relationships to the task and to others. Real challenges are much more fun in accomplishment than are those which can be dreamed up and labeled as adversities.

The real challenges are the achievement of the proper goals that have been established even though those goals are not always achieved easily. The magnitude and complexity of the problems that are encountered in achieving the classroom goals are not to be adversities but simply that they are challenging tasks. Teachers should recognize goals as challenges. Teachers have the talent to resolve many difficult problems. Talent is for using in a positive and developmental way and not just for defense against the presumed adversities that may be lurking around. It is important to look ahead to the achievement of the goals at hand and not to be looking over one's shoulder for the kinds of things that may be following.

Personal goals must be recognized and achieved in order to move ahead to classroom and school district goals. The following *Aids for Self-Development* are structured to help you collect information concerning the tasks ahead of you in achieving your goals.

. . . .

Aids for Self-Development

1 State a personal goal in your work by differentiating the concepts of *job insurance* and *job gratification* for your professional position.
   (a) Determine your position in the achievement of this goal.
   (b) Identify the significant others who can best help you move closer to your goal.
2 State a personal goal in your work by differentiating between *isolation* in your work and *recognition* of your work.
   (a) Determine your progress in the achievement of this goal.
   (b) Identify the significant others who can best help you move closer to your goal.
3 State a personal goal in your work by differentiating the acquisition of *power* and of *authority* in your role.
   (a) Determine your status in the achievement of this goal.
   (b) Identify the significant others who can best help you move closer to your goal.
4 State a personal goal in your work by creating your image as a *teacher* or a *learner* in respect to your profession.

    (a)   Determine your position in the achievement of this goal.

    (b)   Identify the significant others who can best help you move closer to your goal.

5   Plan a strategy to work with those significant others who reappear in your responses above to move toward your goals.

....

Front Office Versus Back Room

Reference has been made numerous times in the earlier sections of this chapter to the problems that can be encountered by seeking isolation from those who might be professional associates within the school. Likewise, references have been made to the advantages of establishing and maintaining an open relationship with others in the school and in the community.

A question might be raised if a choice is necessary as to whether the individual seeks the communication with the front office or with a small clique of dissidents or a small group of positive planners. It appears in common practice, however, that it is a choice between the front office which is the supervisory and administrative offices and personnel, and the place where teachers tend to congregate. The choice often is difficult because in the minds of many teachers the front offices seem unapproachable. The teachers' lounge or other locations convenient for gathering such as at the same luncheon table each noon do provide ready access to colleagues who can share many of their thoughts, ambitions, and problems. An exclusive choice of one or the other probably is wholly unnecessary.

The supervisory and administrative staff exists for well defined functions within the school organization. They can be sought for professional and social associations that can provide some relaxation from the tasks in the classroom. Perhaps, rather than a choice of one or the other, it is wiser to look at it as a possibility of balancing the kinds of contacts that are available so that the individual is not denied any source in the school system as a proper privilege of communication.

The professional teacher associations have become much stronger in recent decades and have provided places for individual teachers to seek council, assistance, and relief that might come from communication with colleagues in the profession. It is not necessarily a matter of the professional association versus the supervisory-administrative offices. Rather, it is the convenience for teachers to be represented in a consideration of those working conditions and benefits (redirection) which the individual teacher might find difficult to initiate without the assistance of the professional organization leaders. Looking at the problem of making a choice between the front office, the backroom, or the independent association forces an exploration of the statuses of availability. These and other sources of influence are defined in the organizational environment in figure 2.

Service can be available from any of the three basic sources. Power is gained from one or the other, and at times emotional relief is available to the individual who is experiencing some frustrations in the tasks at hand. The front office can offer the individual teacher many kinds of support that would be helpful. The interpretation of community wishes is an important thing for each teacher to know. Information for teachers (induction) about the legal prerequisites that are established for the operation of schools is a responsibility of the supervisory and administrative staff. So regardless of which agency is chosen as a means of seeking service, power, or emotional relief, the balance between all of those available sources of assistance should be considered, reviewed objectively, and consulted openly.

The sense of self-sufficiency perhaps is the thing sought in choosing any one of these individuals or groups for reassurance. Support for self-sufficiency can help individuals to the desired self-realization in the professional activity. It is important that the available sources and the unique contributions of each are used to arrive at a balance in the contacts. There must be accepted at the same time the responsibility to use the help that can be secured from any of these sources. Help may exist but it is not there if the individual fails to make use of it. 'Help not perceived as help is not help.' Again, analysis can be very helpful as the individual takes a look at the kinds of origins of help that might be available.

These *Aids for Self-Development* suggest some sources of assistance that exist in most schools and provide an opportunity for your own identification and assessment of them.

. . . .

Aids for Self-Development

1 A general classification of sources of assistance within a local school is presented below. Select those which you see as sources in your situation and add others as well:
   (a) administrative staff;   (c) custodial staff;
   (b) clerical and secretarial staff; (d) lunchroom staff;

(e) regular classroom teachers; (l) teacher aide;

(f) itinerant teacher; (m) psychologists and

(g) curriculum consultants; physiotherapists;

(h) unit or team leaders; (n) school nurses;

(i) department leaders; (o) professional organizations;

(j) counselors; (p) others.

(k) librarians;

2 Determine the helping sources from the list above for the different factors of your professional life. A few specific factors are suggested below; feel free to add your own:

(a) emotional relief; (k) teaching techniques;

(b) knowledge of subject matter; (l) curriculum selections;

(c) attendance regulations; (m) job security;

(d) safety standards; (n) student guidance;

(e) health standards; (o) community approval;

(f) drug abuse; (p) classroom management;

(g) discipline procedures; (q) effective objectives;

(h) attitude adjustments; (r) instructional materials;

(i) classroom atmosphere; (s) legal rights and responsibilities;

(j) inspiration; (t) extracurricular activities.

3 Also determine the hindering sources for those factors you have selected, and determine a way to redirect the hindering sources to become helping ones.

. . . .

.

Interactor-Sufficiency

The concerns in this chapter are indicated in its title as being the various elements related to self-sufficiency. There was much emphasis in the earlier sections of the chapter on the fact that self-sufficiency is not improper but that it must not take one to a position of isolation. Perhaps a more positively oriented identification than self-sufficiency might be *interactor-sufficiency*.

Interaction with others is one of the best means of therapy for undue personal concern. It is not wrong to have personal concerns. Some categories for concern are given in the personal environment sphere of figure 2. Undue personal concern, however, may lead to some attitudes and behaviors that are not as productive as the individual has the capacity to be. Interaction means that openness must always be maintained as a means of contacting others and for others to contact you. The nurturing of reciprocity (renewal) is worth the effort. Just as communication is an interaction between people, so reciprocity indicates that there is a mutual relationship between people that causes them to be helpful to each other.

Reciprocity can be positive or negative. The negative incidence is one in which a person is harmed or believed to be harmed by another and then reciprocates by trying to harm that other person. There is little to be gained from the negative stance in the professional area. Positive reciprocity is one in which each person in the interaction provides some source of help for the other and has the opportunity of receiving help from the other. The increased reciprocity among those on the professional staff, particularly those on the teaching staff, reduces waste caused by duplication. One teacher, who can indicate the characteristics of a student from the previous year's experience, may alert the teacher currently working with that student to some of the ways of being more helpful. Having this indication based upon the previous year's experience of another teacher is much less costly in time than for the current teacher to identify the specific information about the student and then set out to provide some ways of making progress.

Reciprocity increases communication and this tends to differentiate individual responsibility from group responsibilities for the total group outcomes that are beyond the proper expectations of any one individual. Reciprocity can provide the opportunity for identifying the unique things that each individual can contribute to the group enterprise. This can be called the allocation of unique expertise. It takes an openness between people to identify it in the first place and then provide (redirection) the opportunities for putting that expertise to best use. This, in turn, reduces the conflict potential that always exists between peers or between peers and those in the supervisory and administrative positions. Conflict is seldom productive to the desired achievement of goals established in the classroom. It may as well be recognized as interference. Recognize, too, that the power is within our own hands to reduce conflict potential through reciprocal activities.

Reciprocity leads to a mutual reinforcement among individuals that can give a sense of self-sufficiency through this interactor-sufficiency. Giving and receiving help comes naturally for most people who are open in their relationships with others and who are sure of the kinds of goals that they have accepted and the procedures by which those goals can be achieved. Here again an analysis can be helpful in determining the degree of interactor-sufficiency that each one has achieved.

Reciprocity can provide the opportunity for identifying the unique things that each individual can contribute to other individuals and to the group enterprise. These *Aids for Self-Development* give you an opportunity to outline interactions and expertise to build an effective school.

. . . .

Aids for Self-Development

1 Four characteristics of an effective organization are given below. Select a situation from your school experience that is an example of each characteristic:
   (a) cooperation (synergy);
   (b) mutual interest (esprit);
   (c) fellowship (intimacy);
   (d) flexibility (pliability).
2 Identify the staff members who were part of the interaction in each situation you selected above. Name unique expertise of each interactor in these situations.
3 Determine additional ways that these elements of expertise can be combined to create an effective school.
4 Review the facets of the teacher career cycle (figure 2). Which facets represent the significant others you have chosen? Which facets are devoid of significant interactors? What does this mean?

. . . .

Helping Your Helpers

Many people hold the notion that help is available only under special conditions. There are, of course, many special conditions that would make a solution to the situation or problem much easier with the right kind of help. Numerous references have been made in this chapter to the use of help. They are based on the assumption that every person at some time and under some conditions can perform better by having the right kind of help. There is some danger here, however, that individuals may get the idea that when they have put themselves in the mood to receive help that, because of the mood, help will arrive. This is a faulty assumption and requires more analytic realizations with respect to how help occurs.

Early in each teaching assignment, there may be times when a supervisor sees you casually or formally and asks how things are going and if there is anything that you would like done by way of help. Your answer to this in a negative or indecisive manner will not cause the supervisor to impose help upon you. Supervisors and others who are in a helping position (induction) need to know what kind of help you need. They then can search for the right kind of assistance that might be real help rather than just a process of interaction. Self-diagnosis leads to an identification of the kind of help needed.

Self-diagnosis is dependent upon the individual. Numerous references and aids have been provided in the earlier sections of this chapter which are designed to help the individual do a self-analysis. In that way, one can identify the kind of problems that exist, the kind of goals that are to be achieved, and the kind of assistance or help that would be most appropriate (renewal) for the tasks at hand. With self-analysis data, it is possible for that same individual to look around among associates, peers, and supervisory or administrative personnel who might be available. A personal judgment can be made as to which help would be best in the face of the diagnostic or analytic data that have been acquired. The openness and interaction that have been emphasized throughout the chapter are the ways that each individual can find out what kind of potential the other possible helpers might have. Certainly it is necessary to determine the expertise that would be most helpful in a particular situation, then to make some judgment as to where the expertise exists among the environment of the classroom and to make certain that it can be made available. With the kinds of data suggested here and the kind of insights into the potential helpers, the individual is ready to initiate the contact with the potential helpers.

Initiating contacts is not a matter of presenting a demand. It is not a matter of humiliating one's self before a supposed superior intellect. Initiating a contact (redirection) is the matter-of-fact way that each one can approach a potential helper and indicate the problem identified with the information that led to that identification. Realizing that a problem exists is the first step in its solution. Probably anyone contacted would be impressed by the evidence of thorough self-analysis which led to the identification of the need and the approach to those that might be of help. The attitude, at this point, becomes one of the conditioners of the communication's effectiveness. It is not merely the fact that good data are backing up the identification of the problem which requires the help. It is also the attitude in the presentation to the potential helper which makes it easy for that person to respond.

Many teachers take the posture that supervisors are supposed to be able to help with anything. Such is not the case. Supervisors have some areas in which expertise is outstanding and other areas in which they must muddle along just like anyone else. The attitude which indicates that help be provided upon demand can do nothing other than to alienate that helper who might be available. Once the approach has been made on a mutually interactive basis and communications have been effective in stating the nature of the problem as well as the perception of the help needed, the stage is set for the help to be offered.

Suggestions may be presented by positive statement, by query for more data, or by an identification of alternatives or other ways that the helper might be communicating to the individual seeking help. An obligation arises immediately that the one seeking help must be able to interpret the help that is offered. If the supervisor presents a number of alternatives, interpretation of them needs to be achieved in an interactive way in order to make sure that the alternative in the mind of the supervisor is the alternative that is perceived (redirection) by the teacher receiving the help. A great deal of confidence is needed in such instances. Confidence not only in the status of expertise but confidence in the probability of a friendly reaction even though the suggestions made by way of help stimulate questions on the part of the individual being helped.

Once the communication has been completed and the help has been presented and accepted, the implementation of the suggestions becomes the responsibility of the teacher seeking the help. It is well, in talking with the person offering help, to seek any suggestions that might be available by way of the implementation of the suggestions made. If this is not forthcoming, then, as an individual seeking and needing this help, it is important that a plan be developed (renewal) by way of what the individual sees as the best application of the suggestion.

After a reasonable amount of time allocated to the process of implementing the suggestions, there is need for feedback to the person offering the help. At this point, the same kind of self-analysis would be appropriate in determining the kinds of evidence that indicate whether the applied suggestions have been better than the prior activity or whether they have made no benefits at all or even may have brought on other failing outcomes. Feedback is the responsibility of the person seeking and receiving the help. If the person offering the help, likewise, has some follow-up activities in supporting the suggestions made, feedback to the individual initiating the request becomes appropriate.

Feedback responsibilities include some evaluation. It is an evaluation of whether the suggestions helped. It is an evaluation of the help, the helper, and the helped. If the means of communication and the attitudes of confidence have been established earlier in the help effort, it is possible for the evaluation to be used as a data base for joint planning for the next activities in that classroom.

A teacher must be able to make choices that reflect a positive position for both self and school. The next *Aids for Self-Development* are to help with those choices and to establish a data base for evaluation.

. . . . ,

Aids for Self-Development

1   Five statements are listed below that offer you a choice of agreeing or disagreeing. Identify your position on each statement in a short sentence.
    (a)   Extremists take the lead in presenting divergent viewpoints.
    (b)   Creative classrooms are disorderly.
    (c)   Experienced teachers have reached a point of ineffectiveness.
    (d)   All colleagues readily accept my ideas.
    (e)   Classroom interactions should please students.
2   Identify the persons who would be in a position to evaluate your statement in your school situation. Would they agree or disagree with your position?
3   Determine how joint planning with evaluators might be used to improve evaluation on these and other issues.

. . . .

The Laws of Openness

The emphasis in this chapter has been moving from its title of self-sufficiency through self-reliance through interaction-sufficiency to openness. Openness seems to be the key to the achievement of a control over one's self so that one is not deprived of the help that can be made available in the teaching situation. Openness also stimulates the interaction that brings mutual respect and help from others. Since openness is one of the key concepts that seems to provide the avenue for the more rewarding management of self in the teaching situation, it seems appropriate to establish a few of what might be called the *laws of openness*. These are not laws in the sense of legislative demands or administrative impositions but rather the constant relationships among people that provide a way of interacting in the teaching situation. Since these are easily observed in the teaching situation and since many observers have indicated a constancy in these observations, it seems appropriate to say that these are examples of the laws of openness. They might help people in maintaining the opportunity to accomplish the products of their own talents. The laws will be numbered but they are not in any sense to be seen as a priority arrangement. Neither is there any implication that these are the exclusive laws of openness. They are exemplary and it is hoped that individuals gradually will establish their own evolving list.

1 *There are many advantages in participating in goal selection*
   The advantages are in the fact that communication becomes essential in order to get an agreement in goal selection. The involvement here is not one of giving and receiving, but one of sharing — sharing in the judgments that are involved in establishing a mutuality of goal selection.

2 *There must be mutual respect in action planning*
   It is one thing to have involvement and agreement in goal selection but, following that, there must be an action plan. The action plan usually in the teaching situation becomes more individualized so that each teacher's expertise and personality can be expressed in determining the process by which the goals will be achieved. Since there may be differentiation in process among the members of the teaching staff, openness requires that there must be established a mutual respect in order that the interaction involved in process planning will not result in a conflict of interest or purpose.

3 *There must be continuous planned and non-punitive evaluation of the process and product of the teaching activity*
   There has been built into our culture what seems to be an idea that, when the term evaluation is used, it has to have a punitive nature. This is not so. Numerous references have been made in this chapter to the fact that evaluation can be done mutually and that evaluation provides the data base for joint planning of new and continuing activities. The continuous and planned evaluation is essential. The once-a-year snapshot view of what has been accomplished in the classroom was proved long ago to be wholly inadequate to a satisfactory judgment of whether the teacher has taught well and the students have learned adequately.

4 *There must be an identification of all input origins*
   The implication here is that each individual has the right to identify the contributions that are made to the educational program. The identification of all input origins, however, goes far beyond what can be termed the positive contributions that lead to accomplishment. Often there are input origins that are covered up entirely and some of these variables affect what the teacher is doing in the classroom. An input origin can involve other people — what the students bring to the classroom, the materials of instruction, the

working conditions, and many other kinds of things that affect the final product of the classroom which is the learning on the part of the students.

5 *There must be trustful recognition, acknowledgement, and commendation of the contributions made by each individual in the organization*
Emphasis first is on *trustful* because of the seeming attitude of people to think that when some recognition, acknowledgement, or commendation is made, it has a price tag. This has been explored earlier under different kinds of considerations. It is presented here as a law of openness because it is one way of keeping the doors open for mutually supportive types of relationship among the members of the staff, the supervisory and administrative personnel, the students, and the people in the community.

6 *There must be consistency in the development and growth of inter-relationships*
The point here is that it is totally destructive to be trying to perform in the classroom while not knowing what the next moment may bring by way of assignments, expectations, evaluations, and working conditions. Consistency then builds a confidence into individual teachers. It makes it possible for them to feel sure that when some good interrelationship has been established among members of the faculty or between the teacher and the students, this process will not be disrupted at the whim of some other person. Supervisors can sometimes contribute to this but sometimes the teachers themselves bring on the lack of consistency. They may fail to think through the process and to maintain the openness that is required for productive interrelationships of the people on the staff.

7 *There should be periodic reviews of the laws of openness*
The concept here is that each reader should make an evaluation of the laws suggested which seem to support the concept of openness. Periodic review, revisions, additions, and deletions are appropriate. It is better if the laws of openness can be based upon the individual experiences in the teaching situation so that they become completely personalized and openness becomes a way of professional life.

Product is the Pay-Off

These first six chapters might be called the 'getting ready' ones. Getting ready for the major thrust of marching into a continuous developmental status as a teacher. The next chapters will tend to be more specific on the kinds of things that teachers might do to move toward the concept of full status in recognition and respect in the profession of education. No book and no supervisor can put all the things together that are required to achieve maximum competence. The individual teacher is the one who has to put it all together. It is well, then, to begin thinking ahead to the kinds of responsibilities required in putting it all together. The process of teaching may be a rewarding awareness for each teacher. It is action and action is enticing. But to place the judgment or evaluation on the teaching process is to miss the total purpose of the enterprise. There can be only one genuine and final measure of success and that is in the product — the student's awareness of learning and the student's ability to demonstrate that learning has taken place. Success is determined by products and these will be analyzed in chapter 7.

Success: Process and Product

The emphasis in chapter 6 was upon the power potential that exists within each individual teacher. Concern with this power potential was for the purpose of determining the nature of self-sufficiency and the various kinds of safeguards that need to be established to protect such potential. A concern for this power is a concern for the continued success of teachers in accomplishing the purposes of an instructional program. Self-reliance was emphasized but was kept in the context of group activities. The major group activity for teachers is directing the learning opportunities and achievements for students in the classrooms for which they are responsible.

Knowledge and skills constitute a major source of the power that exists within the individuals. For the teachers, it means that the experience in the college level programs required for teaching certification constitutes the basic essentials which make it possible for them to accomplish the purposes of the classroom. Knowledge alone is recognized as important but, in itself, is not enough. Throughout the teaching career there need to be skills, relevant to possessed knowledge, which provide a source of power to the individuals. With knowledge and skills, there still must be a strong purpose for serving the goals established for the teaching profession. The power is within the individual teachers. It is this power, with a major source in the things which are possessed or accomplished by the teachers, that is crucial in directing the learning of others.

A single declaration that the teachers have knowledge, skills, and the understanding of power is not enough. Something must be done with these things. If nothing is done, the power does not exist because it has not been applied to the purposes for which the teaching situation is established. Here again, it must be remembered that the power possessed by the teachers must be directed to and for others. Those others usually are the students in the classroom but it might just as well be to members of the staff, to committees, or to groups of parents in the community showing concern for the educational opportunities of their children.

Many and varied opportunities exist for the teachers to do things with the power possessed as the result of preparation for teaching. The variability of the things to do, however, is less determined by the individuals than by individual teachers' interpretations of the reactions of others to what the teaching act constituted. This may seem to be somewhat in conflict with some of the statements in the previous chapters because the emphasis here is that the achievement so important to the teaching effort must be found in those toward whom the teaching skills are directed. The reaction of the students constitutes the teacher's first and best opportunity to translate the teacher's actions into student accomplishments by watching how they react to the things that the teachers do in the directing of learning.

The emphasis on self-sufficiency and self-management in previous sections of the book must now be tempered by the thought that the self-management must be achieved with the cooperative efforts of others. Self-management is the self-direction that is necessary in order to do those things which cause others to react and, in that way, to interpret their reactions in terms of what are the next best steps in the teaching process. It may be that some teachers feel they are being dispossessed of the power which they have gained by the college preparation program. This feeling may develop primarily because the power must be evidenced not in themselves but in the response of others throughout the teaching career. It is important that a balanced view (induction) be established and maintained so that individual teachers with the best of skills being applied to the teaching tasks can feel a sense of worth and personal accomplishment. The emphasis on the reaction of the students does not mean that the teachers have been dispossessed or deprived but rather that the teachers have achieved more because of the influence exercised upon the students in the class.

This chapter is designed to help individual teachers gain confidence in their success in performing at a high level of teacher behavior in directing the learning of the students of their classes. It is necessary that teachers be increasingly aware of the fact that they have a stake in the progress of students. This progress is the teacher's identification of the success of the teaching skills applied to the students in their classes.

The focus of this chapter is that of achieving an understanding of the inseparability of the person from the process and of the person from the product. In order to achieve this inseparability, the concept of the persons being both the process and the product is introduced. The process might be seen also as role contribution and the product as role achievement. The concepts will be given more explication in the next two sections of this chapter.

Self As A Process

Process can be viewed as a pattern of procedures which results in the accomplishment of the goals established by the individual. This makes the process a purposeful pattern. Purposes must be held by an individual and that individual, upon developing a pattern of procedures, will achieve purposes in the best sense of process. A teacher is a process when determinations are made within self for teaching activities. When teachers are presenting ideas to classes, they are a process. When they are evaluating papers, they are a process. When they plan a field trip, they are a process. These teaching activities are role contributions to the instructional program and, as such, can be identified as an experience of process.

Purpose presumes that there is a knowledge of the goals that have been established by the school and accepted by the individuals who are selected for professional positions in the school. Goal selection and/or acceptance (induction), then, becomes the first step in the process of teaching. The individual teachers possess the awareness of the goal and by acceptance have made that goal a part of the self. Here again, the individual is a process and is engaged in putting many tasks into a pattern of procedures that will accomplish the educational purposes.

The self as a process cannot stop with selection or acceptance of goals but must proceed from there to an assessment of the required knowledge, material, space, and time essential to the continuance of processes toward those goals. The process of making certain that the tasks are associated with the goal achievement requires that someone make an assessment (renewal) of the kinds and the adequacies of the supporting conditions for the teaching-learning activity. Another part of the process which is entirely within the teacher is the determination of the availability not only of the quantity and desirability but also of the availability of the kinds of knowledge, material, space, and time required. This assessment of availability begins to establish the conditions under which the teaching-learning act can be carried forward to a satisfactory conclusion.

An assessment of the things needed for the establishment of purposeful patterns in teaching and learning cannot proceed without viewing the involvements of other people in the total activity. The individuals well might possess the idea of process but soon this must be communicated not only to the students in the classroom but also to those others who can influence the support facility for the classroom activities. The involvement of other people in the pattern of procedures that constitutes the process for the individual requires the coordination of the efforts of those other persons who likewise have knowledge of material, space, and time support requirements just as the individual teacher being considered here.

Coordination is more than just the drawing of a design. It can as well be the demands of influencing others to get the concept of relationship between the pattern of procedures and the goals (redirection) which have been established by the total group or total organizational enterprise. Coordination still constitutes a process in the teaching act but cannot be the sole responsibility of one individual. It must involve the acceptance and support of other persons who are involved in the total school situation. As a part of the process, it is wise to be aware that the maintenance of momentum and direction is as essential as the choice of the pattern of procedures. The coordinating of the actions of others along with the material support elements projects a view that may seem to require control of many people. This it does. The point here is that one individual, as a process, can be the force that initiates and stimulates (induction) others to join in those actions that constitute a desirable program of education.

The more people involved and the more different kinds of support facilities required, the more complex the action becomes. It is easy to see that the processes of teaching and learning as responsibilities of an individual teacher, while shared, still remain a great part of the observed contribution of an individual; as a contributor to the total or complex action. There is nothing about being a process that depreciates the contribution which the teacher makes. Rather, it indicates that the individual has been able to meet the requirements of a complex situation, as teaching always will be, and still not lose the identity with the contribution. In this sense, the self is a process and these processes provide significant role contributions. The next section will point out that being a process alone is not enough. There must be an outcome and attention will be given to that.

The *Aids for Self-Development* given here are structured to help you gain further identity of yourself as a process.

. . . .

Aids for Self-Development

1   The processes of instruction include the pursuit of selected goals.
     Respond to the questions below that deal with different components
     of a procedure based on a goal that you identify.
     (a)   How would you analyze your need for improvement?
     (b)   How would you initiate conversation with your peers regard-
           ing the need you see?
     (c)   How would you stimulate your colleagues to give you input in
           satisfying the need?
     (d)   How would you design a system to improve your instruction?
     (e)   How would you implement your system into your classroom?
     (f)   How would you direct the activities in your improved system?
     (g)   How would you attempt to control the outcomes?
     (h)   How would you appraise your end product?
2   Determine a process that emerges from the stages of this procedure
     and identify how your self is a process within the greater total
     process.
3   Work with your colleagues to design development activities for the
     improvement of the processes you have identified.

. . . .

Self As A Product

The previous section involved an analysis of self as a process. It was
indicated there that the individual teacher has opportunities to contribute to many of the various facets of the instructional program. A
matter of joining others or working alone in the determination of the
kinds of support elements that are required for the teaching assignment
is a process of moving toward the goals which have been selected. In
fact, the very first process suggested was that of goal selection. The
individual teacher is a process in the sense that there is continuous
participation in goal selection.

   The self-as-a-product concept sees the teacher as one who contributed to the goal selection. When the goals have been selected, defined,
and accepted as adequate, there is a product appearing as a result of the
process of goal selection. Just as the pursuit of a chosen goal makes the
teacher a process, so does the achievement of the pursued goal makes
the teacher a product. The role achievement makes the self (teacher) a
part of the experiencing of the product and, therefore, the self is a
product. The degree of contribution of an individual teacher does not

displace the concept of the teacher as a process and now as a product. The contribution to the action of goal selection is the completion of that particular first step in the determination of what needs to be done in order to accomplish successful teaching and learning outcomes.

Goal–product relatedness must exist in every sequence of process to product. The goal must be a supportive way of defining the product that should appear as the final results of a sequencing of processes. If the goal and product are not related, the goal has not served in the selection of processes and certainly cannot possibly claim to have a relationship with the product or outcome of teaching-learning effort. It is important to proceed through the teaching and learning act with full awareness that the goal and products must be related. The self must be seen as a product by virtue of maintaining the relationship between the goal and the outcome resulting from a series or sequence of processes.

The role of the individual in the achieving of product is that of putting things together. A product is just that. It is a result of putting things together. But the putting of things together constitutes the process as was discussed in the previous section. The individual teacher, then, has the opportunity to participate in or to hold exclusive responsibility for a selection of processes that can be goal related. This relatedness leads to the kind of outcomes that are anticipated at the time the instructional program was agreed upon and the processes of achieving it selected for implementation. It was indicated earlier that the process includes many different types of responsibility. It was indicated that knowledge, material, space, and time constituted an illustration of the different resources that must be considered as the processes are designed and carried forward. The individual teacher, in each of these instances, has a role (redirection) in the putting of things together, putting together the kinds of teaching materials available with the needs of the students in relation to a particular goal. The arrangement of the furniture in the classroom and the allocation of time to each of the different activities are illustrations of the kinds of things that are put together. The teacher stands as the prime mover and director of the putting together of these things.

A clear indication was cited above that, with so many different facets of the total teaching act required to accomplish a satisfactory learning status at the end of the effort, many intermediate steps must be recognized. The matter of learning materials requires careful planning and selection (induction) on the part of the teacher. This particular step is one in a series of steps required to accomplish learning adequacy. There must be intermediate products resulting from the intermediate steps which are required in the total program. The matter of goal selection has held priority in the discussion above and it might be used to indicate the nature of the intermediate product. When the goals are clearly stated and accepted and have become the bases for the selection of other aspects of process (renewal), it can be said that the goal selection task has been accomplished. This is an intermediate product. The quality of that product can be assessed in many different ways. It may be judged at the end of total effort to see whether the goal was clear enough to guide the selections of processes throughout the entire sequence of activities.

The individual teacher has much responsibility in the intermediate processes and can recognize contributions by viewing and analyzing the intermediate products. Success at this point simply means success in progressing toward the selected goal. There are many opportunities and necessities for the individual to seek the opportunity of self-improvement (renewal) in role contributions. Role contributions are simply another way of identifying what the teacher decides to do that will contribute to the total enterprise and this becomes an individual contribution and role description for that particular teacher. There must be differentiation, however, between role contributions and role achievements. It is important to keep in mind that the intermediate steps lead to intermediate products and that any one of these, no matter how well done, does not constitute the proof that the goal has been achieved. It is only an intermediate goal that has been achieved and not the goal that has been designed for the direction of the total teaching and learning effort. The part that each teacher plays or the role that each teacher takes in the intermediate processes can contribute only to the intermediate products and must be seen as simply a progression toward the final goal achievement which is the purpose of the organizational effort.

The individual, as well as others associated in the total teaching effort, may have different perspectives of the results. There is a temptation for individuals or even groups to recount the things done in the process, in other words, to talk about how hard one may have worked in bringing progress toward a goal. No matter how one works, the product is not that effort. The product is to be discovered not in the expenditure of time and effort but in the realization that the program of teaching has led to successful learning on the part of the students. This is the product that must determine the ultimate pay-off. It is important that the individual teacher maintains a perspective that gives satisfaction in the contributions during the intermediate steps and in achievement of the intermediate products as the total effort moves toward the final and major goal. The intermediate products, when put together, do add up to the total and final product that is the most important to the educational effort. Role achievement identifies the role contributors and, thereby, makes the self (teacher) a product.

The next step *Aids for Self-Development* gives you the opportunity to look at different processes and determine the responsibility for products.

. . . .

Aids for Self-Development

1 Identify your responsibility in the *selection* process of:
   (a) curriculum materials;
   (b) student assignments;
   (c) physical facilities.
2 Identify your responsibilities in the *guidance* process of:
   (a) student achievement;
   (b) parental awareness;
   (c) staff negotiations.
3 Identify your responsibilities in the *evaluation* process of:
   (a) lesson plans;
   (b) your teaching;
   (c) budget decisions.
4 Determine whether your responsibilities are more intermediate or end products and whether there are areas where your responsibility should be greater.
5 Identify redirective activities to give you success in process areas where you feel the products should be your responsibility.

. . . .

Process — Product Sequence

An understanding of the concepts presented in this section really had their beginning in chapter 2, with the title of 'You and Your Assignment'. The discussion in that chapter dealt with the problem of freeing one's self from many of the cultural handicaps that are so easily carried forward in today's responsibilities. Self-development was one of the continuing thoughts in that chapter and was deemed essential as one approaches any new assignment. The rest of that chapter dealt with the recognition of help that is available to you and your responsibility to receive help when it is available. In other words, the concepts initiated there dealt with the idea of a sequence of your own efforts moving toward an established and accepted goal. This sequence presumed the continuing interaction with other people and an acknowledgement that individuals need help from someone as they move along paths toward success. The previous two sections of this chapter dealt with the teacher self as a process and as a product. The idea of a sequence in the processes was emphasized.

Emphasis, likewise, was on the idea that products tend to move through a series of intermediate products to a final end-product. It is essential to see the sequencing not only within the processes and the products. It is also necessary to recognize that each process can and usually does have a product and that the intermediate steps in both process and product become a result of a well-arranged sequence of activities and outcomes.

The idea of a sequence should have begun to emerge in some of the chapters intervening between chapter 2 and this point. It is hoped that the idea of sequence becomes a part of the thinking of persons concerned with adjusting (renewal) their own selected tasks and modes of action to the idea that there is a continuous merging in this sequence of progress leading to more refined processes and more acceptable products.

Sequence is the progression, the order, the succession, the series, and the flow of activities which lead to the kinds of consequences envisioned in the successful teaching effort. At this point, it might be beneficial to do a quick review of chapter 3 which carried the title, 'Sources of Coordination'. The idea of sequence, whether it be process–product sequence or any other kind of sequencing, infers that coordination is essential or there would be nothing but disruption and no progression. Chapter 3 put the emphases on a number of the conditions as sources of coordination. A matter of security, work sharing, creative subordination, and accountability were the kinds of items used as examples of the sources of coordination. Coordination, then, becomes a way of describing successful sequencing (redirection) of process and product.

Coordination is another way of saying that people achieve the maximum contributions to a selected goal by relating in an orderly way to others engaged in other parts of the total responsibility. It also means a blending or relating of all of the conditions which can weight the success of the teaching-learning enterprise. The idea of sequencing process and product carries with it the thought that, when you start something, it is well to expect something to happen. Watching what you do (induction) can become much more rewarding and accurate by watching how what you do affects the way others do things. This perhaps seems a little confusing but in essence it is simply saying that it is wise to be a careful observer of your activity but, also, it is not enough to watch just yourself to assess that activity. It is necessary for teachers to watch their own activities as they impact others and stimulate a response on the part of those others. When the response on the part of others is not what was anticipated as a way of identifying progress, your process has not achieved a suitable product. For instance, if students are not learning from your selected techniques, there is a process/product dysfunction. This indicates a need to review the entire process and improve components where necessary (redirection).

Each teacher must be a continuous watcher of the sequential relationship between process and product. There are times, of course, when it may not be possible to identify the sequencing of process and product. When such a sequence is not observable, there must be a short-circuit somewhere between the action and the outcome. When this occurs, it is well to stop the activity and to find out why (renewal) the things that are being done are not affecting others in the way anticipated. There are perhaps many types of short-circuits that could be identified such as noise disruptions, breaks in the continuity of the activity of the classroom, a shortage of needed teaching materials, attitudes in the home that send the students to school with no sense of obligation to learn, and many other ways that the sequence between process and product can be disrupted. There is no use saying that continuing the process eventually will make the product show. Gaps in the learning sequence of the students may make it difficult to continue in the well-planned program of teaching and learning activities. The only thing to do, then, is to stop and make an analysis of what disrupted the sequence and seek whatever remedy (redirection) is needed in order to get the sequencing back on the track.

The state of disrupted sequence may signal the point of going back to chapter 2 and reviewing the discussion there on the nature of help and your obligation to find it. Having found the help, it is your obligation to use it in correcting the problems which have introduced a break in the sequence of activities in your classroom. The process-product sequence can present a tremendous challenge to teachers. No teacher is ever free of the possibility that some kinds of disruption may occur in this sequence and it is the obligation of the teacher primarily to find out the nature of that break and to repair it.

Many stages can be defined in working toward goal attainment, and the sequential ordering of these stages creates a process that leads to the product of achievement. The *Aids for Self-Development* given below provide a vehicle to record the elements of process and the evidences of product.

. . . .

Aids for Self-Development

1 Four stages of an instructional process could be (i) developing instructional strategies; (ii) planning teaching behaviors; (iii) identifying student activities; and (iv) monitoring teacher/student interactions. Seven process steps are listed below to carry teaching through to an instructional product. Identify activities you would carry out as you move through this process-to-product sequence for a specific teaching situation within each process stage:
   (a) analyzing the current situation;
   (b) stating objectives;
   (c) listing of available resources;
   (d) organizing resources;
   (e) implementing plan;
   (f) evaluating plan;
   (g) revising plan based on evaluation.
2 Determine the result of completing this process. That is, what is the product of your activities within each of the stages.
3 Relate the use of this process-product pattern to other areas of your assignment and visit with colleagues concerning it.

. . . .

What You Do Is What You Get

The emphasis has been almost continuous in the previous sections in noting that the individual teacher is the most important *self* of concern in this chapter. The individual has been charged with the responsibility of possessing knowledge and skills that constitute a source of power for giving direction to the necessary activities that will lead to the accomplishments of the goals in the educational program.

The responsibilities of the individual have been identified as being a reaching out to others and of seeing in others the results of the personal and professional initiative that is exercised. What you do, then, is a reaching out to these others, either the students in the class or other professional staff members as well as people in the community.

This becomes one of the most important sources of determining the extent to which you are making progress toward the selected goals. What you do in reaching out to these others is the contact with the product of your work and is, therefore, what you get in satisfaction and rewards from the efforts put forth.

The way that you go about this reaching out to others is what you do in carrying out your professional activities and may reveal the kind of person that you are. An extremely selfish person would not be likely to reach out in a helpful way to others especially if the purpose of reaching out is to help those others rather than to use them in achieving personal desires and satisfactions. Reaching out in a realistic, humanistic, and assisting way reveals a kind of person that sees the others as the object and privilege of being a helper to that person in achieving desires and satisfactions. It is well to note at this point that those who reach out have sought an interaction. The doing by the individual teacher alone might not reach to another person and, therefore, it is not an interaction.

The teacher must teach *somebody* and it takes more than simply communicating an assignment and an expectation to accomplish that teaching. Teaching is an interaction between the teacher and the learner. This requires an absolute necessity for the individual teachers to see what they do in terms of getting (induction) the responses from those others whom they seek to teach. The teacher contact with the student is a sequence just as much as sequence was noted between process and product. The interaction can be completed and the concept of the sequence achieved by the learner initiating contact with the teacher as well. The two-way initiated interaction, designed for the purpose of supporting the learning opportunities, constitutes a sequence of relationships that is to be sought and maintained. The efforts of the individual teacher to reach out to others and to secure their responses in order to make a judgment as to what the next action should be constitutes the processes by which the teacher accomplishes the professional responsibilities.

The processes must have products. This is simply another way of saying that, when the teacher reaches out to the student and the student responds, teaching and learning take place. When the teacher receives the response and makes a proper interpretation, the processes and products have been maintained in a rewarding sequence. The response of these others that you seek to teach or assist in some type of activity is the product that results from the things that you do as a professional worker. Stimulating and directing (renewal) others to want to learn and to channel their own efforts in a manner that facilitates learning helps others to do the things that can be called the product of learning. This, in turn, is the product of your doing and the more that you can get others to do what they can do and should be doing is a measure of you and of the outcomes of your efforts. What you as an individual teacher really want is to have success and this success results from the type of activities that you have chosen to characterize your interaction with the learners and other associates in the profession.

These *Aids for Self-Development* give you a chance to look at your selection of professional behaviors in relation to those you teach.

. . . .

Aids for Self-Development

1   State an example or situation that represents each of the following professional behaviors:
    (a)   encouraging students to go beyond a simple answer to a question — *probing*;
    (b)   sharing your own feeling with students — *expressing*;
    (c)   reconciling student differences by allowing them to explore their own differences — *harmonizing*;
    (d)   expressing standards for the class to achieve — *goal setting*;
    (e)   measuring achievement based on stated goals — *evaluating*;
    (f)   being forceful with class to maintain attention — *discipline*;
    (g)   encouraging evaluative statements on your own behavior from students — *self-appraisal*;
    (h)   relieving tension by easing demands that are bothering students — *satisfying*;
    (i)   expressing status to maintain control — *defending*;
    (j)   disagreeing openly in class and encouraging students to disagree with you — *arguing*.
2   Indicate your response to or feeling about each of the behaviors you stated above. Would you handle each situation in the same way?
3   Separate those behaviors that you feel need redirection. Determine a method to refine the behaviors to your satisfaction.
4   Translate the refined behaviors into a repertoire of useful professional skills.

. . . .

Manifestations of Your Priorities

The previous section gave emphasis to the fact that what you do is what you get. The *what you do* are the activities designed to assist students to learn. What you get are the responses from those students which can be interpreted as evidence of achieving the intended learning and development goals or outcomes.

Things that you choose to do to bring about the learning on the part of the student may be an indication of the priorities that you hold in directing your own behaviors. Just as there is concern for what you do, there is now a concern for the extent to which your priorities are related properly to the kind of activities that bring on the best teaching-learning situation. The priorities that you hold are chosen, inherited, imposed, or evolved. Many of the priorities that you encounter in the teaching situation may be the result of the formal action initiated by the people in the community. The actions of the board of education that are resolved into policies make a determination of some of the limits of your freedom to choose your teaching behaviors apart from the expectations that have been placed upon you.

Many of the priorities may be imposed by yourself, by others, or by the circumstances that surround the teaching-learning location. These priorities probably have evolved as your experience progresses in initiating the teaching activities and in watching (induction) the students respond to those chosen activities. It is a happy situation when the priorities that give direction to the ordering of your activities have been chosen by you. It cannot be done in defiance, however, of those who have a right to determine some of the priorities that will be placed upon the school. This provides the limitations of the individual teacher opportunities to deviate from those expectations according to personal whims or desires.

Priorities constitute an evidence that you have chosen some preference from among many of the alternatives that may be available as a way of doing. You have a preference to one way over another and this constitutes a priority. It likewise can be defined as the level of urgency that you feel and which impels you to select certain types of teaching behaviors. As you analyze your own priorities, the chances are that you will draw some conclusions about the superiority of one way over other ways of doing. This evolved out of your experience and has a good solid basis in the opportunities for act by act appraisal (redirection) as you go about your teaching.

What you say and do reveals the priorities which you have chosen. If you are responsible for a group of students in which your top priority is to insist upon strict discipline, you are demonstrating a priority. If you want to give students maximum freedom in pursuing their own activities in the learning responsibilities, that reveals your priority of not wanting to impose your maximum control and direction over the students. You have a choice of dealing with students in a friendly, easy, open manner or in a more austere manner. This again reveals your priority in the selection of the kinds of teaching activities that you choose as your major ways of going about the business of motivating the students to learn the things that have been decided should be learned.

Priorities can be seen as individualized choices or they can be seen as socialized choices or, perhaps, a bit of both. By individualized, it means that you have not had priorities imposed upon you which control your behavior as a teacher. If they have been socialized, it means that an agreement has been arrived at either informally or formally by the group with which you associate or the organization of which you are a part. When the priorities, individualized and/or socialized, come into conflict, there can be a neutralization of progress in the purposes of the educational plan. An example of how priorities can conflict would be the desire to follow a pre-planned order of learning activities with no interruption or modification even though a current happening or an evolving desire on the part of the student is evident.

It is necessary that the conflicts in priorities which can neutralize progress in learning be resolved. These can be resolved by going to the thought presented previously in the variations between processes and products as well as the sequencing of processes and products. The priorities may vary between and within processes and products. There is no reason why a rational point of view (redirection) cannot be applied to the evaluation of priorities of your own behaviors. This can be in terms of the variations that may be necessary in the managing of the processes of directing learning and in the variability of the products because of the variability of the students who are responding to your direction as a teacher.

The rational approach calls for a type of flexibility that must be based upon analysis and decision. Flexibility avoids the probability of encouraging serious conflict in priorities between the teacher and the students as well as between the processes and the products of the learning activities. When the priorities tend to become extremely static and inflexible, it may be related to or the result of the value system which you as an individual hold. It is well at that point to consider whether your value system may be stimulating a conflict in priorities between teacher and learner and, if so, to give a rational analysis (renewal) to the value system itself.

A teacher must be able to recognize the basis for preferring the use of one activity over that of another, as well as knowing the value of each activity in terms of output. These *Aids for Self-Development* should help you develop a fresh perspective of your priorities.

....

Aids for Self-Development

1 List one classroom activity for each of the following descriptions. Write the first activity that comes to your mind, and try to avoid any overlap:
   (a) must be budgeted for;
   (b) individual activities;
   (c) small group activities;
   (d) total group activities;
   (e) requires careful planning;
   (f) may happen on the spur of the moment;
   (g) should happen more often;
   (h) requires some risk;
   (i) students do not appreciate;
   (j) needs refinement
2 Take your list of activities and give a priority (high, medium, low) to each that you have listed.
3 Examine your high priority items. What do the statements that generated these items have in common? Describe the renewal activities that will help order the tasks necessary to complete these high priority items.
4 Examine the low priority items. Do the statements that generated these have any commonalities? Describe the redirection activities that will help reorder the priority of these items.

....

Others Are Your Products

A consistent emphasis throughout this chapter has been on relating self to others. Realization on the part of an individual is the first step in perfecting the knowledge and skills of the teaching act. Working alone does not complete the commitment that teachers assume when accepting a teaching position. The others of primary importance are the students and their learning is the product of teacher-directed effort. This emphasis will continue in that the self-relationship to others must be a basic concern in the teaching-learning activity.

A beautiful opportunity for one to teach one's self is found in the process of directing the teaching efforts to others. Searching for the ways to help others learn provides the teacher with an opportunity for self-analysis, process-analysis, and product-observation. The product-observation is available in those who are the objects of the teaching, namely, the students. The pay-off for the teaching effort must be found in others and those others are the objects of the teaching effort. Improved self conscientiously achieved or gradually accumulated through experience is supportive of helping others to improve their learning statuses. It is impossible to separate self-improvement from the improvement of others.

The test of success in self-improvement is to be found in the improvement of others. This is true insofar as the total teaching act is concerned but not necessarily applicable to each of the segments of the process of the teaching act, for instance, the necessity of developing a curriculum plan or of selecting texts and other learning materials. The excellence by which these things are accomplished is in itself a process that can be terminated and the product observed. That, however, is one of the products that can be termed intermediate and is not to be confused with the end product to be found in the learning of others. The emphasis has been on students, primarily since the concerns have been with the teaching responsibilities. It must be remembered, however, that peers and associates as well as the students are among those others. Sharing teaching experience, materials, or testing procedures with your associates constitutes an opportunity to help others (induction) to learn and, in that sense, they become a part of the product of the individual teacher effort.

The products by project as well as by final and total outcomes are to be recognized in the proper relationships. The project is an intermediate type of action and result, and many projects can add up to that total outcome to be found in the maximum learning on the part of the students. It is impossible to gain the concept of finding your products in others as developed here unless there is a basic liking for people involved in the profession and to be served by the profession. Relationships cannot be established to accomplish the kind of things emphasized here with respect to others unless the individual teacher does like other people. Also, the teacher must find joy in associating with others and with becoming a part of the developmental activities which results in improved educational programs.

Teachers should resist the social-environmental tendency to see personal gain as more practical in this competitive society than the learning progress of those being taught. It takes some effort to achieve and maintain this attitude toward the environment and towards self. It is essential, however, to accomplish this without developing too great a sense of isolation in a society that may appear to have dominance in those who see personal gain as a full justification for living and for acting.

The *Aids for Self-Development* given here will help you assess what you do and how those actions are related to what others do and what others desire.

· ·

Aids for Self-Development

1   Record, in three separate columns, the effect of each listed activity on students, peers, and superordinates. Label each effect as positive (+), negative (−), or neutral (0):
   (a)   I suggest ideas and materials to others.
   (b)   I am efficient and consistent and get along well with the administration.
   (c)   I volunteer to assist in special activities in and around the school.
   (d)   I demonstrate poise and confidence when working with students.
   (e)   I handle problems with originality and flexibility.
   (f)   I allow students complete freedom of action and choice.
   (g)   I show an interest in and enthusiasm for the teaching profession.
   (h)   I am aware of local community factors that influence educational conditions.
   (i)   I provide a flexible, creative classroom environment by grouping students according to individual needs.
   (j)   I measure my own performance by using students' reactions and progress.
2   Compare the peer and administrator columns and explain the differences.
3   Compare the student and peer columns. Are there more similiari-

ties or more differences between peer and administrators? Explain.

4   Select the activities that represent the most positive professional gains and plan a development sequence to increase these activities in your professional life.

. . . .

Self-Management Is Not Self-Containment

The emphases in this chapter, as well as in others, have been upon the responsibility for establishing relationships with others in order to carry out the responsibilities of the teaching profession. These may have led some to an over-emphasis on self-management as it relates to other facets of living and working. It is not the intent to do other than to stimulate the individual readers to give more attention to self-responsibility in the commitments of the teaching profession. If this has caused some to assume that the primary essential to the teaching-learning situation is possessed by the individual teacher, the over-emphasis has gone too far and a corrective caution is offered at this point.

Management is the orderly relating of talent, effort, and support facilities to the requisite tasks of goal achievement. These are the things that have been emphasized in previous chapters and sections regarding the teacher's responsibility to bring about this relationship in order to support the educational program.

Containment is the recognition of and submission to boundaries, imposed by self or others, and designed to limit thought and action. This means that the concept of self-containment would incline the individual to close out the benefits from interactions with others. This would be completely disastrous from the standpoint of the basic concepts presented in the chapters of this book. A pause is taken at this time to take a look at this particular possibility in order that the emphasis has not been overdone and overbalanced with respect to self-management.

Many origins of freedom and constraints can be identified. It has been pointed out frequently that the origin of freedom is found in the knowledge, talent, and skills of the individual teacher. The greater the talent of the teacher, the greater the freedom that can be discovered within the boundaries of the organizational structure and expectations. The origin of constraints is often imposed by self and based primarily on the fears that what you do might not be acceptable to others and, therefore, it is safer to avoid it. This unfortunate limitation of the talent of the individual should be guarded against.

The effect of freedom is to open the way for interaction with others as well as to perform at the creative level. The effect of constraints is to incline the individual to circumscribe the responsibilities that otherwise would limit the excellence of service. True it is that some balance between freedom and constraint is necessary. The balance needed is one of finding an organizational structure and operational pattern that can make it possible for the individual to join others in the organization in accomplishing organizational goals while, at the same time, maintaining the opportunity to act creatively. This indicates that there are negative sides of management and positive sides of containment. The balance suggested here is what is required to keep the negative and the positive of either one from dominating to the extent that a stalemate exists between the capacity of the individual teacher to perform and the achievement of the goals established for the total activity. The self still has a great contributing responsibility and the main point here is the suggestion to pause occasionally (redirection) and to see self-management and self-containment as freedom and constraints that are being kept in a rewarding balance.

The idea of self-management assumes that an individual is responsible for the goals he or she achieves. Self-containment is realizing self-imposed boundaries and adhering to organizational goals. The following *Aids for Self-Development* are designed to help you look at the supporting and thwarting forces of self-management and self-containment.

. . . .

Aids for Self-Development

1 Determine whether each of the listed contributions to teaching is supported or thwarted by the process of self-management:
   (a) I evaluate and analyze my own performance.
   (b) I am thoroughly prepared for the teaching task.
   (c) I prepare special materials to enhance lessons.
   (d) I am able to see problems from the student's viewpoint.
   (e) I praise the accomplishment of students in areas other than academic.
   (f) I maintain control of the class in a relaxed manner.
   (g) I show interest in teaching.
   (h) I am willing to try anything to improve learning.

(i)   I am able to admit my own mistakes.

(j)   I have regular work attendance.

2   Now determine whether the contributions listed above are supported or thwarted by self-containment.

3   Do the examples of contributions that are supported by self-management and self-containment need renewal in your experiences?

4   Do the examples of contributions that are thwarted by self-management and self-containment need redirection in your experiences?

5   Design activities that will give you the professional development outlined in numbers 3 and 4 above.

. . . .

Your Processes Determine Product

This section serves as a summary for the chapter. It seems wise to relate some of the concepts that develop between self and others as well as between processes and products. There was reference and discussion to the self as a process and as a product. It is important to consider this concept in order to have a good basis for assessing the personal contributions to the learning situation in your own classroom as well as to the total educational program for the school.

The processes have a sequence which causes them to be inter-related in a dependent fashion. If they are independent, the sequences probably will not lead to the envisioned product. Products, likewise, were envisioned as having sequences within the area of products. This related the intermediate successes in the total program to the total outcome of the efforts envisioned as an educational program. The sequencing within the processes and products is just as important as the sequencing of processes to products. You should keep these concepts of process and product differentiated as you look at the activities of your classroom and of your school in making an assessment of progress.

The perspective of self-responsibility is exceedingly important. This perspective of self as being either an independent or a sharing individual makes a difference to the degree of contribution that you can make to the activities in your own classroom as well as to the professional activities of your school staff. The emphasis on the individual in the entire book is not to be construed as a *distancing from* or a *rejection of* assistance by others. It has been presented in this manner so that the maximum of self-help can be achieved on the part of each teacher. The specific treatment in some sections of this chapter indicated that the over-emphasis of self-responsibility can bring on a state of isolation that is not rewarding from the standpoint of the contribution that an individual can make to the total enterprise.

Most of the products as well as most of the processes have been shared and it is fair conclusion that most of the products of the school come as a result of the sharing of processes. The most important sharing perhaps is between the teacher and the student but it must be remembered too that a sharing with other professional members of your staff as well as sharing from student to student becomes especially helpful in achieving the desired products of the effort.

Success is individually experienced but it is usually achieved through group effort. This does not diminish the sense of achievement of the individual simply because there has been a sharing. The emphasis given to sharing and caring perhaps can accomplish a sufficient revival of mutual purposes and reciprocal action. Increasing satisfaction in being a part of an ongoing activity and finding the self-achievement satisfactory as a sharing individual makes isolation an unwelcome state. The sharing in the process undoubtedly increases the probability of product realization of the kind envisioned at the time the goals of education are established in your classroom and in your school.

Your World Buzzes On

Chapter 7 can serve as a background to look ahead to the kinds of activities in which the *self* is involved in a much wider range of activities in the environment of the school. Chapter 8 is really an extension of chapter 5 which was an analysis made under the title, 'A Look Beyond The Classroom'. The intent now in chapter 8 is to go much deeper into these activities beyond the classroom and to make a close analysis of what that impact does to your teaching activities as a responsible person in directing the instructional program within the school.

The discussion up to this point has been properly focused on the individual teacher and the in-school environment. But there are many people in the community environment and many of these people have dominant interests in the school and place many expectations upon those who are responsible for the educative activities in the in-school situation. The people in the community provide the origins for the multitude of expectations directed toward the schools. Many of these are in conflict and many of these apparently become part of the inherited culture that teachers find as they move into a new community and/or a new responsibility in the school.

Chapter 8 carries the title, 'Inherited Merry-go-rounds'. It provides an analysis of the nature and impact of the expectations that are generated in the out-of-school environment. These are added to those that originate in the in-school environment.

Part Three
Determining Structure

Chapter 8

Inherited Merry-go-rounds

The title of this chapter may seem somewhat inappropriate for a book designed to offer help to teachers in their professional experiences. Perhaps the title can grow a bit as the chapter proceeds so that the comparison or contrast will help develop a better understanding of some of the things that happen to teachers when they are on the job.

The merry-go-round comes to mind as a part of a county fair or a carnival. It is usually a very colorful machine with riding mounts of inanimate objects of various types and designs. Invariably there seems to be loud and lively music accompanying the experience. The person who gets on the merry-go-round can choose the riding figure that suits the individual fascination. There is no way, however, of controlling the volume or type of music that is played. It is simple to observe that one on a merry-go-round goes over and over the same path because the merry-go-round has been anchored to a particular location. The individual always comes back to where the experience started. The most assuring feature of the merry-go-round is that people can get off when they have had enough.

The pleasures that people have on a merry-go-round and their control over leaving that pleasure and going to some other is a characteristic that cannot be claimed for the teacher's role in the classroom. In the first place, the teacher is not literally taking a ride but, figuratively, may be taken for a ride. The teacher can take an item or plan of special interest and, in this sense, take a ride on the plan or scheme by personal choice. There is little opportunity, however, for the teacher to get off the round of activities, self-initiated or initiated by others, as is possible to do on the carnival merry-go-round. The comparison can be carried to the point that sometimes the things initiated by and for the teachers in the classroom often may come out to the very place of starting. It may appear to be a routine experience but the experience may be one that is chosen by someone else and, in that sense, it differs from the merry-go-round of the carnival.

The term *inherited* in the title indicates that many of the characteristics of the teacher's school merry-go-round perhaps were in the school and its environment before that teacher arrived. Many of the pressures, expectations, assignments, pleasures, and displeasures were created by others. In that sense, it is an inheritance because it was created by others and not by the teacher. The regular merry-go-round figures always remain the same unless changed by the owners. The tendency to remain the same is characteristic of the way people in the school environment may want teachers to be until those people want to change the teacher. There is a tendency for people to take a position representing their personal or special interest and, then, defend that position because they were creators of it. Expansion, of course, can come by those creators but the tendency is to simply hold firm to a declared or stated position. These creators expect teachers to support these inherited positions. A characteristic of the people who provide the teacher's inherited merry-go-round is entirely different from the carnival type. The people who create a particular posture and want it expanded or continued have a tendency to want to destroy the sources that may deter the continuance whether it is round and round or straight ahead for the things that they have developed on their own creative efforts.

Some people believe in maintaining things in the same form that they always have been because of a basic fear of anything that might be different. On the other hand, some people in our society believe that being different is a desirable mark of individuality. These people have the same fear of not being different that many people have of being different from others in their segment of the community. Neutrality is not to be found on the teacher's merry-go-round in the school and in the school's community as easily as neutrality can be observed between the people, the figures, the music, and the round and round characteristics of the carnival merry-go-round. The teacher's merry-go-round emerges from the multitude of demands generated by those working within the school as well as by those working as members of the school community. Further, it is perhaps wise at this point to look upon the community as extending far beyond the school's immediate community because elements of special interest in an entire nation may create some of the things that keeps the teacher going round and round in the same path. It is going round and round to find a way of satisfying all of the conflicting and non-coordinated pressures.

The purpose here is not to frighten the teacher but rather to identify some of the things that can make the task of teaching seem like being on a merry-go-round. The purpose, also, is to give some assurance that each individual has a capacity to exercise much more control than sometimes is evidenced by those who give up easily. It might be appropriate for the reader to look back now to chapter 5 which carries the title, 'A Look Beyond the Classroom'. The substance of chapter 5 was to identify the things that provide conflict potential for the teacher in the classroom. The purpose of this chapter is to discuss some of the ways that these pressures from the classroom and elements in its environment become internalized in the responses of the teachers. It is hoped that through the identification of some elements, which make the school merry-go-round either a controlled or an uncontrollable type of influence playing upon the teacher, you may design an encouraging balance.

Uniqueness of Yourself

An awareness of the people about you can lead to the conclusion that there are very few look-alikes in any group or population. There may be a similarity but to say that people look alike is something that happens to only a few in any population. It is equally true that a look at the people in your environment reveals few be-alikes. There may be some people who seek to be like you or some people that you would like to be like but, when an analysis is made, the uniqueness of the individual always shines through and becomes the strongest point of observation. There is much more to the uniqueness of the individual than just looking similar to someone else or behaving comparably to some other person.

Formal school experiences of each individual produce strengthened individual characteristics. There was a time perhaps when the school tried to make everybody be alike and act alike. It generally has been recognized that, while you can develop people who can perform in similar ways and who can learn similar facts and skills, the individual does not lose the unique characteristics of self. The formal school experiences from the kindergarten through graduate school does not create people who are alike. Each one takes the experience and extends (induction) that into his or her own future in the manner that is unique to the individual. The professional preparation, while controlled in large part by certification requirements, is still not looked upon as something that creates a uniformity in the population of those who enter teaching. Just as formal school experiences tend to strengthen the individual characteristic so does the professional preparation tend to help the teacher evolve (renewal) the uniqueness that eventually either will make the success or failure of the teaching responsibility. The professional preparation can be only a minimal common base and assumptions to the contrary probably cannot be sustained.

The environment in which an individual has grown to maturity is a great influence upon the unique individual characteristics of that person. The thought of this uniqueness is important in the discussion here because each teacher has an assignment that is different from the assignment of others on the teaching staff. The differentiation of assignments relates to the individual uniqueness and it is wise that these uniquenesses are recognized as those specific assignments are made. As teachers look at their colleagues in the school situation, it must be recognized that each one is teaching in a particular assignment because of some recognized unique abilities and strengths observed by those responsible for assigning staff to specific tasks. This gives each one an opportunity to observe self in comparison with others and to see how that relates to the particular and unique assignment that has been made and accepted.

When people see similarity between self and others as a comparison proceeds, they must remember that similarities are not evidence of weakness. There are some so-called strong individual people who think that, if they are behaving as do other people, they are losing their unique contribution because it must be different from that of others. This is one of the little elements of self-imposed merry-go-rounding that needs a dependence upon clearer realities of the situation. There is no need for any individual to be burdened with this thought of a fight against being like someone else. There is nothing wrong with making adaptations (redirection) of what someone else does to the responsibilities that the individual has. It should be remembered, however, that an adaptation to the way someone else behaves in the teaching situation must be analyzed logically and adapted developmentally. In this way, there is little doubt that the individual can become stronger and can avoid the misconceptions that lead to the merry-go-round effect as described in the opening paragraphs.

These *Aids for Self-Development* are structured to help you analyze yourself through the analysis of others.

Aids for Self-Development

1 Give an example of a colleague you have worked with who represents each of the listed traits (one for each):
  (a) competitive;
  (b) challenging;
  (c) independent;
  (d) task-oriented.
2 Give an example of a colleague for each of the following traits:
  (a) imaginative;
  (b) spontaneous;
  (c) outgoing;
  (d) idea-oriented.
3 Determine the persons named in the two lists above who are closer to your own professional style. Are you a *controlling* person (item number 1) or an *advocating* person (item number 2)?
4 What development activities will help you work better with the colleagues who did not choose your style?

Variability of Colleagues

A short step can be taken from the considerations in the last section dealing primarily with uniqueness of self to a more careful look at the nature of the colleagues in your particular teaching environment. First of all, thought needs to be given to just who are those colleagues and how shall they be identified. The first ones to be included naturally would be fellow teachers — those who are teaching in the same area and those who are teaching in fairly close proximity so far as classroom locations are concerned. But there are other colleagues that should be identified and these may be librarians, counselors, supervisors, administrators, secretaries, building maintenance personnel, and many others who serve the total responsibility of the school.

A different perspective may be taken toward each of the groups of colleagues within your environment. You should study what those perspectives are and raise the questions such as does one give greater respect to those who are in positions of authority, to those who are engaged in similar assignments, or to those who can provide a specialized help that is much needed from time to time. It is well to see each of these people in terms of what their unique contributions to the total responsibility of the school may be. Those who are trained in special education can be available to help with difficult cases in your classroom. It is not a major weakness on the part of the individual teacher to call upon these specialists for help. Reference was made in the last section to the concerns that some people seem to have for similarities and for differences to other people. There needs to be a tolerance developed both for similarities and for differences and then apply a rational type of analysis (renewal) for what this does to the collegial relationships.

Inferences could be drawn from judgments that there are assumed or ascribed statuses in the assignment. In other words, does one see those teaching in senior high school as being required to have a higher skill and, therefore, greater respect than those who teach in the lower grades? The very fact of using the terms lower and higher seems to stimulate some people to put a quality or value upon the assignment. It might be necessary to check your own perspective with respect to the statuses of assignment in order to determine how your relationships with colleagues are influenced. There are attitudes toward preferentialism that get into this variability of colleagues and sometimes creates an unpleasant experience on the teaching merry-go-round. Preferentialism often is described as something that somebody else does and, yet, most individuals have an ability to exercise the desire for preferential treatment. There are values in this which are related to the politicization of the powers within a faculty in the relationship of teachers to supervisors and administrators. There are personal and professional ambitions also that seem to get in the way of good colleague relationships on some occasions.

Thinking of colleagues may stimulate concerns for the possible price tags of acceptance and rejection of yourself and of others. By price tags is meant here, that, if you are going to accept or reject the purposes, actions, and accomplishments of others, expectations of others may be granted or imposed upon you for expressing rejection or acceptance. Objectivity in such instances may be difficult to achieve and maintain. Objectivity, nonetheless, is the best therapy for all those involved in such absurd response patterns. Your capacity to be a good colleague of others can depend upon your demonstrated objectivity and ability to deal openly in all interactive situations.

These *Aids for Self-Development* continue the analysis of colleagues begun in the last section.

Aids for Self-Analysis

1   Choose a colleague who represents each of the listed traits:
    (a)   self-sufficient;
    (b)   well-organized;
    (c)   methodical;
    (d)   practical.
2   Name other colleagues who reflect each of these traits:
    (a)   cooperative;
    (b)   reasonable;
    (c)   understanding;
    (d)   helpful.
3   Item number 1 describes an *analyzing* person while item number 2 describes a *facilitating* person. Choose one person from each of your lists who does not work well with others and suggest a method whereby they may be helped.
4   Determine which list is closer to your own professional style and decide on development activities that will bring you closer to people on the other list.
5   Identify the facet of the teacher career cycle (figure 2) where each of the colleagues you selected here and in the earlier aids would fit. Is there a pattern?

Stability Diversified

The inherited merry-go-round has been the concern of the previous sections of this chapter. It must be remembered that there are inherited perceptions held by all people involved in an organization that may contribute to the inherited merry-go-round that is easily credited to the school organization and to the environmental pressures. One of the inherited perceptions is that of incongruity between stability and diversity. Stability is the perception normally applied to security. Those things which are stable tend to stay as they are in the inherited perceptions.

   Diversity, on the other hand, has been related to the distribution of task and to the diversification of assignments. These have been recognized as a way of contributing strength to organizational activities by making the best use of the talents of people involved in those activities. It is well to look at the merry-go-round that comes through the inheritance of the perception of incongruency between stability and diversity. The ability of colleagues, as discussed in the previous section, may be simply an indication that the uniqueness of the individual has been recognized and that these were represented in the assignments to specific tasks made by the organizational management. Variability, in that sense, becomes a strength and should not now be considered a threat to stability because of this observed diversification in the things that people do or even in the ways that they do them. The important thing to recognize is that, if the diversities are goal related, there is a richness added (renewal) to the total operation and it does not constitute a merry-go-round in the sense that it was presented in the earlier sections of the chapter.

Groups are made up of individuals and individuals have the many uniquenesses that were observed earlier in this discussion. Individuals present these uniquenesses to the organizational activities and may represent a variability in what is being done and the ways of doing them. So long as these activities are related to the goals accepted by the organization, the diversities can be seen as strength (redirection) rather than as something threatening the stability of individuals and groups. Groups are made up of individuals and merely becoming a part of a group does not mean that the individual uniquenesses have been sacrificed or changed in order to get a sameness in the operation of each individual.

Groups are strong because of the diversifications of the individuals providing differentiations in uniqueness are applied appropriately to separate parts or sub-tasks of the greater tasks in education. In this sense, difference may be a source of strength. As strength increases, stability is assured. But stability here is in terms of a continuance toward the goal rather than an imposition of meaningless sameness upon the individuals in the total organization.

One of the things that can keep differences as a source of strength is to make certain that the values of the individuals and groups involved in the total activity are kept in focus and that those values are focused upon the goals of the organizational activities. A part of the inherited merry-go-round, based primarily on incorrect perceptions of the participants, is that a certain amount or kind of sameness is wrong and, at the same time, looking at sameness as a major element of stability. Certainly an individual who takes this point of view or people who keep this point of view are putting themselves on their merry-go-rounds and will get no more progress than would be found in the carnival merry-go-round.

School organization provides more than simply doing the things that makes it possible to enjoy the entertainment of the moment. There are serious tasks to be done in education and they should not be handicapped or thwarted by some perspective that puts the things in a questionable order. Sameness is not stability. Sameness may be anything but stability. Under changing conditions and demands placed upon the school, the school's insistence upon sameness would be a deterrent to the progress of the educational program. It is more acceptable, then, to see stability in the diversifications of the unique contributions of individuals to the goals of the institution. It is important, however, to recognize that, when the diversities are coordinated, stability is assured. Coordination is a process that can bring about strength from the diversifications of the skills and creative abilities of staff members as they address themselves to the tasks of education.

These *Aids for Self-Development* are to be used in differentiating between the stability of individual activities and the stability of the total educational enterprise.

. . . .

Aids for Self-Development

1 Select items from the list below that affect the stability of your individual activities and state what this affect is:
   (a)   motivation;   (i)   control of techniques;
   (b)   decision-making;   (j)   control of pace;
   (c)   interaction;   (k)   performance;
   (d)   attitude;   (l)   interruption of tasks;
   (e)   acceptance;   (m) personalities;
   (f)   interdependence;   (n)   reward system;
   (g)   individual differences;   (o)   assignment;
   (h)   specialization;   (p)   social interaction.
2 For those stability items you have selected, state a method or process of coordination between individuals that may lead to stability for the total educational enterprise.
3 Determine how the items that you did not select for stability affect the diversity of individual activities.
4 Develop redirective activities to create stability in those items indicated in number 3 as affecting diversity.

. . . .

Swirling Dervishes of Education

The idea of the carnival merry-go-round calls to mind the fact that one of the mounts for individuals to ride on the merry-go-round is a sort of swirling tub that four or five people can enter and swirl in the tub as the merry-go-round goes round. This perhaps is one of the most critical action points on the carnival merry-go-round.

The merry-go-rounds for teachers in the school are, as described earlier, sometimes unavoidable and sometimes achieved by choice. The advantage of the carnival merry-go-round is that it is entirely up to the individual to participate or not as the pleasures of the moment dictates. The teacher in the classroom, however, may find the general merry-go-round of activities, expectations, and pressures are so continuous that some critical points might be compared to the swirling tub of the carnival merry-go-round. The things that swirl for the teacher in the classroom will be identified here by way of illustration rather than by an attempted listing of all of the special swirls that might be found on the teacher's merry-go-round.

First of all perhaps the altars of innovation may be the special swirl. Somehow, education has followed the idea of commercial institutions, governmental agencies, as well as other public activities, in feeling that innovation gives a mark of creativity and achievement (induction) that nothing else can do. This is an extension of the discussion in the last section in which the matter of stability and diversification was considered. In this instance, the diversification is sought as the primary element of stability.

Stability here means keeping pace with the kinds of things that individuals expect of themselves as well as the expectations that are continuously feeding-in from environmental influence. To do something that has never been done before (redirection) may give a certain thrill to individuals and to groups by feeling that innovation has occurred. But when this becomes the altar before which professional personnel worship and determine the criteria by which future activities will be chosen and carried forward, innovation has abandoned the central focus of the goal of education, namely, to help students to learn. So innovation as innovation has nothing other than the characteristics of a carnival merry-go-round when it is sought for its own purpose and that alone.

Another swirling activity that can characterize this particular kind of a merry-go-round in the school is the conflict between improvements and the attention potential of what is done. There is little doubt that the term innovation as a label appeals to many people because it has attention-getting power and people thrive on attention. Few people in a group activity such as teaching are seeking opportunities to keep themselves and their achievements out of sight of others. So when the attention potential is given greater concern than the innovation or change for improvement in the teaching and learning activities, a conflict of this type will be a deterrent to the progress of the educational program.

One of the things associated with innovation has been the matter of labelling. There is a dominance of labels occurring now which also can be discovered in reading the history of education in this country and perhaps in all countries. There are specially named reading programs, new mathematics, modern science, and open schedules representing some examples of labels. Things apparently have to be named and, when named, they are supposed to carry the total concept of what the very complex teaching-learning program may be. If the central focus is on the curriculum arrangement, the same type of concern can apply. It is that a certain labelled type of curriculum gives the individual a sense of superiority according to the reputation of that particular label of innovation or program.

Special interests are operating within the school and outside the school. Sometimes these special interests are natural groupings of people who want to do things in a particular way. Sometimes special interests come in from the community because they want to impose a particular value system that they hold upon others in the environment. The thing that makes this one of the swirling situations on the teachers merry-go-round is that special interest groups often seem to wear blinders. They are unable to compare their own special interest to the special interest of others or to the common interest of all people. These blinders make it impossible for such people to see alternatives or to analyze alternatives. In this case, it is difficult to achieve the kinds of changes that constitute improvement or even maintenance of the program aspects that are presently very satisfactory.. With blinders such as this affecting people and programs the groups become swirling dervishes in the educational community and they simply go round and round while holding to the same place.

Contradictions and double standards operate within the school and its community. Contradictions can occur when two special interest groups cannot agree, cannot compromise, and thus want to hold to their own special interest while eliminating those other special interests. These special interests often are in contradiction. Sometimes it may be a religious interest that wants to require certain types of value recognitions within the public school that would be a contradiction for those who feel that religion has no part in the public school.

Double standards can occur and do constitute a part of the swirling on this teacher's merry-go-round in that differing acceptances of output may be thought of highly at one point in time and yet rejected in another. This is an instance that occurs if the country goes through severe economic or political swings and conflicting groups within the community and the nation want the schools to perform in one way at one time and another way at another time. In times of threats to a total people, whether it be economic or military, the standards shift quickly and complicate the teacher's school tasks. When the first satellite went into orbit and it was a Russian achievement, many people in this country turned in anger against the schools because they had not provided the kind of an education that would develop the orbiting capacity in this country as it occurred in Russia. In many ways the schools were blamed for this delay, and this single cause was responsible for years of 'innovation for innovations sake' in the schools.

Artificial and punitive criteria can be found in this merry-go-round and they certainly constitute a swirling state that makes it difficult for the teacher to proceed in a rational way with the tasks at hand. An artificial criterion might be one in which, if everything looks good at school and the students can put on a good show in the community, the school is doing a fine job. On the other hand, a punitive criterion might be of the type that, in case of public financial difficulties and heavy taxation, a withdrawal of the financial support not only of teachers salaries but of the materials required for teaching would be judged appropriate. These become substitutes for rationality and, therefore, are listed as a type of the swirling dervishes of education. The artificial and punitive criteria as well as the contradictions and double standards do not constitute a rationality in carrying forward the teaching-learning program that is expected of the schools. And these cannot possibly serve as a substitute for the rational approach to decision-making.

Change is a neutral term. Before techniques, methods, materials, or activities are changed, a teacher should determine positive standards for making that change. These *Aids for Self-Development* may serve as a date-collection approach for the verification of the reason for changing.

Aids for Self-Development

1 Give an example of an educational change that may reflect the listed
motive for change:

Motive   *Change*

Example:

labelling   Remove music or art from the curriculum labelling it 'back-to-the-basics'.

  (a)   change-for-change sake;
  (b)   labelling;
  (c)   attention potential;
  (d)   special interest group;
  (e)   community standards.

2 Select an innovation you feel would be beneficial to your work and
trace your activities through each of the stages of the processes listed
below:

  (a)   assessing needs;
  (b)   developing goals;
  (c)   setting objectives;
  (d)   planning change;
  (e)   implementing;
  (f)   analyzing;
  (g)   evaluating;
  (h)   feedback reporting.

3 Choose the stage from item number 2 where each of the incorrect
motives from number 1 would be taught. Describe how this might
happen.

Bulletins Without End

Some administrators and supervisors may like to write bulletins for
distribution to the teachers because it gives their egos a boost. It
must be remembered, however, that even though the purpose may be
wrong for such people, there is a need to communicate (induction)
some essential information to all members of the staff. While a few may
write bulletins for ego reasons, most people have sincere desires to
communicate that information to teachers which helps to build a well-
coordinated total school activity.

Several varieties of communication needs exist and these do not come in any priority order. Probably the only priority is when the originator of the bulletin feels that it is an appropriate time to disseminate certain types of information. There are information needs (renewal) with respect to schedules, special meetings, regular meetings, committee decisions, board of education policy, legal interpretations, curriculum revisions, special area committee actions, as well as a host of other needs for communicating between the central or building office and the classrooms.

Another reason that the number of bulletins may be increasing year by year is what might be called the 'put it in writing' syndrome. Some people who originate a bulletin feel that, if it is in writing, it gives all persons a chance to review what may have been communicated some days or weeks earlier. It also resolves the problem in the minds of many originators of bulletins that, in case the communication targets say they did not know, the bulletin that carried the information can be used for verification.

An advantage to the teacher for putting it in writing is that the originators of bulletins themselves are not always well coordinated. It is quite possible that one regulation or interpretation of a regulation may come from the system's central office, another from a school building office, and yet another from some of the special areas that may be attached to the central office. It is possible, also, that the ways of stating what is intended for clarification of the same thing may increase the confusion for those at the end of the line receiving the bulletins. In cases of this type, it is well to put the two potentially conflicting suggestions together and consult (redirection) the supervisor or building principal.

Regardless of how carefully and how well the bulletins are drafted and how well and how carefully they are read, there are losses through indirect interaction which characterizes the sender and the receiver of a bulletin. There is often little chance of clarifying meaning with the originator of the bulletin, particularly if it comes from central office personnel. The simple problem of numbers of teachers who might need to enquire of one originator about a bulletin would overwhelm the telephone in that particular office. It is easy for a teacher to say 'Why didn't they tell us what they meant in the first place?'. There might be some truth in that but there also might be some truth in the possibility that the teachers may not have read with the spirit of careful interpretation that may have been assumed by the originator of the bulletin.

Another type of problem that has been developing in recent years is the ratio between telling and asking which characterizes the bulletins. What is meant here is that the original design of the bulletin was to tell but now there seems to be, and properly so, a desire on the part of the originators of bulletins to collect information which can be summarized and used for policy development (redirection) or for evaluating the policy existing as well as their interpretations as recorded in the bulletins. As months and years go by, there seems to be an increasing demand upon the teachers' time to answer questions either as a part of or as addenda to the bulletin or as an accompanying instrument which requires some extended answers. The originators of the bulletins often will summarize the information that is communicated as a result of the request and may, in the summarization, release it to the board of education, or to news media. This may or may not be a scientific handling of the data returned and occasionally there might be some embarrassing angles for the teachers who have supplied the answers to the questions which accompanied the bulletin.

One of the discouraging things for teachers has been the lack of feedback to the questionnaire respondents. This means a direct feedback. Reference made above to the releases to school boards and media does not necessarily mean a feedback directly to the people who were surveyed by the addenda to the bulletin or the accompanying instruments. The feeling here is that teachers or the respondents to questionnaire material are entitled to such feedback and perhaps it would be appropriate to approach the supervisor and principal when input is requested to ascertain the planned use of the responses.

Discouragement is felt by many teachers who are inundated by too many bulletins coming from too many sources and too many of them asking too many questions for data response. A facetious response by many teachers is that what they need most of all is a requisition for larger waste baskets. Perhaps that is symptomatic of the teachers' responses to the over dosages of bulletins and information requests. Antagonistic responses by teachers are not productive and it would be much more appropriate to approach the whole problem more professionally and to avoid letting this develop into conflict between teachers, supervisors, and administrators.

Finally, a reference to the basics at this point seems appropriate since writing has been a *basic* through many decades of education. Some of the bulletins, however, do not demonstrate that the writers of bulletins are really trying to get themselves back to the basics in writing in order to facilitate communication.

Every teaching position has certain administrative details, sometimes called 'administrivia', attached to it. The next *Aids for Self-Development* will help you check how you use the time that is necessary to complete each of the tasks.

. . . .

Aids for Self-Development

1 Select those tasks or data sources from the list below that are important to you in your position:
   (a) attendance procedures;
   (b) special education referrals;
   (c) counseling practices;
   (d) school programs and events;
   (e) school regulations;
   (f) changes in policy;
   (g) school board minutes;
   (h) faculty meeting minutes;
   (i) teacher attitude data;
   (j) curriculum effectiveness data;
   (k) pupil information data;
   (l) pupil progress reporting;
   (m) teacher association activities;
   (n) community activities and attitudes;
   (o) team, unit, or department meetings;
   (p) others.

2 Determine whether the time you spent on those tasks or information aquisition you selected as important was time well spent. If the time was wasted, determine ways to improve upon this.
3 Select the tasks that are unimportant to your teaching responsibilities but on which you feel required to spend time.
4 List ways of communicating this waste of time on unimportant tasks that might result in better use of planning or teaching time.

. . . .

Decision Points and Decision Makers

Any individual or group finds that life involves almost a continuing responsibility for decisions. Each act on the part of the individual is a result of a decision to act. Each plan for the future that an individual holds is a result of a decision in that planning process. It must be recognized that those in organizational positions of responsibility also must determine what their actions will be and those actions represent decisions. Many times the administrators and supervisors in the central office as well as the building principals have the responsibility of making decisions that affect the decisions and actions of others.

The decision points must be identified so that decisions are not made in an off-hand and careless way. Decisions require an approach to planning. The planning process sometimes does not get a substantial amount of time for leading to decision. It means that decision points sometimes arrive unexpectedly and sometimes through the more deliberate process of analyzing and planning. There are at the same time many different modes of arriving at decision points. Sometimes the decision points are identified by another person, either within the school or in the school's environment outside the school and are imposed upon the individuals in the school organization. It is hoped that the mode of arrival (renewal) at more decisions can be that of the more deliberate, analytic, and planning process as indicated above. It must not be interpreted that, when decisions arise suddenly and at the hands of someone else, it has been a plan of some vindictive person to impose their wills upon the individuals who are not responsible for making a decision in that particular area of activity.

Many of the controls over the determination of decision points are a matter of time and circumstance. Time is one element that can offer immediate demands for decision or provide this more rational approach through planning to the decision point. Circumstances, also, constitute whether a leisurely approach can be enjoyed or whether a crisis is at hand, if, when the decision point arrives suddenly, there is no escaping the responsibility of making the decision. There is a limited autonomy on the part of any one administrator, supervisor, teacher, board member, parent or citizen, with respect to the choice of decision-point training. As indicated above, special circumstances often dictate the limit of the autonomy in the choice of the time when a decision shall be made. It is hoped that the timing of decision points will not be resolved by conflict in determining the point recognition. Many people have different pressures upon them and that makes the difference as to what their perception is of the time that a decision should be made.

Much needs to be considered about the relation of the point arrival and the decision substance. Some decisions relate only to routine matters that simply facilitate the activity of a group or facilitate the opportunities for individuals in a group to become a part of the decision-point determination and the type of decision that shall be made. The decision substance, then, must be one of the determiners of who shall have the chance to participate in the decisions that must be made. There are many personal roles in the decision process. The one alluded to up to this point has been simply that of when a decision should be made.

One of the things that needs to be considered at all times (renewal) by administrators, supervisors, and teachers is the matter of identifying who it is that has made the decision or who it is that should make the decision. In those areas where decisions are made without participation on the part of those who are affected by the decision, there can be conflict, lack of cooperation, and other responses that makes the decision of little consequence. It is to be hoped that, in any organizational activity, no decision will be communicated to those who are affected (redirection) by it without a proper and accurate identification of the ones who made the decision. This is just as important in the teacher relationship to the students as it is in the administrator-supervisor relationship to teachers. It is also of great consequence to all school personnel as they relate to the parents and lay citizens of a community who likewise are concerned about the identification of decision makers. Many times the identification may be in a state or federal law or regulation that is much more difficult to identify. But it is important to identify the decision maker whether it be someone in the local community or at some distant legislative, executive, or judicial level of government.

A great problem to be mastered in the matter of the decision points, decision makers, and decision substances is that of uncoordinated decisions. It is to be hoped that most school districts would identify someone to keep a continuous log of decisions that have been made and have been announced for the purpose of influencing others. Many school buildings are fortunate in having principals who take this responsibility for all decisions that originate in the central office of the school organization. It is recognized that there is a differentiating magnitude of decision importance and acceptance. The minor items should remain minor and teachers should accept those as routine until the routine decision seems to have disrupted the teaching-learning process in the classroom. It is at this point that teachers must be willing to report, probably to the supervisor or principal, just what the decision point and the decision results have done to the activities in the classroom.

Many of the decision points and substances do affect the individual teacher's action priorities in the classroom. It is because of this that all teachers must be ready to accept a responsibility for input into the decision-point identification and in the process of assuming a share of the decision making itself. These *Aids for Self-Development* are to help you begin a systematic method of studying this whole area of decision points, decision makers, and decision processes.

. . . .

Aids for Self-Development

1   Eight steps in a decision process are given below. List the individuals who, in your experiences, have been involved in the

deliberations at each decision point. These may be students, teachers, parents, administrators, supervisors, board members, or others:

(a) identifying the need for a decision;
(b) defining the location of the problem;
(c) clarifying the problem situation;
(d) generating alternative solutions;
(e) studying each alternative;
(f) identifying consequenes of each alternative;
(g) making the decision;
(h) evaluating the decision.

2 Identify what your response was to the involvement at each point. Was it positive, neutral, uncooperative, or conflict laden?
3 Select those points that need improvement in the decision-making process and discuss them with colleagues. Determine development activities to improve the process.

. . . .

Commitment to Reason

The previous sections of this chapter could easily lead to the conclusion that there is nothing but confusion, tension, strife, and unhappiness in the teaching situation. Such is not the case, particularly if people choose that it shall not be that way. There are some things about the total situation as well as specific incidences, however, that required the clear appraisal of those individuals who wish to get off the merry-go-round and to get on the better road to reason.

People can solve their problems and proceed with their work tasks and responsibilities but they must choose whether they will be governed by reason, emotion, or incoherence. The theme of this section is that reason is by far the best way (renewal) to make the determination as to how people will handle their responsibilities in an environment that has many pressuring and counteracting influences. Emotion provides little satisfaction except for the moment and incoherence contributes nothing to the happiness, satisfaction, and success of being a part of the educational program.

Irrationality never has been an instrument of support or opposition. It may have seemed so for people who attempted to give support or to provide opposition in an irrational manner. It is to be hoped that, throughout the years of teaching experiences, teachers will find opportunities to view the various aspects of the inherited merry-go-round and to decide that the path of reason (redirection) is the best way to get off the merry-go-round or to create more desirable ones of their own. To do this, there must be a respect for relevant information for every decision that is to be made and every task to be accomplished. It takes practice to recognize relevance in information. For that reason, you are urged to look carefully at the kinds of things you are asked to do, the kinds of problems you seem to have, and the solutions proposed by others as well as your own. Relevance here would refer to that kind of information which helps to solve a problem or to guide an activity. Relevance also can be determined in the light of the individual and institutional goals. These provide guidelines by which reason can bring control over the thoughts and actions of people and educational activities.

Each person should develop a respect for alternatives. There are alternative ways of going about the assigned tasks or alternative ways of solving problems. One of the most helpful things that each person can develop would be the skills of compromise. Compromise is not a sign of weakness. It is a sign that a person can look at alternatives, can value one against another, and can through that process (renewal) be able to achieve a commonality of views and solutions with colleagues. Another perspective needed is to see that concurrence with others is not a major weakness. Relevant information, respect for alternatives, and capacity of compromise make concurrence one of the sources of great satisfaction to the individual.

Thinking about these things should provide a way for teachers to get off other peoples' merry-go-rounds just as individuals can choose to get off the carnival merry-go-round. As individuals get off the merry-go-round that is inherited or that has been created by someone else, they might even want to create their own merry-go-round with better justification and better adaptations to the things that they are capable of doing and want to do. This amounts, then, to disinheriting the inheritances as they have been referred to in the early sections with respect to inherited merry-go-rounds in teaching experiences.

A very important point in the decision-making process is the generation of alternative solutions for the problem at hand. Alternative courses of action or preferred methods of solution are developed through the mental elaboration of decision participants. One active plan or systematic structure for this commitment to reason forms the framework for the next *Aids for Self-Development*.

Aids for Self-Development

1 Trace the selection of classroom materials through each of the listed stages of reasoning:
   (a) *saturation* (know problems from all angles);
   (b) *deliberation* (analyze and review all points of view);
   (c) *incubation* (time for ideas to crystallize);
   (d) *illumination* (emerging of most promising idea);
   (e) *accommodation* (further development of idea);
2 Next trace a situation where you must deal with a truancy problem through the reasoning stages listed above.
3 Identify the similarities and differences of dealing with two unlike problems using the same reasoning process.
4 Adapt this process to your own use in the generation of alternatives for the solution of other problems.

Making Your Own Merry-Go-Round

Reference was made in preceding paragraphs to the fact that individuals can get off the inherited merry-go-round, get off the merry-go-rounds made by others, or create their own merry-go-rounds. This is not to infer that merry-go-rounds are essential nor that they are the best way to organize expertise and effort in achieving the best results in the teaching-learning situations.

Merry-go-rounds usually just happen. They do not have to happen. Those at the carnival are there just as an availability and people can make a choice as to whether they wish to get on one or to stay off it. The inherited merry-go-rounds in the school, however, are not so easily subjected to the response of individual preference. So many elements are beyond the control of the individuals and the result is the conflicting pressures and contradictory expectations that seem to make persons feel like they are going round and round and getting nowhere. It is hoped that in this chapter some suggestions are offered for analyzing the merry-go-round characteristics and giving positive suggestions regarding what individuals can do to disinherit the inherited merry-go-round characteristics. Personally, deliberately, and rationally chosen ones of their own are preferable.

Great therapy can be found in personal planning, that is not a merry-go-round but a straight line challenge. Persons interested in planning their own activities and participating in planning the activities and futures of a group will find greater strength along with the confidence that comes with the assurance of being a part of an activity in which they are respected as a partner (redirection) in the development. While there may be a cyclical nature to events, it is also possible to uproot the merry-go-round effect to create an improvement oriented spiral of events.

Reference was made several times in this chapter to the concern with priorities. This becomes more and more important as one gains in the process of rational decision making. A part of the rationality is the ordering of priorities and letting others know about them. When people's personal priorities are accepted they really are a part of an ongoing group with high respectability. Individuals should discuss their own priorities with those holding conflicting ones. Open discussion, the capacity to look at alternatives, the capacity to make adaptations, and the capacity to compromise constitute a real strength in individuals as they work with priorities that are in conflict with their own.

Teachers should ask supervisors and administrators to assist in unscrambling the inherited merry-go-round ingredients that have been identified in various sections of this chapter. There are many others than those named in this chapter which were offered primarily for illustrative purposes. There is no intent to infer that all of these are subject to the absolute control of someone else and that the merry-go-round is inevitable. It definitely is not and individuals can proceed in an orderly way through the help of those who are there to be of assistance in controlling the merry-go-round ingredients that seem to handicap their own work. Individuals can suggest remedies that would help to achieve clear avenues to the instructional challenge and opportunity to which teachers are entitled.

These *Aids for Self-Development* give an initial structure for the analysis of individual priorities as well as imposed priorities.

· ·

Aids for Self-Development

1   Determine whether each objective listed below is your own or is imposed upon you by someone else:
    (a)   to determine readiness to learn in pupils;
    (b)   to teach children with learning handicaps;
    (c)   to select audio-visual media;
    (d)   to communicate with pupils;

(e) to use effective questioning;
(f) to individualize teaching;
(g) to write specific learning objectives;
(h) to have effective classroom management;
(i) to know the classroom social climate;
(j) to know test limitations and use;
(k) to report pupil progress;
(l) to apply principles of evaluation;
(m) to use self-analysis and appraisal;
(n) to diagnose learning needs;
(o) to determine ways to improve study skills;
(p) to write specific weekly lesson plans;
(q) to know rates of pupil growth and development;
(r) to teach values techniques;
(s) to know legal aspects of education;
(t) to know the expectations of the community role of teacher;
(u) to deal with cultural differences;
(v) to stress the rights of individuals;
(w) to develop logical thinking and reasoning;
(x) to show a concern for the environment;
(y) to know health and nutrition needs.

2 Select those objectives identified as imposed that create a conflict between your priority and that of the person(s) doing the imposing.
3 Identify development activities that will help work toward the resolution of the conflict in priorities.

. . . .

Personalized Management Opportunities

A gradual transition in the earlier sections of this chapter indicates that teaching experiences can be involved in a maze of cross purposing and contradictory expectations. This need not remain so. The ingredients are in the school operation and in the school environment that can encourage the maintenance of many of those conflicting experiences which must be handled successfully or the teaching experience will be neither successful nor satisfying.

Individuals can get off the merry-go-round of the type suggested earlier. Individuals must know where they are going to step. It is not a matter of getting off the merry-go-round and all of a sudden finding a clearly marked road ahead to an absolute certainty of success and satisfaction. Each step must have a purpose. That purpose must be consistent with the individual's own hopes and ambitions and still be well related and supportive to the school's hopes, goals, and purposes. Coordination, then, becomes a necessary part of purposing. Individuals must be able to see what others are doing in order to have some understanding of why they are behaving as they do and to understand the purposes they order as priorities in the activities of teaching.

Coordination requires that people see themselves in relation to those others in the educational operation. How you step in coordination is a part of the expectations that are placed upon you both by yourself and by those with whom you work. Everyone who accepts a teaching contract and the responsibilities of directing the learning activities of students must be willing to see how their own contributions are related to those potential and real contributions of othes. The expectations could be that there need not be another merry-go-round. The facility of skillful analysis and the establishing of sensible priorities can put the expectations into an orderly array that will not be frustrating as are the conflicting and contradicting pressures of the teachers' merry-go-rounds.

Let chapter 9 help you to analyze the problems that are involved in the array of expectations. The title is 'Management of Expectation'. Go from the dilemmas of the merry-go-round to an opportunity to apply common sense and sensible management of the expectations that people place upon themselves or accept from others. They must handle the undesirable expectations that come from within the school and from the school environment if they are to receive the expectations as a challenge to the best use of their own responses to those expectations.

Chapter 9

Management of Expectations

References have been made in some of the previous chapters indicating that the school is primarily a group activity and that group activity cannot succeed without a high degree of coordination. The term *management* is often used to indicate the kinds of arrangements and relationships between people and with material resources that can result in maximum outcomes for the operational intent. Management is a term that can apply to many different kinds of activities of people as well as to many different kinds of material support and environmental input into the school operation.

Management can be viewed as operational strategy. The concern here is primarily with the management of expectations, those developed by individuals as well as by groups. Expectations can be seen as anticipation and contemplation. Self-expectation is the type of status that one imposes upon oneself by way of intent to do things a certain way and to accomplish certain outcomes. Expectations as contemplation means that the individual is thinking about the procedures by which the accomplishment can be concluded. It is equally true that expectations are the anticipations of others who hope that another person, in this case the teacher or other school personnel, will accomplish that which is expected of the school operation and its outcomes. It is often the contemplation of others that individual teachers or other professionals in the school organization shall direct their efforts towards and shall achieve acceptable outcomes.

A prelude to these kinds of thoughts with respect to the teaching staff responsibilities and performance is found in chapter 5 which carries the title 'A Look Beyond the Classroom'. In that chapter there were many indications that the buzzing environment outside the classroom and outside the school might induce a series of expectations that could result in conflict. The conflict could occur between the members of the professional staff but, in this instance, more probably between the teachers and those in the surrounding environment who choose to impose selected expectations upon the professional personnel.

Chapter 8 is also somewhat of a prelude to this chapter. It carries the title, 'Inherited Merry-Go-Rounds'. In this chapter, it was a matter of trying to see why the life and environment of the teacher is a buzzing affair with many expectations, many demands, and very often many judgments with respect to the outcomes of teaching effort. Chapter 8 likewise indicated a number of possible internalized types of responses. This leads directly to the substance of this chapter which is directed to the management of expectations on the part of the teachers.

When the conflict potential and the internalized reponse by whatever manner of description occur, they can be translated into expectations. Expectations can be subjected to personal as well as group management. The discussion involves the matter of where the expectations originate, what sort of nature they possess, what they do to the individuals to whom they are directed, and what ways expectations can be translated into development and positive types of benefits.

The sequential aspects and subject matter of these two earlier chapters provide a basis for the individual teacher to look at the various potentials for managing self and alter expectations. The indications in chapters 5 and 8 emphasize the fact that many pressures develop on the part of the teachers as well as in the direction of the teachers because of the multifaceted impacts that constitute almost a continuous experience. There are expectations from peers, administrative and supervisory offices, boards of education, parents, and students. It must be remembered that the multifaceted impacts directed to one person at any particular time create a pressure on that person. The impacts require skill in finding ways to keep expectations under control. Such control protects the talent and creativity of the individual teacher against the burden of a multitude of targets, many of which can be in conflict.

The individual must find ways of mastering these multifaceted impacts or expectations and, as the single respondent, be able to continue the professional responsibilities of the classroom. The pressures brought about by the multitude of expectations directed to the teacher constitute a strain in maintaining a state of integrity, both professionally and personally, that is not exceeded by many other types of professions. There are many realities related to this maintenance of integrity and many of these will be discussed in later sections of this chapter.

A word of caution is offered to those who think that there might be some way of running away and hiding from this multitude of expectations being directed toward them as a person and as a professional worker in the school. There is really no place to hide from all of these expectations. The impacts of these expectations that originate in other people will be dealt with in a number of different ways and, hopefully, in a positive approach to help teachers find those ways of being able to manage the expectations and perhaps even to use them as a support and stimulant for the teaching and learning situations.

Timing becomes an important point of consideration and will be discussed in subsequent sections. Timing has both benefits and hazards. How long does an individual wait to respond to a declared expectation and what kinds of information are needed at the time of that response? An immediate response, often without adequate analysis of what the expectation constitutes and what kind of information is pertinent to dealing with it, can become a hazard and a disaster for the individual teacher. The point of this chapter is to help individuals find ways of searching for the personalized guidelines that will help them to live creatively and productively in the classroom as confronted by the students who are there for the purpose of learning. If the students seem to demonstrate other types of purposes, the teachers are confronted with those conflicting expectations that require expert skill and management of the expectations in order to proceed with the management of the teaching and learning activities.

Nature and Origin of Expectations

Some indications were given in the introductory statement that expectations can be communicated by many people both within and outside the school. The expectations may be directed by unknown people and those unknown people often do not bother to communicate the expectations to the individuals upon whom the expectations have been placed. This creates a difficult situation for individuals to establish any management of expectations when they are dealing with the unseen and unknown. It must be remembered, however, that there are many vehicles of communication and that the vast majority of expectations will be communicated directly and clearly to the individuals who are the target of the expectations. When this occurs, the origin of the expectations, which is normally a person or an organized group of persons, can be known and can be contacted.

The nature of expectations is often more difficult to determine because the people designing them have their own goals and values and are quite involved in what they expect and how they expect it. It requires a great amount of patience and tolerance in order that the distance between assurance and hopelessness can be steadily increased. The assurance can come from the skill of the management of expectations (induction) and hopelessness comes at that point in which the individual who is a target of expectations gives up trying either to modify them or to measure the things that are expected.

The individual may find it helpful to look upon expectations as a mirror of hopes and despairs of those people who are establishing them. Certainly, within the professional organization, the hopes of improvement, development, and success are mirrored in the fact of working together and sharing the kinds of targets and goals that are chosen for the educational enterprise. The mirror of despair is more easily described by those who may have become discouraged in their personal environment (see figure 1.1) and in their hopes for public enterprises but failed to see the desired outcome as a possibility. This despair may result in directing expectations to the educational programs.

Many times in crisis, people of a governmental unit or of a locality may develop certain types of despair that causes them to develop what they believe can be a mirror of hope but must turn to somebody else to bring about the things that the hope envisions. When it is relating to education or even to youth, teachers are the main targets of those expectations and hopes. Unfortunately, they may turn to those same teachers when the origin of despair in a community or a country may lead to an expectation that the schools can correct almost any threat of disaster that can occur in a society. When there is unemployment, the schools are expected to develop people who are employable. When there is economic disaster, the schools are expected to teach people to develop a successful economy.

It has been unfortunate that the schools have been willing to accept or even to encourage this kind of hopeful status for education. This acceptance has brought on a pattern of expectations that now must be corrected by a realistic appraisal of the limits of accomplishment for educational programs. It is even more unfortunate when conflicting expectations from opposing groups do not allow teachers the opportunity for appropriate management.

The origins of expectations come from many sources as indicated above. When they arrive at the school and are directed to individual teachers, there must be some effort to get a measure of legitimacy of the expectation. The test of legitimacy can be determined in part by gaining knowledge of the reasons why the people have directed the particular expectations at the school. Perhaps for the school, the best measure of legitimacy of expectations which comes from either within or outside the school, would be to determine the relationships (renewal) to the school target or goals. The things the school commits itself to accomplish by the way of teaching and learning must be the most reliable measure of the legitimacy of expectations that are placed upon teachers. This leads directly to the problem of the accessibility of the identification and definition of the expectations that are directed to the school. If it comes from the government, there is a question of how accessible information is regarding the reason for the particular expectations and whether a particular expectation was an expression of the goals of the person or persons originating it.

Here again is a problem of legitimacy which must be tested against the goals and values not only of the individuals originating the expectations but also those individuals in the school situation who receive and respond to them. It is sometimes difficult to find out who speaks and who they are speaking for. In other words, if it is a legislative act, who stimulated the legislature to become interested and to express an expectation to be placed upon the school and why? A pattern of influences and pressures can be originated in a special group, channelled through the legislative process, supported by a court system, and placed upon the school agenda for accomplishment. It is difficult at this point to know who are the originators and what were the particular goals and values that stimulated the development of the specific expectations.

A possible course of action could be to rely upon tradition as the answer to whether an expectation can be considered legitimate and, therefore, a program of action. It is much better to base that decision of acceptance of the expectation upon creative thought, supported by good and reliable information to make the determination of how the expectation will be managed when it arrives at the school and, particularly, at the teacher's desk. It is hoped that the creative and thoughtful approach will be used rather than to assume that each teacher can find some so-called *expectation bishop* and simply consult that individual or individuals to determine whether the expectation is to be seen as appropriate and valid enough to be a cause of action. Self-perception is much more appropriate for the well-prepared teacher to manage expectations (redirection) than to borrow the thoughts from someone else regardless of the seeming superior and solid status of that other person.

Individual self-perception of success in dealing with the expectations of others must find some formal way of being supported by information. These *Aids for Self-Development* give some suggestions as to what kinds of information can be probed.

....

Aids for Self-Development

1 A set of general expectations for schools are listed below. Determine whether each expectation is internal (from inside the school system or profession of education) or external in nature. Add other expectations to the list and determine their origins:
 (a) recognize the importance of individuality;
 (b) bring people into communication with the world;
 (c) respect health and safety;
 (d) establish the relevance and applicability of learning;
 (e) develop group consciousness;
 (f) develop a values system;
 (g) maintain good human relations;
 (h) maintain the status quo;
 (i) advocate the democratic process.
2 Now identify the origin of each expectation for your assignment. Is an individual, a group of individuals, or some amorphous origin responsible for the expectation?
3 Decide whether each of the expectations is valid for your school, and explain why it is or why it is not.
4 Describe how you deal with those expectations you have determined to be valid. Describe your reaction to those that are invalid. Study the nature of the differences in these responses.

....

Life Expectancy of Expectations

Thus far it has been indicated that there are many sources and many different kinds of expectations. These range all the way from those selected by self and those imposed by others. It would seem that, with the multiple nature of the origins and of kinds of expectations that are placed upon the school and particularly upon the teacher, a proper question would be one of determining how long an expectation stands. The answer is about as variable as the origin and nature of expectations. Some expectations seem to last only a few moments and others seem to exist for years and decades.

A number of factors seem to affect the life expectancy of an expectation. One of the most obvious seems to be the amount or degree of power possessed by the originator or author of the expectation. The concept of the authority figure is not new to the current society nor to past societies. The authority power exists in varying amounts. Some variation is due in the real power possessed by an enforcer of the authority and by individual recognition of the degree of that power. The individual in this case would be the target of the expectation. The structured organization of administration poses some authority power in certain positions. The chief administrator of the school system, the principal of the school, and many others have varying degrees of the so-called authority to command over other people. These patterns of authority have been changing in recent years and much more participation has been permitted and encouraged on the part of those who presumably are under the authority of the higher positions. The pressure placed upon the individual who receives the expectations can vary with the authority power of the originator of the expectation.

Another determiner of the life expectancy of an expectation is the stability of the expectation target. This means that a teacher who is well-balanced emotionally can make most decisions on the basis of gathering information (redirection) and making judgments based upon that information thus providing a pattern of stability that affects the longevity of an expectation. If the individual accepts the legitimacy of the expectation and finds that it is in line with personal goals and purposes, the expectation may last longer than in situations where the individual target does not possess the stability. Those who are unable to think rationally in the face of an expectation placed upon them may even withdraw from the position which brought on the expectation.

Another type of condition that seems to affect life expectancy of expectations is environmental in nature. It is possible that a person teaches in a community that is predominantly of one nationality of immigrants. The communities of this type often tend to perpetuate the culture of the country from which they came. This becomes an environment for the teacher that tremendously affects (induction) the kind of expectations placed upon the classroom. A community which has a dominant agricultural crop may have certain expectations because of economic advantages. An example could be that, in the sheep country, the home economics department would find some expectations with respect to teaching the relative qualities of silk, cotton, and wool. Such instances could be extended but it would only continue illustrating the point that the environment has to do with the kinds of expectations that are placed upon teachers and, at the same time, affects the longevity of those expectations.

Expectations may come from organizations that exist within the school or within the community. Within the school the originators of expectations often are the administrative staff members of that school. But at the same time there can be teacher associations or union organizations that also initiate expectations that are placed upon the teacher. The life expectancies of these types of expectations probably are more related to the organization skills and zest which characterize the origination of the expectation as well as the attempt to see it observed. This tends to cause the expectation to last a much longer period of time than if the organization lacks the skill and zest either to enunciate or to perpetuate expectations.

One of the greatest of the determiners of longevity of an expectation is what might be called legal entombment. This means that people have succeeded in having their expectations which are placed over teachers enacted into law. When that expectation becomes a law, it is well-known that changing laws involves a very slow process. When the expectation becomes official, the longevity is extended more than any that might be sponsored by the skill and zest of an organization or the emotional enthusiasm of special interest groups. The teacher who is receiving the expectations and is responsible for managing them needs to develop (renewal) a thought base for dealing with expectations as opposed to the emotional base for managing. The thought base can provide the opportunity to gather information pertinent to the expectancy as well as to its effect upon the teacher and upon the teacher-learning situation. The emotional base has much to do with life expectancy of expectations but there is no way of seeing that these are rewarding in the sense that expectations can be seen as having growth potential.

Many of the less desirable aspects of expectations have been included in the discussion here but it must be emphasized that expectations can be just as positive as they can be negative. The main thing is not to build up a desire to become immune to or fully protected from any expectations which come from outside the self. It is important to see that the expectations can be studied, can be used for the developmental stimulation (redirection), and can provide some of the basis for developing criteria for judging the quality of the work done by the professional in the classroom. It means that the target for the expectation does have an opportunity to exercise management in the direction of planned protection, evolvement, or the demise of the expectation. The protection is the developmental kind which means

that the expectation is proving to be beneficial. Evolvement is developmental in the sense that it becomes adapted to the situation that
becomes more rewarding. The demise means that it has been cancelled
out completely or has achieved a substitution.

The next *Aids for Self-Development* are to help you to study the life
expectancy of professional expectations.

....

Aids for Self-Development

1   Identify one or more expectation that is or has been imposed upon
    you in your current assignment. (The *Aids for Self-Development*
    from the last section may offer some help in this endeavor).
2   For each expectation you identified, determine whether each of the
    possible sources of influence below contributed to the evolvement
    of that expectation:
    (a)   the emotional base of the expectation;
    (b)   the authority of the originator;
    (c)   the stability of the expectation target;
    (d)   the legitimacy of the expectation;
    (e)   the target environment;
    (f)   cultural mores surrounding the target population;
    (g)   the organizational base or support;
    (h)   the legal entombment of the expectation.
3   Decide which of the possible sources listed in item number 2 above
    contribute to the demise of the expectation(s) you have listed.
4   Determine the longevity of your expectation(s) based upon the
    sources of evolvement and the sources of demise you have selected.

....

Response Ranges and Consequences

The preceding section explores some of the factors that affect the
longevity of expectations. These same factors may have much to do
with the kinds of responses that the target of the expectations displays.
At the same time, they may give some indication of the types of
consequences that various responses to an expectancy may generate. It
is certain that expectations can stimulate action in the direction of the
goals anticipated by the originator of the expectations. It is possible also
that expectations can have the effect of paralyzing individuals to a state

of inaction. This, however, is not the usual consequence of the effect of expectation.

Recognition must be given to the fact that there is a great variety and range of response by each individual. Just as expectations can stimulate action, they also can control (induction) action. The reference in the previous section to the authority power of the originator of an expectation represents the influence of pressure that can be exercised by the declaration of expectations of individuals and groups. These expectations which can stimulate or control or can cause complete inaction may be the consequence of over or under responsiveness to the expectation. Over-responsiveness often is exhibited by the immediate and direct protest of the expectation because of its affect upon the individual's freedom of action in fulfilling the employment responsibilities. Under-responsiveness may lead to undesirable consequences such as the increased organization and pressure by the originator of the expectation. It means, then, that the individual in managing expectations must be aware of the fact that there are consequences (renewal) for both over and under-responsiveness when being the target of expectations.

Another factor that is well worth considering is the location of the consequences. The location of the consequences is not always chosen by the individual who has become the target of an expectation. It may be that an expectation is generated by a highly organized group that may have headquarters at some distant point from the locale of the individual responding at a particular time. The consequences in this case are not in the local classroom but rather in the emotional or thoughtful reactions of those who are interested in sponsoring the particular pattern of expectations that will lead to an accomplishment of an organizational goal. This is not to say it is wrong but rather to explore the fact that consequences are not always located where they can be seen by the individual targets of the expectation. In the local community, however, the consequences are close to the classroom and there can be immediate and rather complete interchange (redirection) which helps in the definition, use, and consequences of expectations received and given.

The magnitude of the consequences must be given consideration. If a consequence is something that will offend a large group of people because it violates a long-held goal of that group, the magnitude of the consequences may be greater than when the reacting group is at a long distance or a loosely organized group. Holiday observances constitute a good example of this type of expectation-consequence situation. The individual dealing with all of these problems of response and consequence occasionally samples a variety of temptations. Seeking the route of some of those temptations may accentuate the emotional distance between the originator of the expectation and the person who is the target of that expectation. Temptations must be recognized and, at the same time, explored as to the kinds of consequences that they will generate. One temptation often observed is that of ridiculing the expectation itself. The expectation placed upon the educational program and, therefore, upon the teacher may be such that it violates all of the professional knowledge, experience, and values of the individual targeted for the expectation. But ridicule is seldom the route to compromise. Rather, it might accentuate the determination of the originator of the expectation to make it more potent and restrictive or to seek other avenues of vengeance upon the person ridiculing the expectation.

Another temptation route is that of belittling the orginator of the expectation. This indicates that the person or persons are not competent to initiate expectations which influence the educational program. It belittles that originator's right or competence to initiate the expectation in the first place. Here again, it may lead away from any interaction which might result in adaptation or compromise. It is almost certain to harden the battle lines between the originator and the locale where the education is taking place.

Another temptation to people who are targets of expectations is to shift the responsibility. In recent decades, more expectations have been placed upon the school and upon the teachers than in the past. An illustration of shifting the responsibility (redirection) is to indicate that, when values are concerned, the churches must take as much or more responsibility for teaching youth values than should be placed upon the school. In many of the personal habits of students, there is an easy temptation and an inviting one to indicate that parents have failed to fulfill their obligations as parents and, therefore, have no right to place expectations upon the school or the teachers that relieves them of their failed responsibility. A more recent shift of responsibility is to television which is claimed to take the student's time from the home study and other activities that leaves them incapable of pursuing the educational program with effectiveness.

Another illustration of temptation is that of responding to an expectation with higher expectations placed upon the originator. This has often been true when the expectations require a high degree of expenditure. The retort can be that such expectations can be fulfilled providing adequate funds are made available by the community or district or by those who are levelling the expectations on the school and on the teacher. Many other examples of temptations could be cited but perhaps this is enough to set the reader thinking about the question of whether to choose this kind of response with the probable consequences as opposed to a more positive approach.

Some guidelines might lead to positive (renewal) views of response-consequence relationships. One illustration of a guideline might be that of seeking a clarity of the meaning of the expectation. The originator may assume that the declaration would carry his or her full intent. But the person who is targeted for the expectation may translate some personal perspectives into it that are quite different from those of the originator. The seeking of clarity (induction) can be one way of establishing a solid base for discussion, interaction, and adaptation.

Another guideline might be that of analyzing the nature of the impact of the expectation. What is it likely to do that was not anticipated by the person originating the expectation? Here again, factual data can be put together and presented so that the impact itself might be the best solution to the management of that expectation.

A third guideline can be that of identifying the evaluating stages of the effect of an expectation. Here it is assumed that the target of expectation tries to fulfill the substance of that expectation but, at the same time, establishes the point or check points at which it can be determined whether or not fulfilling the expectation (redirection) will deliver the consequences anticipated.

Still another guideline can be that of exploring the potential of displacements. Many things have been injected into the educational program only to find later that time had been robbed from some other important elements. Many things during the past decade have been added to the school responsibility through the cry of 'back to the basics'. This is a case where displacement was not anticipated but became a reality when other, and often unrelated, expectations were injected.

Individuals need to develop the disposition and skill to analyze their responses to expectations as an essential part of managing these expectations. These *Aids for Self-Development* help to identify a relationship between management and consequences of action.

. . . .

Aids for Self-Development

1 List your immediate response, based on your assignment, of each situation given below:

(a) your supervisor asks you to take part in an experimental program;

(b) you learn from a colleague that other teachers have been discussing your teaching;

(c) your colleagues do not respond to a new motivational technique you have found useful;

(d) you are asked by the principal to attend a three-day workshop on individualized instruction;

2 Identify the location and strength of the impact that the consequences of your response might have. Use the guidelines suggested in this section or develop your own.

3 Study your response/consequence relationship and design development activities that might make it more positive.

. . . .

Relationships to Personal Goals and Values

Reference was made earlier to the self as being one of the many origins of expectations. Self-expectations are often easier to analyze providing the individual has a disposition to do so. The identification, definition, and analysis of self-expectations can become a source of determining the relevance of those expectations. Relevance in this sense is related to the personal goals and values of the individuals concerned. The relevance, however, would be only between the expectation and the personal goals and values and might not be relevant to the group goals and values of the school or of the various individuals and groups in the community.

Relevance, then, can be determined more easily with respect to self-expectations as opposed to the expectations directed toward the individual by others. One of the problems in determining the relevance of expectations of others is that the goals and values of those others may not be known. As a matter of fact, the expectations themselves often are not well known thus increasing the problem of determining relevance in terms of personal goals and values. As individuals go about managing the expectations that have been placed upon them, there is an increasing concern for integrity. The price of integrity certainly becomes higher as one attempts to act upon the expectations of others, particularly when the goals and values of those others are not in agreement with individual goals and values. It is possible also that individuals might have a problem of integrity in following personal goals and values when the expectation itself violates those goals and values.

Integrity is of even greater concern when the individual chooses to resolve the conflict of expectations by joining the cause of someone else. In joining the cause of someone else, integrity demands that the individual learns and assesses the goals and values of the originators and proponents of that cause. To do less than this is to violate the individual standard of integrity in behaving in a way that is inconsistent with personal expectations. Each individual must have some degree of flexibility in order to work in any group enterprise. The flexibility is lost completely when an individual abandons personal decision and joins the cause of another. This is a complete shift from one posture to another. Each individual needs to develop (renewal) some personal rules of flexibility so that expectations can be managed with some degree of integrity and such flexibility must be related to personal goals, values, and self-expectations.

Situations such as the contractual relationships with the school district and, therefore, with the administrative controls and expectations may override some of the rules of flexibility. On the other hand, the teacher enters a contract voluntarily and because of this must accept a reasonable degree of responsibility for conforming to the elements of the contract. If the personal goals and values are being violated by the expectations involved in the contract, there should have been the decision not to enter into the contract in the first place.

The ethical obligations that bear upon the individual begin with the personal goals and values which structure the integrity of the individual. In managing expectations, the ethical obligations would be to treat those goals, values, and expectations of others, which are in conflict with the personal ones, as a desire and requirement for achieving (redirection) some compromise or adaptation. This can preserve one's own goals and values without undue interference or destruction of those held by others. This type of ethical obligation would dictate open interaction with colleagues and with others who presume or assume the right to direct expectations toward the individual. The open interaction, if leading to the better interpretation of the individual contribution to the group enteprise, can be a source of strength to the individual as well as to the group. Open interaction requires a high degree of sincerity and willingness to seek and appraise supporting information. It means that each individual ethically must possess a willingness for self-improvement. In this situation, self-improvement is to be interpreted as a continuing effort to understand and a desire to harmonize the expectations held by others who have been directing expectations toward that individual.

These *Aids for Self-Development* are designed to help you gather information about the relationship of expectations to personal goals and values.

· ·

Aids for Self-Development

1 State what you feel are the expectations of the colleagues described in each of the following hypothetical interactions:
  (a) You approach a teacher with whom you feel quite at ease about a problem you have keeping the students' attention during classes. He/she communicates anxiety and concern about the problem but gives no suggestions as to how to remedy the situation.
  (b) While you are waiting for the teachers to assemble for the weekly faculty meeting, you share the ideas you received at a recent convention with a colleague you have found uncooperative. He/she engages in a two-way communication about the ideas and enriches the conversation with reciprocated enthusiasm.
  (c) You approach a professor at a local college or university and ask his/her opinion on an emerging concept. He/she contributes a new dimension to it, but also indicates not to bother him/her again.
  (d) You discuss an exciting idea that was discussed during your evening college course with your department chairperson or unit leader. He/she welcomes the opportunity to converse professionally, but immediately excludes the possibility of any success in the idea.
2 Decide if the expectations you have listed for each situation are consistent with your own value system.
3 Determine methods to renew or redirect the expectations of others in line with your personal goals or values.

· ·

Relationships to Personal Talent and Assignment

The management of expectations is highly related to the ways that individual talents fit the assignment which has been accepted. Tasks that demand knowledge and skills far beyond or entirely different from those which are possessed by the individual means that the expectations placed upon the person and the position cannot be met and fulfilled.

Most teaching positions and other school tasks have job descriptions. Job descriptions presumably detail some of the things that are expected of the person who has accepted a designated assignment. It is unrealistic, however, to assume that a one or two-page job description can identify all of the specific things that a person is supposed to do. A job description should provide clues to the major areas of function which then can be analyzed into the specific action requirements. The job description, as a basic document, indicates what the person is supposed to do in the position described. This is not always the way it occurs. In other words, what the individual does often may not be included in the job description and, perhaps, not even remotely related to it.

The job description, however, is a logical place to look for the initial identification (induction) of expectations. In that sense, it is an expectation base. It is not to be confused with the expectation origin which resides wth those who drafted the job description. It is an appropriate document to gain the first clues as to the nature and number of expectations placed upon the person in the assignment. It is also a document that can be reviewed from time to time in order to discover whether the functions of the assignment have evolved to the extent that it seems little related to the job description. It would be appropriate in this case for the individual position holder to consult with the administrator and supervisory staff representatives who might best render some judgment as to whether the evolvement in function is appropriate and would fit some revised expectations.

Many elements need to be studied with respect to job descriptions. The reference so far has been to the job description of the person holding a particular position. It must be recognized also that there are many other job descriptions, both within the school and outside the school, which means that those who occupy different positions with different job descriptions may have influence upon any individual who has a different job description. It is well to analyze these expectations which seem to arrive from over the horizon by coming from those descriptions fitting the work of others in related or even remote types of function. The analysis of those can bring insights to the individual as to what kind of pressures might be forthcoming because of the job descriptions that must be observed by others. These take much open interaction when they are discovered and certainly must be subjected to analysis and eventually to compromise and adaptation.

Reference was made above to the fact that the job description often becomes outdated because of the evolving functions that occur with a particular assignment. Personal development of the individual may be one of the primary causes for the evolved functions. It must be recognized, then, that an appropriate related activity will be to update and achieve agreement on the revised job description. As the functions develop or evolve, the expectations (redirection) placed upon the person in a particular position likewise will change. These must be seen also in relation to the kinds of criteria and data that are used in making judgments regarding the quality of performance of the individual. The accomplishment level in an evolved functional situation brings about a renewal of concern for the appropriateness of the job description which gives rise to a series of revised expectations. It is well to keep alert to the clues that would indicate the new or renewed accomplishment level and the bases for making judgments regarding the quality performance.

The responsibilities of analysis as indicated here, suggest a great need for differentiating the identities of subjective and objective judgments. It is impossible to eliminate all subjective judgments and, perhaps, it would not be wise to try to do so. On the other hand, the analysis suggested here can bring about the base for much more objective judgments and more reliable and effective ones than those based only upon subjective feelings while ignoring completely the objective data that might be available or could be made available. The openness of interaction has been emphasized many times and it is again at this point. Openness can lead to one of the better ways that the individual can set about managing evolving assignment and the professional performance. Periodic reviews would involve an evaluation of the applicability of the initial job descriptions and the relationship to the evolving functions of the position. These reviews can become a more profitable way of moving toward the data required for making judgments against the criteria which must have been established at the time the job descriptions were developed.

The following *Aids for Self-Development* provide a structure to discover relationships between personal talent and the expectations of the assignment.

. . . .

Aids for Self-Development

1   Identify a talent that you bring to your assignment that will help
    you meet each of the listed expectations:
    (a)   use of prepared curriculum guides;
    (b)   weekly lesson plans are to be filed in the office;

    (c)   teachers are directed to work in a team;

    (d)   use of the discovery technique is stressed in the school;

    (e)   all materials are approved by the board of education;

    (f)   teachers must maintain regular hours of 8.00 to 4.00 pm;

    (g)   teachers must do student supervision and discipline;

2   Identify an expectation, and who holds it, that makes use of each of the following talents:

    (a)   creativity;

    (b)   adaptability;

    (c)   leadership;

    (d)   subject-mastery;

    (e)   resourcefulness;

    (f)   organization;

    (g)   friendliness.

3   Design development activities that will make use of the talents you have in meeting the expectations of your assignment.

. . . .

Patterns of Non- and Mis-management

An earlier discussion in this chapter indicated that the responses to expectations include a wide range of characteristics. It was indicated also that there is an equally wide range of in the nature of the responsibilities and consequences that are associated with the responses. Expectations have the capacity to stimulate responses and any response is almost certain to have some type of consequence.

    The ranges were identified earlier but it is appropriate now to look at some of the kinds of management tasks that can be applied to the responses and consequences of expectations. The primary management target for any individual must be the self. The person that does the responding to an expectation is the person that has the best opportunity to initiate control over the responses to those expectations. A secondary management target is others or those who establish expectations that have an impact upon the individual. There must be a concern for priorities that are involved in the management of expectations. These priorities at the same time are highly related to the originators of the expectations. This is true whether the concern is with the self-expectation or the expectations established by others.

    Some skills need to be developed in the analysis of the kind and amount of pressures that are exercised through the naming of priorities with respect to responding to an expectation. A framework that might be helpful is to establish pattern categories. The reference is to the pattern of management or of responding to expectations. The five categories for a pattern of management suggested are as follows:

1 identification and definition;
2 impact characteristics;
3 exploration of alternatives;
4 criteria of practicality; and
5 communication of rationale.

Individuals should accept the responsibility for the management of expectations (renewal) particularly those related to self. They can look at these five categories that constitute elements of a pattern of reacting or managing. *Identification and definition* in any type of problem is a first essential. It is important to know the nature of the expectation and to establish some description that makes it easy to think about.

The *impact characteristics* must be studied, particularly when their expectations come from others. The impact can be in the form of directives from an administrative officer. It can be in the form of calm suggestions and requests. It can be in the form of group action, whether deliberate or emotional. It is important to know how the expectations arrive at the individual's entry to responsibility for selecting responses.

The selection of responses leads directly into the third category, namely, *exploration of alternatives*. It has been indicated several times earlier in the text that almost any area of responsibility can be improved by looking at alternatives either as a purpose, a mode of action, or a selection of desirable outcomes for professional effort. Alternatives provide not only a chance to analyze other ways of doing but also to make comparisons (renewal) that might help substantially in selecting the right type of response to an expectation when the impact is realized.

The *criteria of practicality* means that the response needs to be checked against the accepted goals and responsibilities. Often the goals in the school situation are established by the professional group or members of the staff. The practicality is to be determined in terms of the types of responses to expectations which are leading in the direction of both the group and personal goals for the educational program.

Communication of rationale is essential and should be recognized as the basic ingredient in maintaining open interaction. Communication provides the opportunity for sharing thoughts, goals, and concerns, as well as the opportunities to arrive at adaptations of expectations or at modifications that can make them more useful.

Some people may develop the idea that expectations ought not to be managed by the individuals of a teaching staff. This would be an approach that might be called non-management and it has some plus and minus effects. Looking at the pattern categories, non-management can be identified in the individual as a studied response in avoiding the response to the expectation. In this case, let expectations flow where they may while the individuals look to their own business. This often has the impact characteristic of stimulating an antagonistic alter group who may not only develop new expectations but may put pressure on getting conformity to the expectations already established and which have been ignored by the individual. The only plus effect of the non-management perhaps can be the hope for calmness that an individual might realize as a result of not having other people interfere in the work of the position of responsibility since the expectations have already been declared by the school officials. In this day and age, probably few of the plus effects can be experienced by an individual who seeks to respond to expectations by non-management of them.

The possibilities of mis-management are perhaps even more critical to view. Here is a case in which the individual may recognize the expectation, then proceeds to develop some response to it, but the response is not acceptable to those establishing the expectation. Looking again at the pattern categories, it is well to identify and define the nature of the expectation which has been the real cause of a response. The response may be exactly the wrong thing for satisfying the expectation and, in that sense, there is a survival problem for the individual because of the mis-management of the response to the expectation. Here again the impact characteristics become important because the whole means of communication become a part of it. The exploration of alternatives (redirection) perhaps is the one thing that might have avoided mis-management, but that does not always guarantee a good management pattern for expectations. Trouble can only befall the individual who has mis-managed. The criteria of practicality at this point might suggest that to be practical means to go along with all the expectations and that will keep everybody quiet.

Earlier in the chapter there was discussion of the fact that conflict can develop from opposing expectations and, in this case, practicality cannot be determined by the mere fact of accepting all of them. The communication in the fifth category of pattern becomes the most important since rationale probably is the only way that a solution can be developed. The patterns of management and of expectation will be highly related to the purposes of the individual and of the group enterprise.

Help for each individual in the patterns of management may be derived by surveying situations through the *Aids for Self-Development* presented here.

....

Aids for Self-Development

1 Four situations of non- or mis-management are described below. Determine the impact characteristics of each as it pertains to your assignment.
    (a) You misunderstood the directions for collecting book fines from students. You were to collect them and keep a record but you have sent the students to the office for payment.
    (b) All teachers are directed by the local association to be at a school board meeting since a crucial issue is to be discussed. You attend and speak in favor of the *wrong* side of the issue.
    (c) You have volunteered to solicit teachers to become active in a local charity fund raiser. No one signs the sheet you have put in the lounge.
    (d) Students complete their daily work hurriedly in order to make good your promise of an early dismissal. You keep them late because of their action.
2 Describe how a careful exploration of alternatives might have helped each of the situations.
3 Using the same situations, identify a technique of communication of a rationale that might have helped.
4 Design an induction activity for new staff members that will alleviate the management problems outlined above.

....

Responsibility and Expectation Relatedness

Questions of obligation, opportunity, and liability often are raised with respect not only to the responsibility that the individual has to fulfill an expectation or purpose but also questions for the expectation itself. The assumption that a response to an expectation is a fulfillment of a responsibility and, thereby, inherently related is not sound. The responsibility originates from an entirely different source. The individual responding to an expectation may respond out of a sense of obligation or of opportunity but also may view any response as a potential liability. There are limitations, nonetheless, on the freedom of choice. This means that the individual is free to some extent to respond creatively to expectations of all types and from any source. But there are limits to this freedom.

Persons who are chosen to exercise authoritative positions must be seen as those who can define certain of the freedoms of the individual staff members. This does not mean that it is an invitation to abuse but rather that it is a recognition that coordination depends upon some centralized determination of how people and tasks are to be related. In a case where the originators of the expectations are pressure groups or pressure individuals who want to restrict the freedom of others in order to achieve full freedom of their own choice, identification and description constitute different outlooks. There are many variations in exercisable authority. The individual who heads a strong professional community group or strong professional association or union has exercisable authority and there are great variations in how this exercise is expressed.

The originators of expectations often presume that they are free to define the types of responsibility that are to be exhibited in order that the expectation can be fulfilled. There are bonds of professional and ethical action, of course, that must be recognized (renewal) by the staff members of the school system. The bonds of professional and ethical action often are those of becoming a part of the whole learning experience of developing and maintaining the technical skills in being a teacher. These skills themselves are related to a definition of professionalism and the personal sense of the individual becomes the ethics of action.

The primary problem in relating responsibility and expectations is in the fact that the responsibilities inherent in the position held by the teacher may be in conflict with the expectation identified by someone outside the school organization. A clear picture of the difference between authority and responsibility may help to alleviate non-satisfaction of these expectations. While teachers have the responsibility to coordinate certain activities, they may not have the authority to change (redirection) the course of those activities to satisfy external expectations.

One of the most positive things that the individual teacher can do is to develop the skill or the capacity to induce homogeneity in the outlooks (induction) on the purpose and process of education. The criteria of relatedness becomes a matter of negotiating purpose before negotiating process. If there can be some homogeneity by people with differing expectations placed upon the school, the teacher then perhaps can bring about a negotiated agreement regarding purpose. When the purpose has been determined or agreed upon, the process by which the teaching and learning situation shall be directed becomes a much more stable task. It is the only road to peace and productivity (redirection) on the part of those who want to help students learn.

These *Aids for Self-Development* are to help you sort through your position when there is conflict between expectations and professional or ethical conduct.

. . . .

Aids for Self-Development

1 Describe your initial reaction to each of the conflict situations stated below:
    (a) You have planned to meet with a group of students at 4.00 p.m. but other teachers insist that you leave the building.
    (b) Discussion in your class has moved to a controversial topic concerning a local community figure. The students insist on hearing your position.
    (c) A friend on the staff asks you to *cover* for an unauthorized absence during a time you have set aside to plan a special topic.
    (d) Your principal asks a formal evalution of a colleague for the purpose of a merit raise or a promotion. You do not feel this colleague is deserving of this reward.
    (e) A community member who is known for controversial stands asks to address your class on an issue that you have been studying. You anticipate a potential problem.
    (f) A personal friend on the school board makes you aware of some impending action that will adversely affect teachers in another school. You know these teachers do not anticipate the action.
2 Determine whether a formal reaction to each conflict is within your realm of responsibilities.
3 Design a technique to merge your reactions to conflict situations with the responsibilities of your assignment in the best possible way to solve the conflict.

. . . .

Knowledge-Judgment Domination of Emotion

The descriptions of expectations and responses to expectations often involve inferences that emotions can be stirred in the process of relating responses to expectations. Emotion has not been indicated as a satisfactory motivation for directing those activities which can bring about a proper relationship between responses and expectations. Emotion tends to nurture agitation and impetuousness. Such characteristics of response do not support well the kind of adaptations that need to be made among people in order to bring expectations to people as a stimulator rather than as a dominator of freedom of action. Knowledge generates wisdom (renewal) and wisdom is the best route to good judgment. Judgment supports discretion. The discretion is essential in the interrelatedness of people in order to bring conflicting expectations into proper relationships or to bring responses into rewarding relationships to the expectations and the originators of those expectations.

Management becomes an essential to the development of a proper relationship among people where expectations and responses are characteristics of the interaction. There must be quality and stability in the management of expectations and of responses. The effects of management, quality, and stability encourage the pattern of interaction that makes it possible for the conflicts and differences to be resolved and reinforced action to follow. Knowledge and judgment bring about the expectation adaptability (redirection) that can engender a steady pattern of responses. Adaptability of the persons originating expectations is much preferable to a fixation and blind immobility either in holding to expectations or in responding to those expectations. It is important that each individual study the process of adaptation and develop a certain amount of skill in the application of effort to bringing expectations into proper relationships. Also, they must develop those expectations which can stimulate the more rewarding and creative responses in the efforts to sponsor a good teaching-learning situation for students.

Chapter 10 follows with the title 'Mastery of Adaptations'. In this chapter many suggestions will be made for developing the skills which can bring about this most important aspect of management of expectations.

Part Four
Working Toward Improvement

Chapter 10

Mastery of Adaptation

The many and complex differences between people make the processes of adaptation more difficult for each to achieve separately and for all to achieve in a group. The very fact of adaptation indicates that some kind of change has to be made in or by the individual. The adaptation is to one's own different way of doing or to the different ways of doing demonstrated by others.

Many people find it comfortable to continue doing what they have always done and in the exactly the same manner. Others seem to feel that doing the same thing in the same way all the time is an evidence of stagnation and that they must keep doing things differently in order to clear their own consciences of becoming stagnant in thinking and in behavior. These two ways of reacting seem to be extremes. But in a sense they have one characteristic in common. This characteristic is what might be termed living in a straight jacket. It is just as serious a straight jacket to want never to do anything differently than to want to do things differently all the time. In both instances, the motivation is not commendable. There are so many other bases for making the decisions about doing things the same or differently than simply to set up a rigid way of behaving and never deviating from that. Another, and very serious, resolution to either of the straitjackets is that of re-solution by instability. In this instance, it means that people have never come to any decision in their own mind as to whether they want to continue doing things the same or to make changes. This can be due to their self-perceived status or to the recognition that other people also have ideas and ways of doing that may merit careful study and possible emulation. Instability can never be an action strategy any more than the straight jackets alluded to above.

The individuals must possess a high level of self-confidence in order to look calmly and critically at themselves. The capacity for flexibility in creativity must come out of the individuals' own respect for their competence and their wholesomeness of purpose. Chapter 4, 'Bases for Self Confidence', gave an introduction to the conditions which might be helpful in the consideration of the achievement of a mastery of the adaptation process. The capacity, as discussed in that chapter, was to be found in the individual's inclination to make self-assessments. This is necessary to determine the kind of perspectives that influence behavior. It might be well for the readers to review chapter 4 and to find reinforcement there for the concepts that will be presented in this chapter. There is a close relationship also between this chapter and chapter 8, 'Inherited Merry-go-Rounds'. The intent in that chapter was to extend the developed confidence of the individual into a more critical look at the kinds of pressures and influences that exist in every environment. Many of those pressures were in conflict and many of these were illustrated. Here again, a review of some of the presentations of Chapter 8 might help in this chapter as consideration is focused upon adaptation.

The mastery of adaptation can never be achieved by expecting the conflicting outside pressures to chart the course of adaptation. This can lead only to what was indicated above as instability and that can never be an action strategy. A third chapter highly related to this chapter is the immediately preceding chapter 9, 'Management of Expectation'. Perhaps the reader at this point begins to discover the design of this chapter which is bringing to bear upon each individual situation the kinds of considerations presented in earlier chapters that can now be put together as a resource for achieving mastery of the adaptation process. In that chapter, the concern was with managing expectations and here again the conflicting pressures must be subjected to certain controls by the individual. It is not unusual to find inferences in chapter 9 that there are many things that each individual can extend as expectations of self and others but, at the same time, become a target of many expectations that arise within the environment.

Relativity exists in the relationships of strengths and weaknesses. Already, in this introduction, there have been allusions to the fact that, under certain conditions, the individual moving toward the mastery of adaptation is demonstrating personal strength. There is also the inference in preceding paragraphs that instability can occur and that people can hope to resolve their problems by wearing straitjackets. Adaptation must find those strategies which makes it possible for a well-purposed individual to achieve relationships between differing and even opposing points of view and practices. If these differences have an influence impingement upon each other, adaptation is the only avenue to resolution. The achievement of adaptation can be the source of great satisfaction for the individual who is invited in the sections of this chapter to achieve a mastery over the adaptation process. This chapter, then, will be dealing with the nature, processes, and benefits of adaptation.

Reasonableness in Adaptation

The emphasis in the center head is placed upon 'in'. The use 'in' rather than 'of' indicates that reasonableness is related to the process rather than to the product of adaptation. There is *reasonableness* in adaptation. It is required or it would never be adaptation at all. The individuals, who are able to identify and assist their own ways of thinking and doing in comparing those to the ways of thinking and doing exhibited by others, demonstrate an action based in reasonableness. The individual exercises some self-discipline and this becomes the first step (induction) to mastery in adaptation by possessing and demonstrating a 'willingness to consider'.

The willingness to consider means that the way has been opened for a review and study of the relationships between differing and/or opposing ways of thinking and doing. This willingness must be exhibited by any individual who hopes to make some contribution (renewal) in the achievement of the adaptation between what is and what might be. Perhaps some people will find it difficult to achieve a genuine sense of willingness to consider because they may lack experience in relating to others or they may lack confidence in their own thinking power. It is evident that those who will put forth effort in adaptation must have confidence in their own ability to think and to do or they would conclude that adaptation simply means yielding to the ways of another person or another circumstance. The individuals who have exhibited or want to exhibit the sense of willingness to consider are those persons who have confidence in their own knowledge and their capacity to achieve new knowledge.

The willingness to consider is based primarily in a deep personalized outlook toward others and toward other ways of thinking and doing. If personal involvement becomes too self-centered, the individual probably will not be able to free the self to exhibit a willingness to consider and to evaluate the differences that exist between that self and others. This does not mean that individuals must give up all sense of emotion or all sense of self-pride but rather means not to make the personalization a first requisite for resolving differences. Achieving this kind of personalization secures the individual's ability while at the same time strengthening the objectivity of that individual.

Objectivity may release the inclination to be overly defensive and to use an emotional reaction when a thinking reaction would be much more of a contribution. As one looks back over the past, it might be concluded that the creative geniuses who have made the great marks in our society were highly successful adapters. The inventors had to adapt something to what existed in order to develop a new way of doing, a new instrument, or any of the other things that bring about the evidences of change. These are the successful adapters and it is hoped that the individual readers of this chapter likewise will want to have the great experience of mastering adaptation.

Mastery as Proficiency

An inclination to confuse the term *mastery* with control has existed through many years. Mastery is not in any sense used in this chapter as being a control over others either in their thinking or their ways of doing. If there is a control, that control is over self in getting into the position of being able to interact and to bring about adaptations.

Proficiency in the mastery of the skills of change is the key to efficiency. Efficiency is more characteristic of the things that have been changed (redirection) for the purpose of improvement than holding to a certain way of thinking or doing that is declared successful. The holding to sameness seems to see no need of any change or adaptation either to an improvement state within itself or to a relationship with other positions which might be candidates for the shared adapting process. Individual competence in the matter of proficiency of adaptation becomes more of a beginning than an ending. It is the beginning of the opportunity to have a new look (renewal) at points of view and to seek alternatives from which choices can be made and, thereby, resulting in a satisfactory adaptation. The proficiency that contributes to adaptation might be identified as the adeptness of the individual in sharing insights and projections. Being able to self-analyze to the point that the insight as well as the result can be shared with others becomes an adept strategy in bringing about adaptations. It is equally important that those who have insights and a willingness to share them do so. They then can speculate or project what those insights can do to the new and yet unidentified situations of a future or of a new assignment.

A summation might be the view of proficiency as incidental versus planned versatility. The incidental versatility is that which happens more as a result of chance than as a result of an intellectual approach. Planned versatility, however, may be one of the better descriptions of what constitutes an adaptation which brings together the differing points of view and ways of doing. Proficiency, then, is simply a way of identifying a high level of performance and mastery is seen here as proficiency.

Differences Are Not Premeditated Opposition

The thinking habits of human beings have long indicated that differences are either dangerous or obstructive. It is perhaps a part of a culture in which people were urged to be independent and self-reliant as well as a culture that has put a premium on the unique performances of people. Anytime a person performs in a unique manner, it means that individual is doing something quite different from what other individuals are doing. If this were not true, uniqueness would lose its characteristic definition. It is unfortunate, however, that some of the concepts carried on from generation to new generation provide a block against the needs to be adaptive in our approach to those differences.

Differences probably constitute what often is defined as diversity. Diversity in purpose, belief, and performance can be a mirror of the independence of individuals. No one, however, would want to see the independent faker appear to possess a capacity for independent thinking. Neither would anyone want to see a unique performer lose the capacity to be unique in performance. Diversity as a mirror of the independence of the individual is a less combative way of viewing the nature of differences as dangerous and obstructive. It is important that people be able to look upon differences as something occuring either by way of assignment, role expectation, individual ambition, or simply the difference in the ways that people do things. It is more important that the results of independence (redirection) be mirrored into joint action rather than into increased inclination to continue action as separate and sometimes combative individuals.

The thoughts held by one person which lead to a role performance may constitute a contradiction to what another person may think and do. It is probable that contradictive purposes and actions were not designed to contradict. It is more positive to think of them as having evolved through the independence of the individuals who accepted a responsibility and met that responsibility in the ways unique to their own perspectives and skills. It is just as probable that contradictory positions and actions constitute an occurrence much more often than they constitute a plan thwarting action by one person against another. If this outlook could be preserved, it would be possible for the participants in divergent beliefs and actions to make an appraisal of whether the differences constituted influence or if they were non-influencing between the people, positions, or postures involved.

Studying the characteristics of differences makes it possible to identify the elements of difference. In all probability there is seldom 100 per cent differencing. But even if the differencing is reduced to a small percentage, it might identify an element that seems to be indifferent and, yet, might cloud the attitude toward the entire group of elements that constitute a behavior or a posture that could be influencing or non-influencing to others. The inclination to assume or to believe that differences are premeditated opposition between individuals can only lead to conflict. Conflict accentuates rather than resolves differences. If the differences influence the thwarting way, it is exceedingly important that conflict be reduced and that the differences be studied for the elements that constitute the differences. It is not until such an approach to the analysis or diagnosis of differences occurs that the differences can be resolved usually through a compromised adaptation.

It is important to introduce the thought at this point, however, that what may be influencing to one could be labeled as interference on the part of another, yet it might be wholly self-stimulated by the individual feeling the resentment to interference. Each person involved in a difference should be able to make an analysis of self so that it can be determined whether the interference is real with respect to that individual's pattern of performance or whether it is simply a state of mind. It is not a resolution to any difference situation simply to express an annoyance at the fact that someone performs in a different manner and even to a different purpose. It ought not to be considered interference unless it actually thwarts the pursuance of role fulfillment of the person who is influenced by another.

The diagnosis and analysis of self is one of the first ways of finding whether a difference really exists and whether the elements of difference or the characteristic of the elements of difference should be discovered and diagnosed. It is to be hoped that when two people find themselves representing differences that there be a mutuality in the analysis of those differences. This can lead, hopefully, to a resolution which can remove the real or the imagined interference. Mutuality in the analysis and resolution of differences can be a source of positive stimulation. It is a way of studying one's self and one's position. It is a way of studying one's expectations and their fulfillments. It is certainly a source of encouragement to individuals to try to resolve the differences which exist or even to turn them into a positive influence which stimulates more creative and productive action.

The elements of a difference require an analysis of the purposes of each party along with the substance of what the performance is that seems to be different. But why people do as they do becomes one of the very important elements of resolution of differences and, if the purposes can be brought together, the substance of action or role fulfillment may be solved quickly. It is important that persons, as they study their own purposes and their relationship to the purposes of others, try to define (renewal) the personal targets of respect. The kind of people respected, the kind of actions respected, and the kinds of situations that stimulate mutuality of respect become significant areas of analysis. Without a reasonable degree of respect, there is little inclination to set out on any effort to resolve the differences which bring about real interference with one or both of the people involved in the action.

It is important to analyze the kinds of differences that have been resolved and to find those which seem to reinforce more positive action in accomplishing the purposes of the individual and the goals of the organization. The following *Aids for Self-Development* are structured to help you identify influences that exist in a group action of any type.

. . . .

Aids for Self-Development

1   Identify one or more situations where you were in a disagreement with a colleague or colleagues.
2   List the influence items that you and your colleague experienced or witnessed under each of the selected professional factors given below:
    (a)   flexibility;
    (b)   loyalty to school;
    (c)   judgment;
    (d)   ethical conduct;
    (e)   rapport with students;
    (f)   rapport with staff;
    (g)   rapport with administrators;
    (h)   other.
3   Select those influences from your list that became a basis for discussion and describe how this discussion served the purpose of resolution or as a source of stimulation.

4   Would your response to number 3 differ if your colleague were in a different facet of the teacher career cycle (figure 2)?

. . . .

Diagnoses as Therapy For Impasses

Considerable emphasis has been given in the past few paragraphs to the differences in the way that people think about or do things. These differences can be thwarting or stimulating influences. The differences as to which way they will be is to be found in the way that they are managed. Most differences may exist long before the potential discovery that they may have a thwarting effect on others. Most differences are gradual in their development and are equally gradual in developing the awareness of the fact that they exist. There may be situations where sudden changes seem to bring about sudden differences. But many of the differences that are to be dealt with are the kind that may have existed in isolation and grow through a gradual awareness of people.

Awareness of differences sets the stage for the possible reaction in the positive or negative way. The matter of negativeness, however, leads to the feeling by the involved parties that impingement of their own activities or beliefs may have occurred. When impingement occurs, one or both of the interacting parties feel thwarted in proceeding with their role expectations. It is clear that the differences may be independent and at the same time interacting. The meaning of this is that the awareness of the individuals who are parties to the differences are the ones who bring on the interaction. The interaction can be either a matter of opposition to the other position or it can be and hopefully will be a matter of challenge to the participants to seek the ways of bringing about a modification (redirection) of the two positions so the differences are no longer an impingement upon positive action. It is hoped that the individuals can see this as an opportunity to merge their differences and to strengthen both positions. It is for this reason that this section is dealing with diagnosis of the situations which can and probably would contribute a therapy that could avoid the impasses.

Impasses are realized when one or both parties are unable to perceive their obligation in a role or see only the exclusiveness of a position with respect to decision. Impasses mean that progress stops or a blind alley has been found. A blind alley can be there for either one or both of the people involved in differences. If there is an anatomy to the impasse, it should be discovered and the elements of that anatomy be used as a basis for the diagnosis. Diagnosis can constitute the therapy that opens the way ahead for all people involved and permits them to continue with their own perspective of role obligations and their contributions to the institutional goals.

An impasse needs to be viewed from the standpoints of purpose, process, and product. This can be the anatomy of the impasse. Several previous sections emphasized that the status of the difference must be viewed from the standpoint of the purposes which existed to bring about this status. When these are found antagonistic, the first task will be to seek a way of harmonizing purposes by finding how they can remain different and still work in coordination. Hopefully the diagnosis may lead to an agreement on the purpose that can be accepted by both parties to the difference. The process is a matter of what kind of information is needed and what kinds of activities would be affected if changes were made in either one or both of the postures that constitute the difference. Product is of ultimate importance because an impingement affects the progress of each individual toward the fulfillment of the responsibilities and expectations placed upon them.

Studying the anatomy of impasses in terms of purpose, process, and product, provides (renewal) a chance to find out whether another element of anatomy might be ego status. If this is true, the impasse exists as something apart from the substance of the performance involved in the differences and resolves itself into a mental state of the parties involved in the differences. In this case no amount of analysis or diagnosis of the impasse will bring about that needed change in the individual. It might stimulate a suggestion that another kind of problem exists. So it can only be hoped that the impasses are not occurring because of ego status, but rather because of basic differences in purpose, process, and product. These three elements can be diagnosed, can be evaluated, and can provide means for bringing together the differing points of view. It is important for individuals to know the what and the why of their own positions. Here again, while it may not constitute an impasse, it is a good way to collect the data about what is involved in the differences. It is equally important to know the what and the why of the other person's position. This provides the kind of data that may constitute the anatomy of the impasse and provide useful material for resolving the issues.

A similar approach can be applied to the impingement of one person upon another. Impingement can be with respect to purpose, process, or product. If one individual feels that a contrary purpose held by another is thwarting the quality of the purpose by that first individual, the impingement has become real and a point of remedy has been found. Here again, just as with ego status in the anatomy of an impasse, it is important to make sure that impingement is real rather than imaginary. If it is real, it can be subjected to a more objective approach in resolution. If it is imaginary, the correction has to be made within each individual separately. There can be conflict, however, with or without impingement. Conflict exists where people have not decided to use their prerogative of resolving conflict or to take advantage of the opportunities to accept a therapy that offers remediation to the differences which often lead to impasses. It is important to analyze impingement just as was indicated with the impasse.

Impingement needs to be viewed from the standpoint of the importance of the level of impingement to each of the elements involved. Here again, a certain amount of objectivity is required in order that people can view their process and product before the incident of impasse. With the collection of data of these types, it is possible to organize and to view the data and to determine whether the real or imaginary factors are over-weighted in the resolution and the improved relationships of different statuses. People can go from data or information, diagnostic in nature, to a tolerance of the difference or an agreement of how the differences can be brought together in some working relationship.

These *Aids for Self-Development* provide an approach to study the anatomy of impasses that might result in an impingement upon the effectiveness of performance.

··

Aids for Self-Development

1   Identify a difference situation where you were in disagreement with a colleague that resulted in a deadlock or impasse.
    (a)   State your purpose in entering the difference.
    (b)   State your colleague's purpose in the issue.
2   Determine the product you had in mind upon entering the difference situation. Identify the product your colleague may have had in mind. What are the similarities in these products?
3   Design a redirective process to use the similarities of product to resolve the difference and maintain effective performance.

··

Identification of Adaptation Need

Much emphasis has been given in the preceding sections of this chapter to the existence of differences between people and programs. These differences can be either of a stimulating type or of a thwarting type. Regardless of the type, there must be more attention given to the *identification* and description of the needs for adapting to the differences which exist or to program needs that are not yet envisioned.

Emphasis has been given also to the fact that the individuals participating in program action are highly important in defining the kinds of differences that exist and, therefore, the kinds of needs that call for adaptation. It is easy to fall into the trap of thinking that it is all or nothing. In other words, the individuals must have all their own way or there will be no attempt at adaptation at all. As a matter of fact, the all or nothing way of thinking is a sure way of guaranteeing that adaptation cannot and will not be made. It is important to think at the same time of certain prestige effects that exist. For instance, within the local school there is the temptation to give difference according to the hierarchy of authority and controls. It would be so much better to envision this hierarchy not as hierarchy at all but rather as professional colleagues taking the responsibility for different role demands.

Another type of prestige effect that seems to be burdening is the important relationship between the college or university and field school and the perspective of which one is the more important. It is so easy for the field school personnel to look upon the university as being made up of people who deal only in theory. At the same time, there is the inclination of university people in education to avoid contact with field schools and people. It does not take much thought to realize that educational programming needs both theory and practice. It would be better to see an adaptation (redirection) here that brings these two levels of the operation together and strengthens each as a result of it. Here again, the emphasis on prestige gets in the way of an adequate coordination of campus and field, and, therefore, gets in the way of adapting needs in education that could be more successfully accomplished if both were to coordinate and cooperate.

Regardless of the location as being either on campus or in the field, there needs to be attention given to the actor and the action target priorities. When it is more important that the wishes of the teacher take precedent over the needs of the student, one must question the priorities in the attention given to the student as compared or contrasted to that given to the teacher. Here again the adaptation need exists but the target for determining priorities as to what should take precedence over something else must be resolved. In the identification of the adaptation need, it is important to look at some of the adaptation elements. There are many of them and only a few are given here by way of illustrating what an adaptation element is. It is possible to view the personal differences in concept, in practice, and in goals by looking at the school goals. Here is the organizational or institutional reason for existing. All members of the professional staff, as well as the supporting laymen in the community, need to give attention (induction) to what the school goals are. When differences appear that seem to call for an adaptation, this adaptation should be accomplished in the light of the goals that are to be accomplished by the school as an organization.

Another element is that of individual purpose. The individual participants in the total educational program often vary according to the demands of a particular situation but also according to the individuals. The individual purposes may be highly conditioned by the previous experiences or even the kind of environment in which growth has taken place. These purposes must be scrutinized in relation to another element, namely, the group purposes. The group purposes are represented by the professionals who have been employed by the school district to direct and carry out the educational program. The individual and group purposes of the professionals in the school organization must at the same time be contributory to the institutional goals which have been determined not only by the professionals but by the lay people of the community as well as in various legislative, executive, and judicial offices in the state or in the nation.

Another adaptation element is what might be called proximity statuses. Certainly in our past there was a difference in the views that people took toward a first grade teacher and the senior high school teacher. There are even some statuses recognized within the high school, for instance, those who teach the 'solid academic subjects' and those who teach the 'supportive or even the vocational'. These statuses have existed primarily as an inheritance from the past and have never really been supported by logic. The proximity status is also important in adaptation when talking about the local school system in its relationship to the state and federal government. The organization of professional educators into associations or unions likewise provides a proximity status problem.

Proximity is highly related to another adaptation element, namely, communication facility. It is important that the people who view adaptation needs and apply their abilities to achieving adaptation must be able to communicate with each other efficiently. Another element is that of involvement of others. How many people will be involved beyond whose who are initiating the adaptation adjustment? The involvement of others often can be taxpayers, other educational organizations, or special interest groups. It is important to know how these will become involved in the adaptation of existing differences.

Another important element is that of the displacement potential. It is possible to alter one element of difference and bring two differences into agreement by common planning and action. But at the same time, if it will displace some other subject, some other need, or some other program, it is important to know at the time of difference resolution. In recent years, there have been instances in which the federal government has stimulated new programs in the local school. Often this so-called matching-money results in some of the subjects normally chosen to be taught in a local school, for instance art and music, to experience budget losses that target them as displacements. When changes are made, another element that must be considered is that of facility and material adequacy. The plan can be made but perhaps it cannot be supported. This is a part of the other element, namely, implementation processes. The support facilities must exist in order to bring about the adaptation that is required to eliminate differences that seem to be thwarting.

Another and final element to be included in this illustration is that of the evaluation review schedule. Whatever changes are made, there must be plans at the same time for an evaluation design as well as an evaluation schedule. If these elements are acceptable, they can be looked upon as need characteristics. Other illustrations could be extended almost without end and could be adapted to each individual or local community. These, then, become the prelude to a more specific concern with the strategies of adaptation which will be presented in forthcoming sections.

The next *Aids for Self-Development* suggest some adaptation needs that may exist as a result of differences between colleagues.

. . . .

Aids for Self-Development

1   Identify and describe a difference situation, or disagreement, that you have had with a colleague in the adaptation of each of the following areas:
    (a)   school goals;
    (b)   individual purpose;
    (c)   your status;

(d)   communication in school;
(e)   outside involvements;
(f)   displacement potentials;
(g)   program implementation;
(h)   program evaluation.
2   Add other areas where adaptation needs are evident. Determine which of your identified differences were stimulating and which were thwarting influences on the educative process.
3   Develop renewal activities to restructure the thwarting influences into stimulating ones.

....

Personal Adaptive Strategies

The previous section on the identification of adaptation needs emphasizes that the individual is always the starting point in whatever adaptations are to be accomplished. Analysis first of the individual and then of the group with respect to the adaptive strategies that are to be used should be done. In this section, attention will be given to the personal strategies that each professional member of the school staff should consider. In viewing *personal adaptive strategies*, it is well to look first at the role position of the individual.

A characteristic of aloneness typifies many role positions. It is true, of course, that many teachers, administrators, and supervisors in the school system are involved in tasks that are comparable to many others in the school organization. There are positions, however, that do not have counterparts in any other sector of the school organization or in another part of the school district. There is, then, a relative aloneness that needs to be considered as personal strategies are studied. It is more difficult for the person in a role position, unduplicated in the school organization, to bring about an involvement of other people in the adaptation needs and processes. It is important that this is recognized at the outset and that strategies be developed which are appropriate to the relative aloneness of such a position.

Each individual should identify and appraise the alternative ways of fulfilling the role expectations. This does not mean that each individual must find a certain number of substitutes for the various elements of the role expectation. Rather, it means that the process of adaptation to others as well as to new or emerging needs stimulate the inclination to look at alternative ways of going about the tasks. The individual who is willing to look at the alternatives with respect to a specific role assignment will initiate (redirection) experiences in implementing changes in the practices that are characteristic of the current time. The process of implementing changes can bring about a fresh way of studying current procedures.

The implementation of changes themselves opens up new avenues of thinking and new opportunities to evaluate the current practices. When changes are implemented, however, it is most important that the results of that implementation be evaluated and judgments be made as to whether the change procedures or purposes are filling the role expectations better. Evaluation of the results provides a basis for the judgment as to whether the adaptation is worthy of being retained or whether it should be discarded and another alternative investigated and tried. When practices are changed and the evaluation of results has been accomplished, it is helpful to communicate with others (renewal) about these changes and results.

The mere fact of communication causes one to think through more clearly the things that used to exist, the kinds of alternatives that were explored, and the support for the judgment that was made in selecting the new procedure. In the process of communication, it is equally wise to seek out expert opinion. Expert opinion with respect to the change practices can come from administrators, supervisory personnel, and colleagues. The communication (induction) of these to others can stimulate a response that does not necessarily constitute evaluation but rather that explores some of the facets of the new practice that would need to be subjected to scrutiny, evaluation, and maintenance. Another excellent source of expert opinion would be the college and university specialists. Almost every school has, within easy contact distance, a college or university with people who could react to the kinds of things that have been changed and the reasons for instituting those changes.

It must be recognized, nonetheless, that in communicating with others regardless of their status, there might be adverse comments coming from some quarters. One must be ready to resist anger and vindictiveness in the fact of adverse comments. When adverse comments appear, it is important to increase the opportunity to exchange ideas with the source of adverse comments. Adverse comments themselves constitute excellent identification of the things that could have been included in the evaluation of the change procedures. When adverse comments appear the rationale of all such reactions needs analysis. The comments constitute, at that point, a difference or conflict in point of view.

The analysis of the rationale of both parties in such a conflicting position can be an excellent source to identify (redirection) the strengths and weaknesses of the newly tried procedures. This, then, becomes one of important personal adaptive strategies that needs to be not only assumed by each individual but pursued as well. When the individual is evaluating the change processes, it is wise at the same time to evaluate the strategies by which those processes were selected and initiated. The mere fact of studying the strategies might facilitate another attempt to increase the adaptive activities but more importantly to provide added opportunities to evaluate the things that have been changed.

This entire section on adaptive strategies assumes that the individual can gain and hold to an outlook that means trust in self and in others. There are plenty of opportunities to reassess whether the trust is well placed but it is hazardous to enter into any sort of a relationship with others who might help in the adaptive process if antagonism or lack of trust exists at the time that the initial contacts are made.

These *Aids for Self-Development* offer help in making an evaluation of personal adaptive strategies.

. . . .

Aids for Self-Development

1 Identify the most influential colleague in your role position who can help with the adaptation of each of the listed items:
    (a) lesson plans;
    (b) discipline techniques;
    (c) curriculum development;
    (d) instructional methods;
    (e) understanding individual differences;
    (f) working with teacher associations;
    (g) planning parent conferences;
    (h) other.
2 Describe how the colleagues you have selected helped to generate alternatives for you to implement change in the areas where they had influence.
3 Outline your strategies of adaptation based on your decision to retain or discard the results of evaluation input given.

. . . .

Interactive Adaptive Strategies

The previous section dealt with the personal adaptive strategies and kept the focus on the individual's contribution. This does not mean that individual contributions will not result in an interactive situation. It means rather that the individual has strategies that can improve not only the individual performance but also strategies which make it easier for interactive situations to occur successfully.

This section presumes that strategies are appropriate to interacting individuals. This means that both individuals in a situation have a responsibility to arrange their personal strategies in such a way that the interactive situations will become more productive. One of the basic ingredients in the interactive situation is that of practicing open friendliness rather than aloofness. This means that all parties to the interactive situation must practice this friendliness. Aloofness on the part of only one can thwart the success of the interactive process between two people or between individuals in a group.

A good strategy is to initiate group discussions on role similarities and differences. This can open the way to making an assessment of the nature of the differences and similarities. This assessment can reinforce the similarities and convert the differences into the maximum productive results. Each individual in an interactive situation must support group discussions of the individual perspectives that may affect participant harmony or conflict. The perspectives held by individuals so often are the conditioners of their behaviors. These perspectives must be identified and related to those behaviors which perhaps do not gain maximum productivity in the interactive situation. Harmony between individuals is just as essential as open friendliness. Conflict may come from the inclination toward aloofness. The various strategies involved here are interlinking and all of them need to be given careful consideration in order that the best selection of activity can be used as a basis for the productivity of all the interactive parties.

Individuals who have handled their personal perspectives and attitudes successfully as outlined above can develop (renewal) the art of commendation. It is important that sincerity in giving and receiving compliments exists between all parties involved. It is difficult to cover up insincerity in a commendation or a compliment because of the tone of voice, the choice of the words, the look on the speaker's face, and perhaps body activities that become part of communication. It is hoped that sincerity can be built into the *interactive adaptive strategies* so that it not only produces better strategies but also maintains them into a future of productive results.

Individuals can relate to each other in the ways suggested here and open the avenues to coordination providing people apply the same sincerity and goodwill to the study of those avenues or strategies toward coordination. This would involve all of the role activities, whether they are similar or diverse. Coordination is essential to any group action. School situations cannot be isolated actions in most aspects of their operation. If the avenues of coordination are studied and some priorities given to those that are more productive, then suggestions can be treated as a resource (redirection) rather than an insult.

Many people have developed the unusual and unhappy trait of looking upon suggestions as a built-in criticism. Many people also are unable to take criticism graciously. The suggestion here is that suggestions be looked upon and offered as a resource to an individual. If a misunderstanding seems to develop, it is as much the responsibility of the person receiving the suggestion as it is of the person offering the suggestion to try to penetrate the nature and intent of the person making these suggestions. With this kind of interchange, the resources to each individual become much more productive from the standpoint of fulfilling the role expectation in the educational program.

Many teachers seem to avoid or to resent the invitations to participate in organizational activities. It is often referred to as doing somebody else's work or a shifting of the load from those in the higher bureaucratic echelons to those in the lower. It is worth repeating here that it is much more productive for all areas in the bureaucracy or hierarchy of responsibility to view themselves as colleagues with each having a unique contribution to make. When this can be done, the organizational participation can be seen as an opportunity to participate. Many types of interactive strategies are adaptive strategies that can be identified and carried through to fruition. It is much better to be a sharing and helping colleague than to be an obedient servant.

People in the educational profession have the training, the ability, and the responsibility to be sharing and helping colleagues to all persons in the varying roles needed for carrying on the educational program. The next *Aids for Self-Development* provide a measure of your personal contribution to interactive activities.

....

Aids for Self-Development

1 Identify a sharing potential of thought and talent with others as you pursue the following activities:

(a) committee work;
(b) faculty meetings;
(c) informal gatherings;
(d) team planning.
2 Describe how you adapt the results of the interactions you identified above to your own specific assignment.
3 Determine renewal activities to make the interactive activities even more useful to your situation.

....

Enhancement Potentials

Many specific suggestions have been made in the previous sections of this chapter regarding the selection, use, and mastery of the adaptation process as appropriate to the individual and group activities in the school. A number of strategies have been suggested as well as various ways of studying the worth of those strategies and the activities which they generate. All of these can be summarized now in terms of the great benefit that can be realized not only by the professional staff members but also by the students and the people of the community who sponsor the maintenance of the educational program.

The first category of enhancement potential is that of adaptation intent. This calls for open minds on the parts of all individuals when working alone or in a group. It calls for respecting the views of colleagues and of dealing with those views objectively. There is much to be gained (induction) by way of new knowledge from colleagues but it must be viewed as a resource and not as something to tolerate. Another adaptation intent is that of seeking new learning opportunities. Very often this comes from the benefit that can be received from colleagues but it comes also from one's individual efforts in trying to understand the thought and practices of others which have been recorded in published form or which can be observed.

Another important adaptation intent is that of placing merit above political advantage. It is an easy and selfish reaction for individuals to look to advantages that might give them increased prestige or more financial stability. This is a type of political advantage that does not produce increased quality of output on the part of the professionals on the school staff. So the intent must be that of seeking to achieve merit as well as to recognize merit and not to see personal advantages over someone else as being the intent of the adaptation process. Another adaptation intent is that of reducing the inclination to be offended. The willingness to hear and to see what others are saying and doing becomes one of the resources that each individual can claim. The suggestions that come as indicated in previous sections ought not to be looked upon as a criticism or an insult but rather as a resource. The intent here must be that of rejecting offense as one of the convenient responses to what may be the action of some other person that is not in agreement with what the individual is doing. Above all, adaptation intent must provide the opportunities for the adaptive process to provide added excitement to the work of teaching students and of managing the educational program.

A second category of enhancement potential is that of the adaptation skills. Examples of these can be increasing the enrichment capacity of each individual as well as of the program. These skills can stimulate (renewal) a continuing self-evaluation. The self-evaluation becomes one of the best ways of achieving and of maintaining the adaptive strategies that can be most rewarding. Adaptive skills improve group participation. The willingness to offer suggestions and to receive them, the willingness to commend and to receive compliments provide a progressive relationship among all individuals that can improve the quality of group participation. The adaptive skills can upgrade the anticipation of progress. With a mind open to a study of the differences and similarities with others, it becomes clear as to what constitutes the progress. If that becomes clear, it is easier to anticipate the kind of outcomes that chosen behaviors can yield.

The adaptation skills stabilize the role perception of other people. It is just as important to understand the nature of the role of colleagues as it is to understand your own role. It is also important to help that colleague understand your role. The adaptation skills reduce the desire to develop special interest groups within the staff. Too often this has been done for a personal purpose, and sometimes to gain control over certain aspects of the educational program. But the adaptation skill does not support that kind of behavior. It encourages a better one by clearing the way for a total group interaction rather than for special interest group interaction. The adaptation skills also sharpen the anticipation of accuracy. It is important that people increase their ability not to be satisfied with minimum effort nor with low quality outcomes. The adaptation skills are the best guarantee that the anticipation of the outcomes of effort will be predicted with much greater accuracy.

The third category of enhancement potential is that of adaptation benchmarks. This gives the individuals involved in interaction an opportunity to know what to look for in order to decide whether the adaptive process was worth the effort. One of the benchmarks is that of cooperative group action. When the openness of the exchange between members of the group can be observed to be rewarding in the purposes for which the school was established, the benchmark is visible. Another benchmark is that of acknowledgement of program quality. This acknowledgement can come from colleagues, from students, from the people in the community, or from the official agencies of government. That acknowledgement means that the adaptation effort has succeeded. Another and very important benchmark of successful adaptation is that of security in creative action. So many times individuals seem to avoid creativity because it might turn out occasionally to be wrong. The important thing is to have a relationship with colleagues and with the people of the community so that if creative efforts fail, they must be evaluated as unsatisfactory and revised.

There must be security to the individual who has released this creative balance. When there is no adaptation it is always possible that some aspects of the program can become imposed upon other aspects of the program to the exclusion of the opportunity for those aspects to be changed and/or improved. Another and final illustration of the adaptation benchmark is that of the high interrole coordination. This has been referred to many times in the previous sections of this chapter. The interrole coordination is what makes a school a successful group effort. A school cannot have a group of individuals going their own ways for their own purposes, while disregarding all other role demands and expectations, and still have successful group effort. So interrole coordination must be one of the most important benchmarks of the success of the mastery of adaptation by individuals and by groups.

Interrole activities are the key to the next *Aids for Self-Development*. Think of the discussion of enhancement potentials as you respond to the items.

. . . .

Aids for Self-Development

1 Describe your views of your colleagues in each of the listed positions:
   (a) teachers in your school;
   (b) teachers in your district;
   (c) principals;
   (d) central office administration;
   (e) supervisors;

(f)   support personnel.
2   Identify an important interaction with each of the colleagues you
    have listed above and the result of that interaction.
3   Show how the roles of your colleagues can be blended with your
    own to redirect the activities of your assignment.

....

Contributors and Contributions

The substance of the entire chapter has dealt with the mastery of
adaptation. This means that the individual has an important responsibility in the interactive situation. The focus has continually been on the
fact that adaptation can result in an improvement of the individual
productivity as well as an improvement in the quality of the educational
program. It has been mentioned a number of times that there must be
a mutuality of acceptance of the need for adaptive activity and it is
summarized here again that adaptation at its best is effective mutuality.

Helping is reinforcing rather than weakening. Here again is an
attitude toward one's own work as well as toward the cooperative
activities that are so necessary in organizational activities. Recognition
of what an individual is contributing is more than a reward. A
satisfactory exchange may be ruined when recognition is thought of as
being only a reward. And so recognition of contribution to the
program and to the interactive activities is a way of putting together the
contributors and the contributions.

Many of the adaptation strategies involve the capacity of individuals to adjust and to compromise. There is strength in compromise
(redirection) when it is done for the right purpose. The right purpose is
that of improving individual output as well as group productivity.
Selfishness can be a state of inclusiveness rather than exclusiveness.
Mutuality denies the opportunity or even acceptability of exclusiveness
in a school situation. The teachers cannot exclude the students and they
certainly ought not to exclude their professional colleagues. So selfishness likewise can be seen as a state of inclusiveness in which each
individual may want to achieve some dominance or at least high
influence over all other persons and program activities. Selfishness has
no place in a situation in which the adaptive opportunities exist and in
which the adaptation strategies are focused upon successful enterprise,
successfully completed.

Awareness of one's own contribution and of the contributions of
others not only to one's self but to the program is a virtue in the

intellect. That awareness can support many types of effort that assist the adaptation needs to be recognized in the strategies designed and carried forward successfully.

Participants when viewed as contributive make contributions that can be seen as a source of enthusiasm for all who engage in the total activity. This is one of the most important outcomes and benefits of being able to master the processes of adaptation. These will be summed up in terms of continuing strength to the individual and the organization in chapter 11. This chapter carries the title, 'Continuing Development'. It is to be hoped that the first ten chapters provide a good foundation for an acceptance of the responsibility for continuing development.

Chapter 11

Continuing Development

The declaration was made at the outset that this publication was designed to increase the knowledge base for individuals in the profession of education through a review of their own experiences. This review can be used to bring about continuing improvement in the educational services to which each individual is committed. Many factors exist, both within the school and the school's environment, that must be reviewed in order to make a proper identification of the things that individuals should learn about themselves. They must develop the ways by which these things can be learned. The thrust of this chapter is to offer specific ideas as to how the suggestions in the preceding chapters might be focused upon the individual's opportunity to develop as well as the individual's desire to bring about continuing self-improvement.

Development is growth and maturation. Growth must be related to an increase in the amount and quality of knowledge possessed by individuals. Maturation indicates that the individual has been able to interrelate the knowledge of various types in order to reinforce the goal achievement which each individual is entitled to identify and describe. A basic assumption is made that a static state is a state of decay rather than of growth. The assumption indicates that the individuals who will profit from the suggestions in this book will be those who have a desire not to remain static but rather to move ahead.

The concept of development that characterizes the preceding chapters includes the activities of *induction*, *renewal*, and *redirection*. These three action thrusts are not sequential in nature. There may be periods of sequencing but there will be more occasions when they will be alternating or joined in reinforcing movements. *Induction* is an entering activity and there are continuing entering opportunities and requirements throughout a teaching career. *Renewal* is the expanding of individual expertise and each step of progress is instituted through an induction approach. Through the mutual reinforcement of induction and renewal, redirection opportunities evolve. *Redirection* activities progessively reveal the identity of in-process improvements. These, in turn, invite more assistance from renewal and induction activities. Clearly, then, continuous development is a purposeful interlacing of induction, renewal, and redirection. These concepts bind together to accentuate the existence of career-long teacher education.

Some supportive assumptions are offered as a basis for envisioning the continuity of development and career-long teacher education. These assumptions can be identified as (i) quality in performance is worthy of pursuit; (ii) individual capacity relates to the needs envisioned in the work commitment; (iii) progress is a human characteristic; and (iv) other people will respect the growing expertise of an individual. These assumptions can run contrary to some of the facetious and sometimes dismal attitudes toward individual development which are extant today. This book, however, is based upon supportive assumptions rather than the kind that can assure defeat. It is for the individual who has aspirations to make contributions and for the individual who wants to find a sense of self-worth in the tasks to which commitment has been made. There is much reassurance to be gained through the evidence that is easily available to almost everyone. The emphasis in previous chapters indicated many times that self-development is an appropriate goal and commands the expertise best related to individual improvement.

Goal achievement can be evaluated. When goals are realized and accomplished, there is a reassurance to the individual who has been directing expertise and effort to the achievement of those goals. Evidence can reaffirm progress. This, in turn, is a reassuring element for the individual worker. Success is an enthusiasm stimulator. A realization that success has been achieved causes individuals to work harder and to develop new and better ways of achieving the goals to which commitments have been made. The sense of worth in helping others is one of the unique elements in the educator's experience. There also is much reassurance to the individual who can observe that individual effort has resulted in helping others to achieve their full capacities to accomplish their self-selected as well as jointly-selected purposes and goals.

The presentations in this book indicate that the individual cannot be separated from the group. Education is primarily a group enterprise. It does not mean that individuals cannot and should not have unique contributions to make and to feel the sense of individualized responsibility in accomplishing the tasks that are characteristic of the teacher, supervisor, and administrator. The emphasis at the same time has been on the fact that the individual cannot be all things to all tasks. There is, nonetheless, a personalized logic for action. There is no need to be merely a cog in the wheel just because the individual is a part of a group enterprise. Knowing why one does or why people do as they do is most important. This is the personal logic that each one must achieve or be characterized as merely a cog in the wheel without the individualized expertise that is hoped for, that is absolutely requisite to each person in the educational task.

Logic is personal but it is not necessarily private. Each individual can share the logic for action with others and, in turn, have the privilege of realizing coordination in group achievement. Self-improvement is emphasized throughout this book and particularly in the aids for self-development by which an individual can do a self-analysis. Personal logic that one possesses includes values and perspectives. These values and perspectives, in turn, affect not only what people do but the way they go about doing it. Each one must want to improve in order to develop the ways to improve. This does not mean again that it cannot be a group action as well as an individualized one.

This chapter brings together the previous chapters in short summary. The summary is achieved through the projections of suggestions which can stimulate the desirable outlooks not only of current development but also of continuing development. Thus, the title of this chapter indicates *continuing development* and the following sections of the chapter will keep this in focus. The center for each section will bear a relationship to an earlier chapter and reference will be made to the appropriate chapter. The intent here will be to draw a brief summary from that chapter not by way of a review and duplication but by way of a focusing on the use of those suggestions for the purpose of continuing development.

Creativity Generators

The tasks associated with teaching originate in self-chosen or accepted assignments that identify the teacher's responsibilities. The term *task* is used because it implies less restrictiveness than general usage imposes on the term *assignment*. The presentation in chapter 2, 'You and Your Assignment', includes details of assignment variability which were previewed in the section, Discovering Evolving Expectations of chapter 1, 'Teachers and Learners'.

Improvement in one's approach to or completion of any task can be the way of identifying the development as discussed in this chapter. Creativity can be the chief instrument for stimulating not only the desirability for improvement but also the genius that can provide many alternatives which can make the action rewarding and worthwhile.

Purpose has much to do with how one goes about the task as well as with a choice of the tasks themselves. Much of the literature contains discussions of purpose. There is little doubt that purpose provides definable goals and provides at the same time some stimulation that causes the unique expertise of individuals working alone or in a group to apply their talents to a particular task. Purposing is not a way of controlling the direction for the action of the individuals or of groups. Purposing has purpose, not only for the direction and choice of actions but for the stimulation that can be gained from the fact of being conscious of the purpose and the need for it.

Purpose is one of the best ways to keep people fully aware of the kind of task commitments that have been accepted. Awareness of the task commitment can give direction and purpose to the individuals who are engaged in the activities related to the task. To be unaware of the task commitment is to be a drifter in an agency filled with people who are aware of task and have made commitments to it. Lack of awareness is one of the surest ways of failing to stimulate the creativity that resides within people. The awareness of the task commitment leads to the expectations of one's self with respect to choosing directions. The task commitment itself can increase the amount of self-direction not only that an individual might wish but also that an organized group might grant. It is important that each individual establishes a set of expectations for self so that direction becomes a part of the stimulation to be creative in the approach to the carrying out of the task to which a commitment has been made.

It was indicated earlier that certain rewards can come from establishing compatible relationships with peers and other specialized workers in the school organization. Intra-group compatibility not only provides a personal reward for the individual but also provides a stimulation to develop the unique expertise of creativity that a person possesses or can develop and apply to the committed task. There are many situations in which compatibility cannot be achieved either within the immediate working group or within the environment. Environments have many points of uncertainty, sometimes primarily because they have never been identified and defined. The environment can contain what might be considered potholes in the road to educational planning and expedition. The individual can identify these and can apply a certain amount of remedial application to whatever the distress or disturbance seems to be as it impinges upon the instructional program of the school. Success in bringing together some of these influences in the environment and assisting in their adaption to a supportive role of instructional programs can be stimulating to an individual. Success in one instance may lead to an awareness of other situations or instances in which similar school community therapy might be appropriate. In this sense, the success in remediation of some of the conflicting stresses upon the educational program can be a stimulator of the creativity of individuals in the group constituting the professional workers of the school.

The success in identifying and offering assistance to these conflicting environmental impingments can develop a sensitivity to the fact that there are observers and there are observations. The educator who has some success in mending the environmental school conflicts sharpens the sensitivity to the fact that there are observers of almost everything. Their observations often can be described and traced to an origin. When the origin is identified, it is more probable that the mending processes can be appropriately chosen and be applied successfully.

Successes in mending the school environmental irritations will aid in the development of a recognition and realization of the individual who has achieved this correction through the uniqueness that is possessed. When recognition of uniqueness is realized in one's self, it is much more probable that, whatever the nature of that virtue, skill, or creativity, it is likely to be applied more often and more effectively. The figure presented depicting environmental influences and facets of a teacher's career can be used to aid this recognition. This, then, becomes another generator of the creativity in an individual.

The past several paragraphs cannot be read without becoming aware of the fact that there is mutuality in almost all of the relationships within the school organization and its service area. Mutuality can be most simply and perhaps most accurately described as assistance without resistance. Mutuality has to begin with a spirit, not only of help to self but of help to others. It is equally important that those who give help are just as ready to receive help when the receipt of that help can improve the quality of the performance and the degree of success in achieving purpose. If mutuality can be of this much assistance, it follows that each individual should seek and find appropriate helpers for all of the task that are recognized as needing to be shared because of the great variety of activities and expertise required.

Imagination can support all of the kinds of independent and group interactions described here. Imagination stimulates origination. An origination in this case would be to initiate those kinds of contracts and those kinds of individual and group activities that would serve as a stimulant or a generator to the creativity possessed by each individual. The generation of creativity provides great assurance that development will be continuous because the activities of induction, renewal, and redirection are maintained with maximum effectiveness.

Lights on the Road Ahead

Coordination is often looked upon as an administrative or supervisory procedure by which the efforts of many people can be focused upon the goals of the school and school system. Coordination can be viewed more as a result than a process. The presentations in chapter 3, 'Sources of Coordination', kept the emphasis on the fact that coordination was the result of people being able to look upon individual and group activities in a way that does not conflict and thwart the efforts of individuals as they work together in the educational enterprise. Emphasis was placed upon the fact that policy has a purpose and that the policy can be identified. There are relationships between policy and regulation.

Policy can be the product of an individual act or a group act. There is an increasing inclination to determine policy through the interaction of all personnel involved. This has removed much of the misperception of policy being a procedure for regulating. The coordination of individual effort is more effective when achieved by procedures acceptable to all involved personnel. It is to be hoped that the participation of involved personnel will be one way of keeping policy more active as a means of providing the ways that people can work together and accomplish the group accepted purposes. A suggestion was made in chapter 3 that individuals who work in a school system which lacks coordination would be more frustrated than those experiencing coordination that was achieved through the joint determination of policy.

Recognition must be given to the fact that the road ahead requires some adaptation. Many of the adaptations imposed upon the individual may come as a result of changes in environmental purposes and procedures. It means that, as purposes change, the procedures have to change. This often means that an adaptation by the individual must be made to the revised system by which the educational enterprise can move forward. The recognition of the need for collaboration with those assigned to specialized responsibilities such as supervision or administration is a basic need. Collaboration perhaps is simply another way of referring to the achievement of coordination in effort. It infers, however, that the collaboration is a voluntary procedure for coordinating the individual's choice to work not only agreeably but also in a rewarding and reinforcing fashion with others in the school organization.

Individuals can be better collaborators and work in a more coordinated fashion providing they maintain an alertness to the directional clues that can be observed in the environment of the school and within the educational enterprise itself. Directional clues can come from the changing purposes of a society or from the changing conditions under which society provides educational opportunities. At the present time, there is much concern about changing enrollments. Student enrollment shifts have required many adjustments. There have been concerns also for a long-neglected segment of society, namely, those who are handicapped by some condition which causes them to be dealt with in a more specialized way than is found necessary for the so-called normal students in the school. As society became more cognizant of the specialized needs of certain types of individuals, there came the need to adjust and to adapt many of the processes and procedures of the educational activities. Individual alertness to these things may affect the educational work of the total organization as well as of individuals. Everyone should be preparing themselves to fit into the changed needs and to support a collaboration that brings the best of expertise from each individual in the organization.

Another item on the road ahead is a matter of having confidence in the responsiveness of peers, in the specialized assistance from the school organization, and in the people influences of the school community and broader environment. The importance in maintaining a confidence in responsiveness is paramount for one prime reason, namely, to find it as a means of self-stimulation to bring the individual's best assistance to the total organization and operation. As individuals look ahead to need or continuing professional opportunities and responsibilities, they should recognize that there are many rewards of compatibility. Teaching or any other task in the educational program need not be a lonely and isolated experience. Each individual must recognize that his/her professional peers, while having individual responsibilities, also have ways of collaborating and, thus, bringing their own expertise to the operation in a way that will make each individual's part in it more effective.

Continuing development, as viewed in this chapter, as well as the emphasis in all of the chapters, assumes a policy-based type of improvement. Here again, with policy developed by sharing with all of those who must carry responsibility in the total operation, continuity can be assured on a much more logical and effective basis. It is believed too, that there is much reinforcement for each individual in the collegial relationships. Compatibility achieved under the policy-based continuity will provide each individual an opportunity to find many ways and opportunities to appreciate colleagues and peers. With conditions and expectations changing as much as they do, it is necessary to watch for those signs ahead which may require some adjustment to individual aspirations. The individual is encouraged to find ways of individual realization in self-controlled expertise. On the other hand, some of those controls may have to be shared in the future in order to bring about the continuity of improvement that is envisioned here.

The accountability of each individual has been bandied about as a very rigid type of standard imposed upon each one in the school organization. This is unfortunate. The definable accountability also must be adaptable accountability. This does not mean that the individual can ignore the supporting agencies in the community nor the other people in the educational enterprise and develop a personal accountability imposed upon the individual. It must be definable in terms of the relationships not only to others in the school organization but also to the varying conditions that surround the school and the ever changing expectations placed upon education. It is important to look ahead with the thought that coordination must be realized if individual satisfaction can be achieved. Coordination in any action is complex and education will require the contributions of many different types of expertise brought together in a reinforcing manner. In other words, each person in the process of coordination should emphasize the 'co' because that involves each individual along with all others who bear a similar relationship to the task and goals which have been established.

The lights on the road ahead reveal opportunities to do new things and differing ways of doing them. Induction to these opportunities can be a continuing experience of challenge. These challenges lead to many in-service activities that result in the development of new abilities and renewal of previously unchallenged expertise. The entering opportunities usually call for decisions that require a redirection of professional talents. The road ahead, then, offers the essential ingredients to continuing development.

Mirrored Rather Than Conjured Images

Much emphasis has been given in this chapter and throughout the book to the importance of the individual's recognized personal abilities and to developing the ability for self-analysis. This becomes the first step toward the establishment of a self-confidence that is so supportive of creative action. Much of this is dependent upon how individuals see themselves, thus, the concept of the mirror as one place where a personalized identification can be located. It is personal because it is recognizable. It is personal because the individual who is mirrored is the one who is doing and reacting at the same time. It is not a matter of audiences being involved with the reaction to self. The personal identification can offer much help in the establishment of appropriate bases for self-confidence and, therefore, for the self-development through improvement activities.

Conjured images are those that have developed without any direct viewing but depend almost entirely upon mental images. These images are non-analyzable with respect to the source. Most individuals who conjure images of themselves are not able to trace the origins of such images. A source may not be present and perhaps not even definable, yet, the individual has been influenced greatly.

Chapter 4 deals with 'Bases For Self-Confidence' and, in that chapter, a number of elements are discussed which involve the matter of justifiable self-confidence as well as some suggestions for studying the appropriateness of the bases of that confidence. It is hoped that individuals will seek more of the *mirrored* type of images than the *conjured* type since they are analyzable and can be traced to sources. In this way, if they are not supportive of the professional activities of the individual, they can be adapted, retained, or discarded.

The question often arises as to whether the image of one's self or even the fact of self-confidence is benefitted by the continuity of that image. In other words, are there benefits to stability insofar as self-confidence is concerned? It can work either way. In some instances observations of stability in the images of self might give reassurances that, somewhere along the line, good choices were made and they were worth keeping. On the other hand, if the stability is fixed over too long a period of time it may cause the individual to lose both the desire and the ability to analyze sources of images and go directly to corrective actions whether they apply to purposes, procedures, or products.

Stability when applied to describing the most appropriate and desirable type of action patterns, can be worthy of retention. It is important, however, that the relationship between stability and creativity be explored. Creativity is the ability to see alternatives, to define them, to analyze them, and to adapt them to the ongoing activities. Stability if placed ahead of all other characteristics can work against the development of creativity within individuals as they apply their talents to the educational tasks at hand. There is little doubt that perspectives held by individuals influence the kinds of choices of purpose and of action that they make. In other words, the images screen the knowledge choices. Images screen the knowledge application choices and images may screen the procedures selected for pursuing the requisite activities leading to task accomplishment. Individuals may find that images stimulate both creativity to the task at hand or the tasks that can be envisioned ahead.

The anatomy of ambition can be identified in part by the fact that it involves (i) the acceptance of responsibility; (ii) the recognition of contributions; (iii) the expansion of purpose; (iv) the sense of accepted achievement; and (v) the mastery of alternative choices of adaption and application. These are the things that when put together in the awareness of the individual, can cause that individual to be ambitious in improving both the purposing and the procedures requisite for the achievement of the goals identified. It must be recognized, at the same time, that there are many external impacts on the self-assurance of the individual. This, in turn, may have a great influence upon the status of self-confidence. Many of these external impacts might be originating from peers and specialized services within the school system and, more assuredly, from the environment of the school and from public opinion in general.

Approbation often leads to self-assurance status on the part of the individual. Denigration of the outcomes of the educational enterprise can destroy any self-assurance that may exist. The images which develop as a result of this can have much to do with the desire to continue improving through either renewal or redirection types of activities. A part of the outcome of self-assurance would be the individual's image of a personal future. If the images of past experiences have been stimulating, have caused creativity to be generated, and have provided the experience of accepted performances, they will affect the future in a favorable way. On the other hand, if the images of the future look hopeless, frustrated by the impacts from others, and the mirror that one has for one's self, they can do nothing other than result in defeat. Defeat leads to a loss of self-confidence and, consequently, of the vigor by which the individual applies expertise and creativity to the task at hand.

The images of the future are influenced by other people. Those other people can be the mirrors apart from the individual mirror or conjured images. People react to the individual and the individual ought to be aware than an interpretation of how other people react can be suggestive of what is being done wisely and what needs to be improved in personal behaviors and accomplishments.

Objectivity has to be the overall essential to self-mirroring whether the mirror be the one on the wall or the conjured images. The images of the future may be affected by one's past and by other people who have been reacting to the relationship and the performance that could be observed. Objectivity is essential and it needs to be analyzed in terms of whether the purposing was right, whether other people had a basis for significant mirroring of the individual, and whether the purposes still are acceptable as directors or guides to the efforts of individuals. These are the image controls an individual needs to consider. Primarily, the consideration must be directed to the origin of the images that an individual has of self. It is then possible to make an objective decision as to whether the images will control the future and whether they will offer the directions by which a new future can be influenced and controlled. Futures can always be new if the images provide purposeful access to many induction, renewal, and redirection activities. This guarantees in-service improvement and career-long professional development.

Daring To Be Challenged

The previous section dealt primarily with those elements of the inner-self that make it possible for individual evolvement as a creative worker or as one who neglects the opportunity to find self-confidence in successful development. This section shifts the emphasis more to the impact that others have upon the individual. These others extend the consideration beyond the peers of professional workers in the school organization. There are many influences coming from a great variety of sources both within the school and within the community that can present an opportunity to be challenged or can present a situation in which defeat can be assumed. Many of these sources were identified and discussed in detail in chapter 5, 'A Look Beyond the Classroom'.

The thrust of this section is in the direction of being ready to accept challenges. Most people are confronted almost daily with someone who will ask whether you can do this or that. The mere fact of the question may be an indication of confidence of those people in the individual so queried. It could be seen as an opportunity to dispose of some task that otherwise might befall those persons who directed the query. The problem to be considered here is that of finding a challenge in all of these types of situations that can lead the individual to find opportunities for personal renewal and redirection merely by the fact that a challenge opportunity is presented.

A human inclination to be somewhat adventurous generally exists. It often is said that timid people are less adventurous than are bold people. Probably neither of these two statuses explains much about how a human being can feel toward an adventurous situation. It is believed here that the challenges can come because they are challenges to the individuals through the testing of personal qualities and capacities in the achievement of a goal that has been inferred by another source. The inclination to seek adventure is more than an avoidance of boredom. It is more likely a response to testing out one's own ability in the face of a defined task or problem situation.

The inclination to adventure also can be described as being easily stimulated to be competitive. The competition inferred here is not limited to people competition but to the competition which is a test against the demands of a task and the ability of the individual. Most people like to try out their strength to see if they can overcome a problem or achieve a stated goal. It must be recognized that the stimulation to competition can be wholesome in the sense that, if it is competition toward goal achievement, it is much better than the personal rivalries that can develop. See competition as a test — a comparative test of one or more people seeking to achieve a common goal. This is the most satisfactory position because it is competitiveness not in the sense of trying to defeat the other person. It is competitive in the sense that, whether it be a person or a task, the challenge is to accomplish. This is one of the best ways for each individual to develop competencies that have not existed before or to sharpen those which have existed.

Much depends upon the attitudes of people toward other people involved in similar tasks or in the strength of the challenge that comes from a stated assignment or problem situation. These can be described as the perspectives held by the individuals who are so challenged. Many times, whether facetiously or not, politicians are referred to as practising the art of the possible. Perhaps a more positive reference would be that it is an effort to practice the arts of development and accomplishment rather than simply to look for the easy way of achieving the goals, either in whole or in part, depending upon the demands and the task situation. These perspectives toward competitive situations affect the insights that describe the images held by the individual in terms of the deepest meanings of involvement in challenging situations and task commitments. These perspectives might have much to do with how people gain an image of what they want to be when confronted with a task situation. They may, on the other hand, turn it to the influence of the selectivity of the origin of the challenge that will stimulate response.

Induction, renewal, and redirection are related closely to this inclination to be selective with respect to the challenge origins. If the origin is in a political situation, wholly unrelated to the educational task commitment, a challenge can be set aside in favor of some of the more solidly related challenges that can be involved in teaching and learning. This selectivity does not mean that people are avoiding the challenge of accomplishment but rather that the challenge is placed in a priority system so that it can build toward the development of the individual as a more competent and creative worker in the field of education. Even though the individual is being emphasized here, it must be recognized that the freedom status of that individual may have a great deal to do with the challenge acceptance. This means that the organizational support and restraints existing in the school as an agency may have much to do with the individual's response to challenges. It is important, however, not to make assumptions about the organizational supports and restraints but rather to seek the solid facts about that support and/or restraint.

The individual who has accepted a challenge to improve certain aspects of the educational program must have support facilities. The organization must provide the freedom status to the individual through the provision of the support facilities. On the negative side, which must not be neglected in the consideration here, it might be termed the sell-outs to security. When the challenge is avoided for some reason that is not particularly well-founded in fact, the individual is avoiding the challenge in order to gain or maintain security of personal advantages and future economic welfare. Often the discouragement that can come in the challenges to security is the work of a third party. The third party here is a person not directly involved in the cooperative efforts of the teaching and learning programs. The complications can come from a third party challenge who may in a certain manner provide deterrence to the individual by a challenge to non-factual assumptions that have implications for the quality of the work and the level of outcomes.

Challenges are not always individual in nature. Challenges can signal group involvements in many different ways. Challenges are not lost as a result of the inclusion of other people in the tasks at hand. It is important, when groups are involved, to develop the skills of being a liaison. This means that the skills are developed for helping people to relate not only to their goals but also to their activities which are chosen as the ways of goal achievement. The skills that the individual has in providing the liaison between people and the task will bring about the challenge of effectiveness that can be most enlightening and certainly developmental in nature. The application of the skills of being a liaison can be understood best and can be developed along with those skills which are most effective in the directions of learning and in the provision of the design for an educational program. The liaison efforts of individuals can stimulate increasing acceptance of the concepts of continuing development.

Evolving Personal Adequacy

The discussion presented in chapter 6, 'The Nature of Self-Sufficiency', indicated that no individual has all of the competencies required for most any task at hand. Our society is so structured that people work in association with others with many varying degrees of interaction leading to the accomplishment of common goals. The most important thing indicated in chapter 6 was that all teachers in their own work need to recognize when help in needed. This thought was extended in this chapter in terms of the personal competencies that the individual can recognize and use as a basis for planning personal relationships to tasks and to other people in similar or supportive roles.

Adequacy can be seen best as need fulfillment. This is practically synonymous with the achievement of goals. The important thing to see is that adequacy is an ongoing type of characteristic and involves the continuous improvement of the individual in confronting the tasks accepted and which serve as the target of responsibility. Need-fulfillment may not be a completely individualized responsibility. The adequacy and need fulfillment, nevertheless, will be dependent upon individual capacity to seek and to find the help that can be made available by others. Those others can offer help either directly or in the form of reports of publications. The main thing is to recognize that, when there is assistance which can be used profitably, the fulfilled need does not deter satisfaction.

Personal responsibilities and adequacies that must become involved in the accomplishment process is that of achieving needs definition or assessment. The most crucial needs require the most carefully delineated description or definition. The impact of what is needed upon the tasks of teaching and learning become the responsibility of teachers. Teachers must not wait for others to define the need but, nonetheless, should seek the help of specialized personnel particularly in identifying the need and achieving the definition. It is only when this need–definition has been accomplished that a resolution to the securing of the fulfillments can move ahead and be successful. This interdependence among individuals in working in the educational program can stimulate the surveying of the support adequacy that can be available. If specialized help is needed for unique types of learning problems, a support facility would be to have that specialized person available to advise and to suggest. At the same time, the support adequacy may be measured in terms of the ability to determine whether the goal has been achieved. The evolving personal adequacy as seen here is a part of the induction, renewal, and redirection of the teacher's responsibility. Finding out what the problems are and, through the need–definition, knowing what support facilities are required constitute the prelude to making the judgment regarding adequacies. Once the need has been carefully defined and the support facilities have been determined adequate, purposeful implementation becomes one of the creative tasks of the individuals involved.

Personal implementation means that the efforts and support facilities are directed to the refined need and that all effort is focused upon the organizational or individual purposes and goals. Evolving as an individual in developing the adequacies to bring about the joint expertise of many individuals makes it clear that *evolving includes involving*. It was emphasized in the previous section that the skills constituting a liaison between people or between people and a problem become one of the great responsibilities of each professional worker. The involvement of other people brings about strength through a combination of varying types of expertise. Here again the personal adequacy in making certain that these are directed toward an accepted goal becomes the crucial consideration. As a person works with needs and with the development of support adequacy, it becomes clear that the parallelism existing between individuals in a group activity becomes a part of the important activities that lead to goal achievement.

Parallelism is not a status, it is a process and it is a process rather than a goal. Parallelism is the way that persons can go about their own unique and accepted tasks while others do the same thing. Yet, those involved in parallel but separate activities eventually arrive at a commonality of goal that is reinforcing to each and to the goal achievement. In the sense used here, group action can reinforce or subdue individual developmental contributions. It can reinforce when the skills of the individual keep the needs well–defined and in sight while searching for the support facilities and bringing them to the stage of adequacy. These support facilities can be achieved throughout the implementation processes inferred above. Group action in this sense is positive and reinforcing. Group action at the same time can become rigid. When this happens it may subdue the individual developmental activities which could constitute improved contributions to the problem at hand.

Flexibility in group action is important providing that flexibility can be seen as the review of alternatives in the important decisions being made. It means that there will be occasions when group action may not reinforce but rather may subdue involved individuals. In this sense, there may be a feeling of personal failure. It is suggested that there may be some positive aspects of failure. If individuals involved in that failure are willing to analyze the inadequacies that occurred in the interaction and those requisites of a non-people nature, judgments can be directed to the essentials for the accomplishment of goals and purposes. Just as there may be some positive aspects to failure, there can be some negative aspects to achievement. It is an easy invitation for the individual who has experienced a high level of achievement to develop the feeling that perhaps the goal has been reached and further creative effort is not required. In such cases, there is no longer an evolving personal development of the individual's capacities to bring successful activity toward goal achievement.

Good enough is not the conclusion to high level achievement. *Good enough* must be progressive rather than static. *Good enough* must say to each individual that the evolving personal responsibilities must continue because there will be higher goals and greater demands for the developing expertise to be applied to the newly selected and defined goals in induction, renewal, and/or redirection.

Climbers Out-distance Coasters

Numerous references in the preceding sections of this chapter have been made to the desirability of generating creativity as one goes about accepted responsibilities in the educational program. Emphasis has been given also to the advantage of being susceptible to challenge. Challenge is a stimulator of the creativity that is so important to the improvement of educational services. In all of these instances, the responsibility for development has been placed primarily upon the individual. It is the individual who must do the improving in order to have continuing development.

This section deals with yet another aspect of this continuous improvement program. Climbing is two-directional. The individuals can climb up or climb down. It is important to recognize that there are times when the direction of the climbing is a matter of choice and wise determination. Coasting, however, is one-directional, at least in the accepted earthly concept it has to be down. Coasting can be usable as a concept for studying the problems of continuous improvement.

Individual purpose, knowledge, and effort are the dominant determiners in whether one climbs or coasts. This was discussed as a personal responsibility in chapter 7, 'Success: Process and Product'. It was discussed there as the matter of extending self-analysis beyond the point that had been indicated in some of the earlier chapters. The most important emphasis in chapter 7 was that of establishing a continuing attack upon the process of maintaining and improving one's own efficiency in the classroom or in that particular phase of educational program accepted as an assignment or responsibility. The individual purpose, knowledge, and effort become the determiner as to whether there is a desire to climb regardless of the way but that the way or direction should be determined on the basis of analysis and desirable product. The individual purpose, knowledge, and effort can also lead the individual to coasting in one direction. This occurs if there is no incentive, existing or developed, on the part of the individual to be established in the educational program as a person meriting recognition for a high degree of competence in the assigned or assumed task.

Equally important is that, after the initial stages of teaching experience, the continuity goes from successful induction to progressive renewal and/or redirection. In this way, individuals will continue to climb and to climb in the direction of improved performance. The purpose, knowledge, and effort indicated here can be summed up in the thought that knowing is implemented by doing. Individuals should put their purpose, knowledge, and effort wisely to chosen activities that lead to the accomplishment of the established goals. The doing is highly important because it gives a first hand opportunity to analyze not only the procedures but also the products of educational effort. This thought is focused primarily upon the individual teacher but it must be remembered that purposeful and coordinated helping and being helped make effective work processes. Placing this high responsibility on individuals to be interactive does not negate their own purposes of seeing the need for added application of human creativity and effort as an individual responsibility. It is equally true that, when others have identified an area of help, still other individuals must be willing to offer help. It is coordinated effort that results in both helping and being helped. This is a sure way of maintaining continuity in the efforts toward improvement and will result in the continuing development of the individuals involved in the educative activities.

Climbing as indicated above can be subjected to choice by the individual as to what the direction shall be. Regardless of whether the direction is up or down, climbing is progressive. By progressive is meant here that, whichever way that the climbing is directed, it can result in an improvement of the educational services as individual and as group effort. Emphasis above has been primarily on the climbing up aspect but it is important to recognize that climbing down may be just as important as climbing up. Climbing down may mean abandoning some of the kinds of strategies that have been used and modifying, adapting, or replacing them with others. In this sense, climbing down can be corrective in nature and, being corrective in nature, may bring about a revision of the individual procedures which provides a direct pathway to what is termed renewal and redirection.

Renewal is not necessarily returning to something that has been done and abandoned before but rather a renewal of enthusiasm. Renewal is the recognition of personal contributions and a regaining of enthusiasm to seek the manner and ways that will result in educational improvement. While climbing up or down can be developmental and renewing in nature, coasting is purposeless and regressive. Coasting means that the individual has abandoned the responsibility to seek those analytic directives which can put creative and unique abilities to the use that results in improved educational programming. The choice of climbing or coasting is an inescapable individual determination. Each person must decide what direction to go and how to get there in order to have the marks of continuing development as an educational program operative.

Mastery Preferred to Coping

The term mastery seems to strike fear into the minds of many people. It has gained a traditional interpretation as being a state of perfection. Thus, those who claim mastery in some or all aspects of a professional task infer that there is no more improvement needed since the individual has already attained the absolute in the perfection of performance. It is well to recognize that mastery in that sense is a product but it can be a process. The concept of process is more pertinent to this section of the chapter than product which means completion.

Mastery is proficiency in achievement. Thus, as individuals choose the behaviors appropriate to their concept of contribution to the educational program, the idea of proficiency must be maintained. This means that whatever effort is put forth, it moves in the direction of the achievement of purposes and goals. This is a sense in which mastery is used in this section.

Coping on the other hand has never had a very clear traditional meaning to most people. Coping has been looked upon as simply tolerating, not necessarily taking the responsibility for making adjustments either one one's self or in the situation. Coping in this section is seen as sparring with real or imaginary problems and situations. In other words, *coping is getting along with situations and expectations.* Coping is turning this way and that in the face of problems and situations, hoping at last for some personal satisfaction and, perhaps, professional status. It is not a concept, however, that denotes a person who is interested in continuous improvement either in self or in the programming for higher achievement of educational goals.

Mastery and coping, then, are appropriate to the organization of discussion in viewing the many cross-currents of belief and action that can signify either treatment failure or neglect. The cross-currents referred to here are the ones that may be generated within a teaching staff, within any agency that has impacts upon the schools, and within the community, which relate to the manner in which education is conducted and the success of those ways.

The discussion in chapter 8, 'Inherited Merry-go-Rounds', is pertinent to the concepts here. In that chapter, there was an extensive review of the differing kinds of impacts that play upon the teacher from organizations both within the profession and in the environment of the school. These cross-currents are challenges to the teacher who must find ways of resolving them or recognizing that they could induce failure. They must not reside in the state of neglect, for neglect could be a deterrent to educational development of those who work in the educational program.

Differences identified in the cross-currents can be viewed and treated as alternatives. In this way, a more positive approach is taken toward any distortions in the agreements between the oppositions constituting the differences. If the differences are viewed as alternatives, then alternatives become the vehicle to which analysis can be applied. If all of the people involved in the cross-currents can be made parties to the analysis of alternatives, they can find mutually accepted goals for the resolution of the differences. This resolution would be a commonality of selection of the best alternative that is offered.

The analysis of alternatives must result in data and information that can be related to the various aspects of the educative process. The alternatives should be prioritized according to their probable contribution to the educational improvement. The logical step and the mastery inferred would be in the process of using the highest priority of alternatives in the structuring of trial applications of the alternative as a solution or resolution. It is wise to structure the trial on a reasonable basis with respect to numbers involved and with a time limitation. Here again is a mastery of the procedures of being able to join in considerations even with those who differ and to select alternatives according to the purposes. Any trial application should be accompanied with a time schedule for analysis to discover whether the alternative resulted in an improvement of the points that gave rise to the differences.

Some prime skills need to be taken into consideration in this process of mastery for this kind of involvement with others in the resolution of cross-currents of belief about action. These prime skills are (i) ordering of effort; (ii) differentiating responsibility; (iii) applying evaluative strategies; and (iv) designing next steps. This constitutes really a summary of the preceding paragraphs by way of what to do in the face of conflict situations. These prime skills would result in the identification of a mastery approach rather than a coping approach to the resolution of problems.

The prime skills application, even in the state of mastery, by all of those who are involved in the action assumes that there must be history-free decisions. History-free decisions means that the decision will be made upon the basis of the analytic data produced from studying the alternatives and that there is no hang-over of previous belief or posture that will overrule the evidence produced in the analysis of the alternatives. This leaves the involved individuals free to make goal-related decisions and to maintain greater objectivity in determining whether the trial efforts are leading toward a better chance of achieving the chosen goals.

Goal-related mastery as described above is true professionalism. It can be achieved by individuals, whether in the early stage of induction into the teaching experience or as a mature educational worker who has not lost the desire to put effort into continuing development. Mastery achievement is a developmental status. Mastery effort can lead to improvement of the program as well as to the success of the induction, renewal, and/or redirection desires and efforts of the teaching staff.

Measures of Responsibility

The emphasis upon the individual's creative activities has appeared frequently in each chapter of this book and each section of this chapter. This is evidence of the importance that the author places upon the individual action in the school program which is looked upon as a group activity. A group can perform little except through the quality of the individuals providing the group support to the action toward accepted goals.

Responsibility is a trust rather than a performance. It is almost impossible to give instruction to people as to how they can be responsible. If the idea of responsibility as a contributor to the individual and group successes holds, perhaps the *balance* concept of the term can be achieved. It is what the individuals do in the performance of the assigned and accepted tasks that gives a measure of the responsibility of the individuals as they go about these tasks.

Responsibility, then, is a trust that is placed in the individual. The trust is placed there by self and in part by others. It must be recognized that the perceptions held by other people about the individual's contribution to the total activity and to the achievement of goals is directed to the individual as a responsibility. The extent to which the individual can internalize this trust is one of the first measures of responsibility. In the sense presented here, a trust is a personalized credence. It is what the individual can show in performance by way of responding to the trust that others have designated as being appropriate to the individual contributions.

Responsibility relates to both successes and failures. The discussions in chapter 9, 'Management of Expectations', can provide a good platform for the concept of responsibility. It is the individual's obligations to identify, describe, analyze, and manage the expectations that are placed upon them either by themselves or by others. The instance of success is always inviting to use as a chief measure of responsibility. It can never be forgotten, however, that failure too has come about as a result of the way that somebody has or has not performed. The responsibility for failure is not necessarily a measure of defeat but an acceptance of the fact that the activity did not lead to the anticipated state of contribution to the achievement goal. To be responsible for a failure is not to indicate that the individual has failed but rather has the courage to face up to the fact that some changes, adaptations, or replacements have to be made in the program of activities which did not lead to the success that was desired.

This concept of responsibility brings about a merging of purpose, process, and product. This concept has been indicated in numerous places in this book. It is mentioned here in passing merely as an item in the measures of responsibility. These items are not the only ones but they are important ones that are to be scrutinized and observed. It was indicated above that, since other people are so much involved in the placement of the trust in individuals which is the identification of responsibility, these perceptions are influential in determining the kinds of trust but more particularly the kinds of responsibility that could be deemed of high measure.

The perceptions held by each person affect that person's way of behaving. The same is true of those who are observing that person. These perceptions are important in the assessment of a degree to which responsibility has been achieved. Here again, it is done through the merging of purpose, process, and product. The perceptions held by self and by others may be sufficiently different to bring about different conclusions or even different goals as well as ways of achieving those goals. It means that all individuals need to develop a generous amount of flexibility and adaptability both in responding to the demands of others but more particularly in placing demands upon others. This becomes an integral part of the concept of responsibility as a trust placed in the individual.

Flexibility-adaptability demands and responses are important not only in the definition of responsibility and in measuring it but also in making certain that responsibility is accepted and assessed in terms of the individual's personal capacities as they relate to the task commitments. It must be recognized too that, just as individuals change with experience and learning, tasks have a way of evolving from one state to another during the process of activity. There needs to be a conscious awareness of a balance between personal capacity and task evolvement. Were it possible to say that the task will always remain the same, the problem of balance could be adjusted at the outset but such is not the nature of work and work purpose. A balance then is essential as one of the commitments to a measure of responsibility.

A previous chapter indicated the high number of impacts that can come from within the school and from outside the school. These change from time to time and sometimes require sharp adaptations on the part of the teachers in the educational process. It is important that each individual possess a value-integrity so that the environmental fluctuations can be seen from a firm purpose. The educational task and mode become an area in which the value-integrity of the teacher is highly essential in order that variations do not get out of control and no longer are subject to management or adaptations. All individuals need to develop a systematic self and task scrutiny. This has been empha-sized a number of times and is offered now as one of the measures of responsibility that can support the idea of continuous improvement in the teaching and learning processes.

Systematic self and task scrutiny if successful provide the basis for learning and relearning on the part of the professional worker. This capacity to learn and relearn grows as the practice of learning and relearning takes place. The learning and relearning can provide much of the flexibility and adaptability that was indicated as highly important in the above paragraphs. Clearly, learning and relearning are the essence of renewal and redirection. The outcomes of renewal and redirection call for carefully planned induction procedures so that development will be a continuing experience.

Substance of Ingenuity

Reference has been made many times in the preceding chapters and in this chapter to the fact that the most important thing to achieve is the development of creativity which can apply appropriately to the accepted or assigned tasks. Ingenuity is another way of describing the application of expertise, talent, and creative ability. Ingenuity is resourcefulness to find the ways of doing the things that need to be done so that they will fulfill the envisioned purpose.

The inference of substance of ingenuity presumes that there are in existence some constituent elements. These elements have been iden-tified at numerous points in the text and in this chapter. These are the things that need to be subjected to scrutiny and analysis to determine whether they shall be retained, adapted, or replaced. The constituent elements can be created, modified, or disregarded. This possibility was discussed in chapter 10, 'Mastery of Adaptation'. Here again the responsibility is placed upon the individual who in turn must use creative ability to gain a mastery over the elements that are involved in accomplishing the tasks at hand. There is a high demand placed upon the individual's purpose, reason, and skill — not only in analyzing one's self but in all interactive situations as well.

The assumption has not been made at any point that teaching responsibility can be achieved without the involvement of other people. This indicates the involvement of other professional workers but the most basic element would be the interaction of the teacher and the learner. This provides the first analysis of the elements involved in the teaching-learning situation. These must be viewed from the interactive point of view or teaching becomes a matter of pouring-in rather than of stimulating and developing. It is important that the teacher sees all of the things that can be seen among the elements that are involved in the selection of those activities which will accomplish the purpose. Many times there will be situations in which the greatest requisite is to discover the unseen. It is important to identify the forces which are operating in the teaching-learning situation even though they are not overt and even though they have never been identified and defined. The discovery of some of these things that have not been seen before often calls for a shock-resistant learner or learning procedures because some of the elements of the inherited merry-go-rounds may be of the nature that do shock. It is important to see this kind of an element in the ingenuity required in the teaching situation.

Another element is that of optimism in and maintaining that optimism in viewing the distasteful opposition and divergencies that are to be encountered on the part of anyone involved in directing the learning of others. There will be opposition of some types all along the way. There will be divergencies and the individual must develop the ingenuity to deal with these rather than try to overpower or divert them from enthusiastic work attacks at the task of the learning situation. This calls for a mastery of developmental and adaptive thinking. This is another way of saying again that improvement must be continuous from the point of first *induction* to a position until the time of *career exit*. This total span of time will be interspersed with many occasions involving induction, renewal, and redirection activities.

Days Need Not Be Done

A concluding thought is appropriate for this chapter and for the entire book. Perhaps it is used facetiously but unfortunately not always, that Friday is looked upon as the greatest day of the teacher's week. The TGIF (Thank God It's Friday) attitude can be an escape route for cowards and lazy people. It is more appropriate that people do not seek the end of the week but rather to look forward to the beginning of a week and anticipate all of the activities of involvement for that coming week. Sunrise anticipators are productive contributors and are far more valuable in the educational process than members of the TGIF club.

Goals are the substance of the future as you look to the sunrise and anticipate the expected as well as the unexpected tasks and expectations of the next day and the future. It must be remembered, however, that the past is not one big scrap pile. The past is worth reviewing occasionally to see if something has been discarded which all of a sudden might find a new use and a new application in the ongoing educative process. It is this ability to look to the future, to analyze the past, and to make the adaptations that constitutes the real challenge for those who are willing to make a commitment to continuing development.

Outlearning the learners is a developmental experience. Most teachers discover this early in the teaching experience. It is a thrill to be able to stay well ahead of all the learners as a learner. This does not mean staying ahead of the learners at their level of the subject matter involved at a particular moment but rather at the goal of learning itself and of advancing in learning at each level of a particular time. Reviewing and redoing is professional renewal. This calls for the adaptation of what may have been concealed in the past and perhaps forgotten, yet, a review of redoing is a professional action that can be a renewing experience to the individual involved in it.

Continuing is a concept used in this book as increasing the levels of competence wherever and whatever the competence demand is. It is continuing and that means growing, learning, and developing. It is unfortunate when people have to be called a 'has been' because they no longer put forth any effort to grow and develop. Perhaps it is more accurate to say the 'has beens' maybe never 'were' if they have the inclination after some years of experience to say this is far enough so far as competence is concerned. This may signify that their competence never was surprisingly high. The pace of progress may vary, but standing still is going no place at all and, when the 'has beens' are so declared because they are standing still, the pace of progress has stopped. This status may be either the *stable and stagnant* or the career *frustration* facet of the teacher career cycle. It is more encouraging to see people be conscious that progress has a pace and exercise some control over it both for their own benefits as well as for the educational service that can come from it.

Continuing development provides the reason for effective service and professional satisfaction to which each individual is entitled upon having achieved the recognition of being a contributing worker in the educational program. Professional satisfaction is not the signal of completion. It is viewed more appropriately as a stimulant to continuing development. The author hopes the substance of this book will be supportive of such stimulation. Your notes relating to the *Aids for Self-Development* may be even more supportive at the close of each school year. Review your notes, categorize their substances, and establish priorities. Use the high priority items to focus your improvement thrusts for the beginning of the next school term. This approach provides each one with a progressive career assessment as an integral part of self-improvement. It will help to assure that *induction, renewal,* and *redirection* activities provide substantive resources for *continuing development* and career-long teacher education.

Bibliography

ADLER, M.J. *The Paideia Proposal*, New York, Macmillan Publishing Co., 1982.

ADLER, M.J. *Paideia Problems and Possibilities*, New York, Macmillan Publishing Co., 1983.

ADLER, M.J. *The Paideia Program*, New York, Macmillan Publishing Co., 1984.

ANDREWS, T.E., HOUSTON, W.R., and BRYANT, B.L. *Adult Learners (A Research Study)*, Washington, D.C., Association of Teacher Educators, 1981.

APPS, J.W. *Problems in Continuing Education*, New York, McGraw-Hill, 1979.

Association of Teacher Educators, *Developing Career Ladders in Teaching*, Reston, VA, Association of Teacher Educators, 1985.

BALDRIDGE, J.V., and DEAL, T. (Eds.). *The Dynamics of Organizational Change in Education*, Berkeley, CA, McCutchan Publishing, 1983.

BEEGLE, C.W., and EDELFELT, R.A. *Staff Development: Staff Liberation*, Washington, D.C., Association for Supervision and Curriculum Development, 1977.

BELLON, J.J., EAKER, R.E., HUFFMAN, J.O., and JONES, R.V. JR. *Classroom Supervision and Instructional Improvement: A Synergetic Process*, Dubuque, Iowa, Kendall/Hunt Publishing Company, 1976.

BERK, R.A. (Ed.). *Educational Evaluation Methodology: The State of the Art*, Baltimore, MD, The Johns Hopkins University Press, 1981.

BERMAN, L.M., and RODERICK, J.A. (Eds.). *Feeling, Valuing, and the Art of Growing: Insights into the Affective*, Washington, D.C., Association for Supervision and Curriculum Development, 1977.

BLOOM, B.S. *Human Characteristics and School Learning*, New York, McGraw-Hill Book Company, 1976.

BLUMBERG, A. *Supervisors and Teachers: A Private Cold War*, Berkeley, CA, McCutchan, 1980.

BOLDEN, J.H. *Developing a Competency-Based Instructional Supervisory System*, Hicksville, NY, Exposition Press, 1974.

BOYER, E. *High School*, New York, Harper and Row, 1983.

BURKE, P.J., FESSLER R., and CHRISTENSEN, J.C. *Teacher Career Stages: Implications for Staff Development*, Bloomington, ID, Phi Delta Kappa,

1984.

BURKE, P.J., and HEIDEMAN, R.G. (Eds.). *Career-long Teacher Education*, Springfield, Ill, CHARLES C. THOMAS, 1985.

CARVER, F.D., and SERGIOVANNI, T.J. (Eds.). *Organization and Human Behavior: Focus on Schools*, New York, McGraw-Hill Book Company, 1969.

CASE, C.W., and MATTHES, W.A. (Eds.). *Colleges of Education: Perspectives on Their Future*, Berkeley, CA, McCutchan Publishing, 1985.

CHAMPAGNE, D.W., and HOGAN, R.C. *Consultant Supervision: Theory and Skill Development*, Wheaton, Ill, C.H. Publications, 1981.

CHRISTENSEN, J.C., BURKE, P., FESSLER, R., and HAGSTROM, D. *Stages of Teachers' Careers*, Washington, D.C., ERIC Clearinghouse on Teacher Education, 1983.

COMBS, A.W. *Educational Accountability: Beyond Behavioral Objectives*, Washington, D.C., Association for Supervision and Curriculum Development, 1972.

COMBS, A.W., AVILA, D.L., and PURKEY, W.W. *Helping Relationships: Basic Concepts for the Helping Professions*, Boston, MA, Allyn and Bacon, Inc., 1971.

CONANT, J.B. *The Education of American Teachers*. New York, McGraw-Hill, 1963.

COOPER, J.M., HANSEN, J., MARTORELLA, P.H., MORINE-DERSHIMER, SADKER, G.D., SADKER, M., SOKOLOV, S., SHOSTAK, R., TENBRINK, T., and WEBER, W.A. *Classroom Teaching Skills: A Handbook*, Lexington, MA, D.C. Heath and Company, 1977.

CORWIN, R.G., and EDELFELT, R.A. *Perspectives on Organizations: Viewpoints for Teachers*, Washington, D.C., American Association of Colleges for Teacher Education, 1976.

CORWIN, R.G., and EDELFELT, R.A. *Perspectives on Organizations: The School as a Social Organization*, Washington, D.C., American Association of Colleges for Teacher Education, 1977.

CORWIN, R.G., and EDELFELT, R.A. *Perspectives on Organizations: Schools in the Larger Social Environment*, Washington, D.C., American Association of Colleges for Teacher Education, 1978.

DAILEY, C.A. *Assessment of Lives*, San Francisco, CA, Jossey-Bass, 1971.

DAVIS, R.C. *Planning Human Resource Development: Educational Models and Schemata*, Chicago, ILL, Rand McNally and Company, 1966.

DeROCHE, E.F. *An Administrator's Guide to Evaluating Programs and Personnel*, Boston, Allyn and Bacon, 1981.

DILLON-PETERSON, B. (Ed.). *Staff Development/Organizational Development*, Alexandria, VA, Association for Supervision and Curriculum Development, 1981.

DREIKURS, R., GRUNWALD, B.B., and PEPPER, F.C. *Maintaining Sanity in the Classroom: Illustrated Teaching Techniques*, New York, Harper and Row Publishers, 1971.

DUCKETT, W.R. (Ed.). *Planning for the Evaluation of Teaching*, Bloomington, IN, Phi Delta Kappa, 1979.

DUCKETT, W.R. (Ed.). *Observation and the Evaluation of Teaching*. Bloomington, IN, Phi Delta Kappa, 1980.

Bibliography

DUMONT, M.P. *The Absurd Healer*, New York, Science House, Inc., 1968.

EDELFELT, R.A. *Rethinking Inservice Education*, Washington, D.C., National Education Association, 1975.

EDELFELT, R.A., and BROOKS SMITH, E. *Breakaway to Multidimensional Approaches: Integrating Curriculum Development and Inservice Education*, Washington, D.C., Association of Teacher Educators, 1978.

ENGLISH, F.W. *Fundamental Curriculum Decisions*, Alexandria, VA, Association for Supervision and Curriculum Development, 1983.

EPSTEIN, B. *What is Negotiable?* Washington, D.C., National Association of Secondary School Principals, 1969.

EYE, G.G., NETZER, L.A. and KREY, R.D. *Supervision of Instruction*, New York, Harper and Row, 1971.

FANTINI, M.D., and YOUNG, M.A. *Designing Education for Tomorrow's Cities*, New York, Holt, Rinehart and Winston, Inc., 1970.

FEISTRITZER, C.E. *The Making of a Teacher*, Washington, D.C., Center for Education Information, 1984.

FRIEDMAN, M.I., BRINLESS, P.S., and DENNIS-HAYES, P.B. *Improving Teacher Education: Resources and Recommendations*, New York, Longman Inc., 1980.

GAGE, N.L. *The Scientific Basis of the Art of Teaching*, New York, Teachers College Press, 1978.

GAMBRILL, E., and STEIN, T.J. *Supervision: A Decision-Making Approach*, Beverly Hills, CA, Sage Publications, 1983.

GARLAND, C. *Guiding Clinical Experiences in Teacher Education*, New York, Longman Inc., 1982.

GLATTHORN, A.A. *Differentiated Supervision*, Alexandria, VA, Association for Supervision and Curriculum Development, 1984.

GLICKMAN, C.D. *Supervision of Instruction: A Developmental Approach*, Boston, MA, Allyn and Bacon, 1985.

GOODINGS, R., BYRAM, M., and McPARTLAND, M. (Eds.). *Changing Priorities in Teacher Education*, New York, Nichols Publishing Company, 1982.

GOODLAD, J.I. *A Place Called School*, New York, McGraw-Hill, 1984.

GORDON, T. *T.E.T. Teacher Effectiveness Training*, New York, David McKay Company, Inc., 1974.

GRIFFIN, G.A. (Ed.). *Staff Development*, Chicago, Ill, University of Chicago Press, 1983.

HARRIS, B.M. *Improving Staff Performance Through Inservice Education*, Boston, MA, Allyn and Bacon, 1980.

HECK, S.F., and WILLIAMS, C.R. *The Complex Roles of the Teacher*, New York, Teachers College Press, 1984.

HENRY, M.A., and BEASLEY, W.W. *Supervising Student Teachers the Professional Way*, Terre Haute, ID, Sycamore Press, 1982.

HEYWOOD, J. *Pitfalls and Planning in Student Teaching*, London, Kogan Page Ltd., 1982.

HOSFORD, P.L. *Using What We Know About Teaching*, Alexandria, VA, Association for Supervision and Curriculum Development, 1984.

HOUSE, E.R. *School Evaluation: The Politics and Process*, Berkeley, CA, McCutchan Publishing Corp., 1973.

HOUSTON, W. ROBERT and ROGER PANKRATZ *Staff Development and Educational*

Change, Reston, VA, Association of Teacher Educators, 1980.

HOWEY, K.R., and BENTS, R.H. *Toward Meeting the Needs of the Beginning Teacher*, Minneapolis, MI, Midwest Teacher Corps., 1979.

HOWEY, K.R., BENTS, R. and CORRIGAN, D. *School-Focused Inservice: Descriptions and Discussion*, Reston, VA, Association of Teacher Educators, 1981.

HOWEY, K.R., YARGER, S.J., and JOYCE, B.R. *Improving Teacher Education*, Washington, D.C., Association of Teacher Educators, 1978.

HOWSAM, R.B., CORRIGAN, D.C., DENEMARK, G.W., and NASH, R.J. *Educating a Profession*, Washington, D.C., American Association of Colleges for Teacher Education, 1976.

JELINEK, J.J. (Ed.). *Improving the Human Condition: A Curricular Response to Critical Realities*, Washington, D.C., Association for Supervision and Curriculum Development, 1978.

KIRST, M.W. *The Politics of Education at the Local, State, and Federal Levels*, Berkeley, CA, McCutchan Publishing Corp., 1970.

KIRST, M.W. *Who Controls Our Schools?*, New York, W.H. Freeman and Co., 1985.

KNOX, A.B. *Developing, Administering, and Evaluating Adult Education*, San Francisco, Jossey-Bass, 1982.

LANG, D.C., QUICK, A.F., and JOHNSON, J.A. *A Partnership for the Supervision of Student Teachers*, DeKalb, Ill, Creative Educational Materials, 1981.

LEEPER, R.R., and WILHELMS, F.T. *Supervision: Emerging Profession*, Washington, D.C., Association for Supervision and Curriculum Development, 1969.

LEWIS, J. JR., *Appraising Teacher Performance*, West Nyaack, NY, Parker Publishing Company, 1973.

LORTIE, D. *Schoolteacher: A Sociological Study*, Chicago, University of Chicago Press, 1975.

McCARTY, D.J. (Ed.). *New Directions for Education: Creating Appraisal and Accountability Systems*, San Francisco, CA, Jossey-Bass, Inc., 1973.

McGREAL, T.L. *Successful Teacher Evaluation*, Alexandria, VA, Association for Supervision and Curriculum Development, 1983.

McKIBBIN, M., WEIL, M., and JOYCE, B. *Teaching and Learning: Demonstration of Alternatives*. Washington, D.C., Association of Teacher Educators, 1977.

McNEIL, J.D. *Toward Accountable Teachers: Their Appraisal and Improvement*, New York, Holt, Rinehart, and Winston, Inc., 1971.

MARKS, SIR JAMES ROBERT, STOOPS, E., and KING-STOOPS, J. *Handbook of Educational Supervision (3rd Edition)*, Boston, MA, Allyn and Bacon, 1985.

MELSTEIN, M.M. *Impact and Response*, New York, Teachers College Press, 1976.

MILLMAN, J. *Handbook of Teacher Evaluation*, London, Sage Publications, 1981.

MOLNAR, A. (Ed.). *Current Thought on Curriculum*, Alexandria, VA, Association for Supervision and Curriculum Development, 1985.

MOSHER, R.L., and PURPEL, D.E. *Supervision: The Reluctant Profession*. Boston, MA, Houghton-Mifflin Company, 1972.

NEALE, D.C., BAILEY, W.J., and ROSS, B.E. *Strategies for School Improvement*, Boston, MA, Allyn and Bacon, 1981.

NEEDHAM, C.W., and MORRIS, B.C. *A Systems Model Approach to Accountability*, Belmont, CA, Fearon Publishers, Inc., 1976.

NETZER, L.A., EYE, G.G., DIMOCK, M.E., DUMONT, M.P., HOMME, L., KAST, F.E. and KNEZEVICH, S.J. *Education, Administration, and Change: The Redeployment of Resources*, New York, Harper and Row, 1970.

NETZER, L.A., EYE, G.G., GRAEF, A., KREY, R.D., and OVERMAN, J.F. *Interdisciplinary Foundations of Supervision*, Boston, MA, Allyn and Bacon, Inc., 1970.

NETZER, L.A., EYE, G.G., STEVENS, D.M., and BENSON, W.W. *Strategies for Instructional Management*, Boston, MA, Allyn and Bacon, Inc., 1978.

PETERSON, P.L., and WALBERG, H.J. (Eds.). *Research on Teaching: Concepts, Findings and Implications*, Berkeley, CA, McCutchan Publishing Corp., 1979.

RINGNESS, T.A. *The Affective Domain in Education*, Boston, MA, Little, Brown and Company, 1975.

ROTH, R.A. *Individualized Staff Development Programs for Competency Development: A Systematic Approach*, Lanham, MD, University Press of America, 1980.

RUBIN, L.J. *Artistry in Teaching*, New York, Random House Inc., 1985.

RYAN, K. (Ed.). *Don't Smile Until Christmas*, Chicago, University of Chicago Press, 1970.

RYAN, K., NEWMAN, K.K. MAGER, G., APPLEGATE, J., LASLEY, T., FLORA, R., and JOHNSTON, J. *Biting the Apple: Accounts of First Year Teachers*, New York, Longman Inc., 1980.

SCIARA, F.J., and JANTZ, R.K. *Accountability in American Education*, Boston, MA, Allyn and Bacon, Inc., 1972.

SERGIOVANNI, T.J. *Supervision of Teaching*, Alexandria, VA, Association for Supervision and Curriculum Development, 1982.

SERGIOVANNI, T.J. (Ed.). *Professional Supervision for Professional Teachers*, Washington, D.C., Association for Supervision and Curriculum Development, 1975.

SERGIOVANNI, T.J., and STARRATT, R.J. *Emerging Patterns of Supervision: Human Perspectives*, New York, McGraw-Hill Book Company, 1971.

SIMPSON, R.H. *Teacher Self-Evaluation*, New York, MacMillan Company, 1966.

SIZER, T.R. *Horace's Compromise: The Dilemma of the American High School*, New York, Houghton Mifflin, 1984.

SUDMAN, S., and BRADBURN, N.M. *Asking Questions*, San Francisco, CA, Jossey-Bass Publishers, 1983.

TUCKMAN, B.W. *Evaluating Instructional Programs*, Boston, MA, Allyn and Bacon, 1979.

TYLER, R.W., GANGE, R.M., and SCRIVEN, M. *Perspectives of Curriculum Evaluation*, Chicago, ILL, Rand McNally and Company, 1967.

VROOM, V.H. *Work and Motivation*, New York, John Wiley and Sons Inc., 1964.

WATERMAN, F.T., ANDREWS, T.E., HOUSTON, R., BRYANT, B.L., and PANKRATZ, R. *Designing Short-Term Instructional Programs*, Washington, D.C., Association of Teacher Educators, 1979.

WITTROCK, M.C., and WILEY, D.E. (Eds.). *The Evaluation of Instruction: Issues and Problems*, New York, Holt, Rinehart and Winston, 1970.

WYANT, S.H. *Of Principals and Projects*, Reston, VA, Association of Teacher Educators, 1980.

Index